ESSAYS IN POLITICAL ECONOMY

About the Editors

Both the Editors have put in more than 35 years of experience in the fields of teaching, research and educational administration. They worked during their long academic career in various capacities such as Lecturers, Readers, Professors, apart from holding the positions like Heads of the Department, Chairman of the Board of Studies etc. Both of them are the Research Supervisors guiding research scholars for both M. Phil and Ph. D. Degrees in Economics since seventies. A number of candidates have taken their Doctoral Degrees under their guidance. They have completed a number of research projects sponsored by the State and Central Governments, Planning Commission, UGC, ICSSR etc. They have published quite a number of books, research papers, book reviews in both the national and international Journals.

Prof. Satyanarayan was invited as a Visiting Professor by the Illinois Institute of Technology (Stuart School of Business), Chicago, U.S.A. for a period of three months from July to October 1994. He is presently holding the position as Coordinator/Director, Special Assistance Programme (Sponsored by the UGC), Department of Economics, Osmania University.

ESSAYS IN POLITICAL ECONOMY

(Selected Papers of Prof. Gautam Mathur)

Editors

PROF. B. SATYANARAYAN

PROF. CH. RAGHURAM

Department of Economics, Osmania University, Hyderabad (India)

CONCEPT PUBLISHING COMPANY, NEW DELHI-110059

ISBN 81-7022-781-X

First Published 1999

Published and Printed by
Ashok Kumar Mittal
Concept Publishing Company
A/15-16, Commercial Block, Mohan Garden
New Delhi-110059 (India)

Phones: 5648039, 5649024
Fax: 091–(11)–5648053

Dedicated

to

The Memory of late Professor Gautam Mathur

ACKNOWLEDGEMENTS

In an endeavour of this type, it becomes necessary to solicit academic cooperation from various sources. It is our privilege to acknowledge the cooperation which we received from such institutions and persons whose help was immense in completing the present task. At the outset, we would like to express our thanks to Mrs. Sudharani Mathur w/o Late Professor Gautam Mathur, for having given us the copyright to get the papers published. In finalising the Editorial remarks, we had the benefit of discussion on a number of issues with our colleague Prof. Tippa Reddy in the Department of Economics. Likewise, Ms. Sarah Varkki and Mr. G. Ramalingam have helped us in the work relating to comparison of the draft and typing work. Our thanks are due to all of them.

The Advisory Committee of the Department of Special Assistance (Sponsored by the UGC) in its Meeting held on 19th November 1996 has resolved to publish Late Prof. Gautam Mathur's Research papers dealing with various aspects of Planning and Development Economics (presented at various Symposia, Seminars and Conferences) under the joint Editorship of Prof. B. Satyanarayan and Prof. Ch. Raghuram. We would like to express our thanks to Prof. V. Ramakistayya, Vice-Chancellor of Osmania University, who is also the Chairman of the Advisory Committee of the Department of Special Assistance, Department of Economics. The authorities of Osmania University are always helpful in encouraging academic activities. We would like to place our sense of appreciation to Prof. M. Bhagawantha Rao, Registrar and Prof. P. Jayaprakash Rao, Dean, Development and UGC Affairs, Osmania University. Last but not the least, all our colleagues in the Department of Economics are always cooperative and helpful. We express our thanks to all of them.

PROF. B. SATYANARAYAN
PROF. CH. RAGHURAM

CONTENTS

INTRODUCTON

I

The present volume consists of a collection of nine research papers written by Late Professor Gautam Mathur, and published in several leading journals and edited volumes during the seventies and eighties. However, surprisingly, the polar shift in perceptions and prescriptions in the economic field has not outdated any of his views. If any thing, many of the ideas of Prof. Mathur have actually gained in relevance. This may look paradoxical, considering the fact that Professor Mathur's major work, *Planning for Steady Growth* assumed total planning as its theoretical scaffolding.

Notwithstanding the theoretical rigour and a high degree of formalism adopted in "Planning for Steady Growth," Professor Mathur never lost sight of the fact that it should serve as a guide to development planners. To this end, he preferred to underplay the substantial contribution the book made in the field of Capital Theory and Development Planning. If he wanted it, he could have highlighted these in his subsequent writings and stood out as one of the foremost exponents of Capital Theory and Factor Pricing and joined the select band of economists who were involved in the "Cambridge Controversies".

II

Professor Mathur believed that an economy can be made to experience rapid econon ic development, if only proper choices were exercised. These "basic choices" as he described them dealt primarily with what to produce and with what technique. All other choices like consumption, savings etc., would flow out of the basic choices. He thought that economic growth and development rightly belonged to the real system, and hence, production sectors and their inter-dependence were central to his writings. He found the Leontief system to be too restrictive since it does not easily accommodate choice of techniques.

He, therefore, turned to von Neumann's model, which was much more versatile and accommodative to issues which he wished to address. While trying to make the von Neumann model operational, he used the concepts of sub-economies, and basic and non-basic goods to decompose the Neumann system into a string of sub-economies, which was capable of satisfying any choice criterion.

While it is true that Professor Mathur wrote *Planning for Steady Growth* in an environment of a totally planned economy, such an extreme form of centralisation was not needed to appreciate his contribution. Actually, he used this extreme market-form as a means to isolate his model from the complexities of actual market place so as to highlight the importance of identifying proper choice of strategy of development.

It is fruitless to criticize his model on the ground that it is far removed from reality and that it cannot be implemented—a point of view often expressed by those who did not care to read his later works. Two arguments that can be marshalled in his defence are : (a) his transparent concern for egalitarianism; and (b) his later works which mainly dealt with the instruments of implementation.

Professor Mathur's approach to economic development was essentially humanitarian. Egalitarianism was an article of faith for him. He never liked the slogan, "produce! produce!". Instead, he asked, "produce what? and for whom?". An egalitarian society, for him, was coterminous with a just society, and all the economic policies must be trimmed in that direction.

Professor Mathur was convinced that an egalitarian society does not conflict with high rate of economic development. Actually, his Heavy Investment Strategy of Development shows that a high rate of economic development is not only compatible with egalitarianism, but the latter is a precondition for the former.

The concept of economic justice, defined this way, should not be confused with equalitarianism. Actually, to his great credit, while using the von Neumann model (for a purpose other than the one intended by the original author), he surmounts the temptation of making the assumption of equalitarianism which is implicit in the von Neumann model.

If the objective is to establish an egalitarian society, certain preconditions have to be satisfied. These take the form of Basic Choices in economic development. They are : (a) choice of goods dealing what goods should be produced; and (b) what techniques to use in their production. While in a perfect command economy, these are directly implementable in a market economy, they remain as mere prescriptions unless the necessary navigational tools and techniques are developed.

It is this which became the exclusive preoccupation of Professor Mathur during the later part of his illustrious academic career. In his next major work, *Disparity Taxation in a Composite Economy,* he dealt extensively with the requirements of an egalitarian society, and more importantly with the tools needed to navigate, what he called a Composite Economy.

A mixed economy becomes a Composite Economy when two major economic participants, the Public and the Private Sector, work together towards a common purpose. This is unlike the compartmentalised mixed economy (as was witnessed in India till recently) characterized by mutual suspicion and exclusion. The only major precondition for the establishment of a Composite Economy was the presence of a Firm State, which is an intermediate between the Hard and Soft States, described by Myrdal.

A reading of this and the later works shows how far-sighted Professor Mathur was. The prevailing philosophy of coopting the private sector in economic development under the present liberalisation regime is precisely what he advocated more than twenty years back. Actually, the essence of his argument was that if the private sector was barred entry into critical areas, it would be forced to invade inessential sectors and distort the production spectrum. It would have an inhibiting effect on growth as physical resources get diverted from use in the priority sectors. He tended to blame the policy makers for the low growth and under performance muddle in which the economy found itself, before liberalisation *mantra* was discovered.

Professor Mathur's argument was that the productive capacity of the private sector should be used to attract additional capacities in the essential and infrastructural activities. This can be done by offering suitably tailored incentives and disincentives. A Firm State should and can develop such navigational tools, which is a mix of fiscal and monetary instruments. Reliance will be placed on using the market as an allocator, but the market itself will be made to tilt the profitability in favour of activities considered essential for economic development.

By doing so, Professor Mathur replaced a centralised State machinery with a more sophisticated one capable of using the strengths of the market for common good. This is still far ahead of the present day liberalisation attempts, since his scheme revolves around allocations which satisfy the basic choices and which help economic development. Throughout his works, he never lost sight of the need to eradicate underdevelopment.

Professor Mathur always held that it is the real resources which are vital for economic development and not monetary ones. This is not to plead for barter. It is also not a plea for underplaying the importance of finance. What he sought to do was to place finance in its proper role, namely; a facilitator. Not surprisingly, therefore, he relied more on fiscal instruments to trigger changes in the rates of profits and motivate investment flows in desired directions. This is in contrast to the present day liberalisation with its accent on financial markets. In other words, one has to appreciate the difference between purposive and directionless liberalisation.

Professor Mathur believed that even when reliance is placed on the market forces, the basic problems stemming out of under-development should not be lost sight of. Hence, the Firm State must have a proper strategy, which is itself-dependent on the endowments a country has. A strategy based on the endowments is advocated since there would be fewer bottlenecks on the path and growth could be faster.

It is not easy to capture the essence of Professor Mathur's contribution to economics in a short space as this. However, we have endeavoured to present his views with the objective of stimulating interest in his works rather than to give a comprehensive idea. If our write-up acts as an *appertif* we will have succeeded in our effort.

III

The paper entitled "The Economic Policy Choices" (1971) contains eight sections. The first three sections are devoted to a discussion on the issues faced by the pre- and post-Independent India. The author is of the firm opinion that there is no choice for India except opting for a strategy which yields a high rate of growth with social justice. According to Prof. Mathur, the choice is between Heavy Investment Strategy for Growth as well as Social Justice on the one hand, or a complete breakdown of the economy on the other hand. The strategy needs a proper hausbanding of resources and their use in socially appropriate sectors and curbing the tendency of the upper income groups to indulge in unproductive and conspicuous consumption. He suggests that this form of consumption should be discouraged by the use of progressive taxation. This idea was further developed in his ''Disparity Tax for a Composite Economy.''

Prof. Mathur feels that the physical resources and the skills available are the real bottlenecks at the national/macro level. The role of money is downgraded, as it is expected to facilitate the mobilisation of real resources. What matters most is the allocation of resources for non-inflationary, high growth situation. Given that such resources are available, the Government should not pause for want of money, since its supply can always be changed to suit the needs of the real economy. On the other hand, no amount of monetary conservatism is going to save the economy from bottleneck-ridden inflationary growth, if the real resources are not properly allocated.

The second paper entitled "The Regime of the Large Corporation", (1974), extensively discusses the pros and cons of the large houses within the country as well as the multinational corporations. Prof. Mathur was of the opinion that these big houses have a tendency to produce non-essentials which normally give them relatively high profits, thereby adding to the existing inflationary tendencies. The big houses are also prone to use capital-intensive techniques which normally do not create adequate employment opportunities.

In this Paper, the author tried to explain the causes for price inflation in the economy. The traditional theory attributes price inflation to an increase in the quantity of money (read Fiscal Deficit). On the other hand, Prof. Mathur attributes inflation to the unbalanced allocation of expenditures in the economy. If the resources are diverted from the production of necessaries and their equipment, to either long-gestation projects or to the production of luxuries, semi-luxuries, conspicuous consumption and wasteful expenditure, the general price level is bound to rise. No amount of curbing of deficit financing would cure inflation if the ratio between inflation-creating and inflation-dampening expenditures remains lopsided. The use of highly-mechanized techniques in the consumption-goods sector eats into the growth of the Heavy-investment sector and jeopardizes the present and future growth of the economy, besides reducing, considerably, employment opportunities in the Heavy-investment and Consumption-goods sectors.

The later part of the Paper deals with Distribution and Wage Disparities. If a country is economically advanced, its real wage at the threshold of employment is normally high. The distribution of income would not be very unfavourable. In a developing country like ours where the entry level wage is very low, usage of highly mechanised techniques aggravates the skewness in the distribution of income. The author feels that the regime of dependence on the large corporations (whether controlled from abroad or from within the country) militates against the spirit of equalitarianism.

The third paper on "The Rule of Order" was based on the Presidential Address which he delivered at the Diamond Jubilee Session of the Indian Economic Association held in 1978. The paper is divided into eight sections. The first two sections are devoted to dealing with the theories of Capital theory in their historical perspective, which, as described by him were as "full of cobwebs". The paper attempts to clear the confusion surrounding the concept of "Savings". Prof. Mathur feels that it is Investment which creates Savings, and not the other way round. The third section discusses the concept of "The Glass Curtain Economy", in which consumption inequities not only exist, but are there for any one to see. If austerity is imposed, the probability of building up capital accumulation gets enhanced. The austerity concept is also a part of Gandhian economics. The other Gandhian aspect is the need for equality.

Development strategy can be based either on the principle of Percolation or Permeation. In the former case, the beneficial effects of growth on the standard of living of the majority can be accessed through a slow process of trickle-down, while in the latter case, the majority itself will be the direct target group, and production is planned keeping their needs in mind. The former necessarily adopts capital-intensive techniques, which have serious implications for income distribution. The latter approach, on the other hand, can use labour-intensive techniques, wherever available, thus maximising productive employment.

This argument is used to establish the importance of proper allocations, according to a pre-determined strategy. His case for Heavy Investment Strategy is primarily built on his concern for realising the highest rate of economic development, in an equity-compatible ambience. The resultant income distribution will be less unequal. The production will be anti-inflationary in character. It will cater to the massive supply of necessaries of consumption and create large employment opportunities. Some of these factors are discussed in Section IV, which is captioned as "On Multi-Generational Survival".

Section V discusses the role of what he calls, the "Visible Hand". The author sought to dispel the notion that social justice cannot be realised in an economy where the principle of the co-existence of private and public sector is followed. According to him, freedom to run private enterprise is concomitant with freedom to make at least normal profits. Of course, the private sector must be made to fall in line with the national policy by evolving a suitable Permeation policy based on inducements and disinducements.

Section VI deals with Sterilization of Ransoms. Here, the effort is to ensure that income earned are not channelled into conspicuous consumption. The author deals with the instruments pertaining to a Composite Economy. For this purpose, Income Tax is shown to be an inappropriate instrument, since it does not enquire into the nature of activity which gives rise to income. Further, he takes his stand along the side of Hobbes, who argued that it is those who deduct from commonweal who should be taxed and not those who add to it. Given this stance, it is not surprising that Professor Mathur advocates Mis-expenditure Tax wherein each investment is weighted by a factor of approval depending upon the social necessity of the investment and then deducted from income to yield the quantum of notional mis-expenditure.

The fourth paper, "The Tangled Skein: Planning for a Mixed Economy", is based on a lecture delivered by him at the Nehru Memorial Museum and Library, on 26th May, 1982. The paper is divided into thirteen parts. The initial parts of the paper were devoted to analysing the change brought about in India under Nehru. The subsequent parts deal with the concepts like socialistic pattern of society, Fabian socialism etc. He attempted to identify factors that lead India into a grossly inegalitarian stage, which he described as the 'The Glass Curtain Economy', a state in which a small proportion of the total population (say, 10 % or so) enjoy the consumption standards available in any developed economy, while the rest helplessly watch them doing so. Such a lopsided development process would also lead to intra-generational gap and inequity.

The fifth paper by Prof. Gautam Mathur, "Capital Theory and Political Economy" sought to elaborate his strategy model further. It restated his firm belief that unless an economy like India builds up Heavy and Basic industries sufficiently, it cannot achieve the policy of self-reliance. Besides this, social justice cannot be achieved unless poverty is eradicated. He attributed mass poverty to the conspicuous consumption of the affluent.

The author was of the opinion that the Optimum Strategy of Development should integrate the physical and financial aspects together through an integration of Effective Demand and Effective Supply. Reliance on high taxes alone cannot curb conspicuous consumption, as long as the taxed segments can shift the burden to those who cannot shift them further. He proposed a novel tax, named Disparity Tax' with the disparities in consumption as the base.

The sixth paper is on 'Precepts of Traditionalism for Aims of Modernity' dealt with Economic Justice, Austerity and Trusteeship. Here, he tried to synthesize the Gandhian Economics of Austerity with that of the Nehruvian Modernity. It is austerity in physical terms, through restraint in real standards of consumption, which ultimately provides the basis of ensuring growth (by preventing malallocation of physical resources in luxury products). He felt that the manner in which we have implemented our planning has not taken into consideration the basic aspects of Gandhian economics. Nor has it taken into account the basic aspect of planning which the former Prime Minister Nehru wanted, namely: that planning must give us long-term growth in addition to social justice. We neither got a high enough level of growth rate of capital goods for the future, nor did we get enough social justice on any of its criteria—namely; of higher employment-creation, greater equality of personal income distribution, more favourable functional income distribution, reduction of disparities in consumption, absence of shortage of necessaries, absence of monopolism and of metropolitanism, spatial diffusion of industry in rural areas etc. We have thus, lost on both the counts—of growth and of social justice.

The seventh paper entitled "Equitable Transformation for National Integration" is divided into twelve sections. According to Prof. Mathur, whatever may be the emotional appeal of National Integration, it should always be supported by proper economic action. The important points which are to be taken into account are as follows:

(i) It should generate more employment opportunities;
(ii) It should reduce visible inequalities (in holding of land, in consumption standards);
(iii) It should control real inflation;
(iv) It should reduce disparities between regions;
(v) It should try to build up capital for future generations;
(vi) It should give entrepreneurs, as well as managers and workers, the feeling of participation in the national investment and its management;
(vii) It should provide educational opportunities equally to those who require it and can benefit from it; and
(viii) It should provide a comparable basic standard of living irrespective of educational qualifications, and higher talent, or productivity, apart from what is required for each specific job for functional purposes.

The author felt that all these aspects are captured in the 'Ten Prescripts of Equity'. These Prescripts—five of Consumption Equity, three of Production Equity and two of Distributive Equity—are presented in detail in this paper. With their help, the emotional appeal of National Integration will be strengthened and whatever sacrifice of individual benefit is required will be forthcoming because it will be for the social good rather than for promoting disparate living standards.

The eighth paper 'The Analysis of Responsibility of Poverty' argued that poverty is mainly the result of :

(a) Continuance of non-employment; and
(b) Real inflation.

Poverty continues to exist as long as non-employment is not reduced. The reasons for the slow reduction of non-employment in an economy are as follows:

(a) Selection of Inappropriate Strategy of Development;
(b) Adoption of Orthodox Public Finance and Monetarism.

It is necessary to think of measures which will prevent the spread of poverty by appropriate and radically different State action from that undertaken in the past. The composite instrument of firstly, the Strategy for Inter-generational Equity and, secondly, of Allocative Public Finance ensures:

(a) The accelaration of employment;
(b) Of not permitting lack of finances to be a bottleneck to the higher growth rate; and
(c) The eradication of Real Inflation by curbing parasitical consumption.

The last paper on "Social Relevance in Transfer of Technology" dealt with the problems of transfer of technology to a developing country like India. For such a policy to be successful, the criteria laid down were:

(a) What goods are to be manufactured with the help of the new technology?
(b) What is the capital intensity to be chosen?
(c) What place has each of the above in the Optimum Strategy of Development?

But most of the experts do not look at the economic effects in the context of long-term planning. Nor do they study the subject from the angle of social profitability. In most cases, private profits may be positive but social profitability may be negative. The criteria which one should adopt must relate to social optimality—long-term benefit to society as a whole. The author then explains the features of "percolation" and "permeation" strategies. He also emphasizes that the transfer of technology is not a matter of physical duplication alone.

The editors have attempted to capture the essence of Professor Mathur's contribution to development economics through the medium of papers included in this volume. No claim is made for either exhaustiveness or complete fidelity. It is impossible to outline the life-work of an active academic like Professor Mathur with the help of a handful of papers. Considering that he has been a prolific writer, it would be pretentious on our part to claim that our work is any where near being comprehensive. Indeed, that was not our goal when we started this work. We wished to highlight the increased relevance his works have acquired because of the recent "rediscovery" of the market forces and the need to navigate the economy through using the market mechanism. We also set before us the more simpler task of arousing enough curiosity of the reader in Professor Mathur's works, so that the interest in the issues discussed in these papers would become durable. We are reasonably confident that it would achieve this limited goal, since the problems tackled by Professor Mathur during his life time still plague the economy, notwithstanding the gloss provided to it by Liberalisation.

March 31,1998

PROF. B. SATYANARAYAN
RROF. CH. RAGHURAM

1

THE ECONOMIC POLICY CHOICES

I. THE REDUCTION OF DEGREE OF CHOICE

A quarter of a century ago, in the year 1946, our country achieved self-government with an Indian as premier and a Constitution-making body inaugurated. A year later we formally entered the comity of nations as an independent country, with our vote in the General Assembly beginning to be exercised on the same term as any other free country through representatives chosen for the first time by our own National Government. The political equality with most other countries had been attained, but not with all, for India did not have, nor does it still have, a permanent place in the Security Council on the same term as those powers which were considered to be industrially, militarily or traditionally more important to be given that place.

For a long while, the towering moral stature of our First Prime Minister in international politics gave to our country and the ideals upheld by it, a pre-eminent place in international affairs. There was a time when Indian served as a bridge and the only means of communication between two contending power blocks, and a lot of credit is due to our foreign policy at that time in averting some serious world crises and a third world war.

But gradually with the thawing of the cold war (for which state of relative deconfrontation, Indian leadership in International stability itself was a contributory factor) the importance of the country in preventing international conflagration was reduced. The moral stature of our distinguished national leaders, and high ideals would not by themselves carry us far in international affairs for long, especially when it seemed to the outside world that we ourselves, for reasons of grave expediency, had not hesitated to transgress them.

Published in *Young India,* Republic Day issue, 1971.

The stark reality has now stared us in the face that our position in the international field is not any longer dependent upon what we professed, but we could be effective at an international plane only through exhibiting successful domestic economic action. The nation itself has lost faith in pronouncements, when it found a gap between statements which purported to very rightly guarantee that not a single inch of soil that belongs to us legally would be allowed to go under the occupation of others, and the sad results of the experiment in making this plea come true in the case of our northern frontiers.

The other nations have also been watching how we have to strain our economy to be able to ensure vigilance over our borders, how we had been trying (but rather unsuccessfully), to keep up the external and internal values of our currency, how we have not been able to solve our food problem even within one generation-span of self-rule, how we have not seen our way to breaking the population explosion or cured our unemployment of highly-skilled and less-skilled man-power. They could, perhaps, also have noticed that the average degree of utilisation of the heavy investment equipment has been low and that its rate of growth has been at a pace incompatible with the declared national policy of priority to that sector.

In the field outside economies, it is also being observed, how the parochial loyalties of region, language and sectarianism have been growing and engulfing the spirit of patriotism for the country as a whole, how the civil service cannot in general boast of integrity or the educational institutions of profound scholarship, and how a large number of the political leaders have given an image of the working of democracy that is derogatory to its dignity. They have also watched the breakdown of law and order in certain parts of the country and of discipline throughout the civilian sector.

It is a time when serious rethinking has to be done by the few political parties which have an All-India character. This process of thinking should be aimed at taking certain fundamental decisions, which have been shelved up to this time, as we have allowed matters to drift, thinking that time will somehow solve the problems by itself. For facilitating this discussion in the light of the above background, we have to be aware of the issues on which decisions are to be made and this essay tries to describe some of them.

We have, first of all, to decide whether we shall be a strong independent united India or a conglomeration of states each weak in itself with the centrifugal tendency of drifting away from a weak Centre. The consequence of choosing the latter alternative is not difficult to foresee—India will be in the danger of not remaining for long, either politically or economically, a free country; for foreign domination, either through military means of political infiltration (whether from the leftist or the rightist foreign powers), will completely overwhelm us. This is not the wish of any true Indian; yet many of us are busy digging the path to this destination by the most potent instrument known to us, namely; the paramountcy of regional loyalty or community or caste in suppression of the unflinching duty to the idea of 'One Nation in One Country'.

We cannot allow sub-nations within the nation, nor political parties representing the sub-national interest, nor can political expediency justify alliances of All-India parties with others having sectional allegiance, and to the extent they have been made, their character of progressivism gets denuded. There is no choice for the nation but to forge out one nation without any interference of personal, religious, racial, linguistic, cultural or regional differences in political matters of the country.

A few years back we had wider choices also in the economic field, but we exercised them in a way which has led to the present situation of little economic growth and hardly any social justice. The crisis of non-employment and poverty which twenty years of non-rigorous planning has occasioned, will not now allow us many real choices in the ways and means of tackling them. Apparently there will still be many open choices of varied fields—regarding degree of mechanisation, about the rate of ploughback of Heavy Investment, in respect of the type of commodities to be manufactured, dealing with size of firms and scale of plants, among types of taxes to be levied, pertaining to monetary policy, or to rise of wages, between continuing or restricting disparities of consumption, of the vector of allocations to investments, etc.

But all these choices become circumscribed by the necessities of efficient growth compatible with securing distributive justice. Choice in one field has to be made compatible with the constraints in the other fields, so that the system as a whole is consistent. The broader are the terms of reference of our choice, paradoxically, the lesser is the choice which can be exercised, because the wider are the dimensions of the problem. The possibilities do open up but the constraints enter in a larger measure, reducing the degrees of freedom.

II. MICRO AND MACRO CONSTRAINTS

As an illustration of the above paradox one may say that there is a choice between large and small scale production in the consumption sector. In this, one has to weigh the advantages of economies of large scale and consequent lowering of cost of production, higher surplus potential and greater growth-orientation against the employment creating potential of the small-scale type of production. However, this type of argument is based on a micro-economic view. Which type of technique out of these maximises, at the given wage rate, the long-run rate of growth of the economy ought really to be the criterion.

In applying this, it is found that in the Indian context large-scale production exhibits three properties—though they are not necessarily associated with it in theory.

Firstly, large scale production uses a high capital intensity per man. This is not an essential property of large-scale production, because one can have a thousand handlooms in a large shed, and keep capital intensity per man low. But the equipment used in actuality is highly capital-intensive.

Secondly, the high capital-intensity techniques use the products of the H-Sector to a large extent. This also is not an essential property as one could have giant water-wheels of Samarkand, of medieval type, which, if prebuilt now, would perhaps require some steel, but much less than electric turbines and tube-wells do.

Thirdly, the large-scale plants in the consumption sector have tendency to make luxury articles. This is also obviously not germane to large-scale production, as the large scale plant can make chaff-cutters, rather than refrigerators.

Hence, in the Indian context, large-scale manufacture of luxuries by techniques with high degree of capital intensity creates low employment per unit of investment, on the one hand, and uses up the resources of the H-Sector away from its own reproduction, on the other hand, thus decreasing the potential for long-run growth. Looking at one industry by itself gives the illusion of choice between growth and social justice. But looking at the economy as a whole shows that large-scale production in the consumption sector (as has taken place in Indian Industry) gives neither growth nor social justice, while the industries of low degree of mechanisation for consumption necessaries (or their equipment) yield to the economy both growth and social justice. The choice disappears in that context, as one of the alternatives becomes inferior to the other on both criteria of choice.

When one decides to survive as an independent country, then one must decide to be an economically strong country where both growth and social justice are ensured, and there is no choice in this case except opting for a strategy which yields both these results. The apparent choice gets limited by these constraints.

III. THE CHOICE OF STRATEGY

Our economic strength depends upon the stock of capital per man which we are able to accumulate over a long span of time. It is this which will give, at a future date, full employment to our people and which will assure for them a standard of living which workers in advanced countries enjoy. The task of accumulation has to be performed now, in anticipation of the rise of the standard of living, for once the real wage of the employed workers rises before accumulation has preceded it, it makes self-reliance and the achievement of the high standard of living at full employment impossible; for it frustrates the growth of capital which alone can satisfy the demand for a higher standard of living at full employment.

The process of accumulation requires that the key industries should be allowed to grow at the fastest pace technologically possible. This further requires that the products of the Heavy-Investment sector should as far as possible be ploughed back within that sector itself to increase its rate of self-reproduction. Any diversion of the output of the H-Sector to Investment in the light-machinery sector which produces consumption goods, decreases the rate of growth of Heavy Industries.

This method of development necessitates that the requirements of consumption goods for the country should be met from a sector which does not require substantial inputs from the H-Sector. On account of a large degree of non-employment in the country, the adoption of techniques of a low degree of mechanisation which do not use foreign exchange or Heavy Investment products to any large extent is possible. This strategy (called the Heavy-Investment Strategy of Long-term Development), allows the necessary consumption and employment to grow fast, but emanating from a sector using capital-saving and H-conserving techniques. It allows the Heavy Industry base to expand fast, but without depressing the standard of living of the employed workers, at subsistence level, that is without causing real inflation.

The nation's choice is not any longer between the above suggested paths or development through the Heavy-Investment Strategy, or alternatively the Mechanised Light-Machinery Strategy. The latter uses techniques of high degree of mechanisation in the fields both of Heavy Industries and industries for consumption goods and also of agriculture. This requires so much capital and products of heavy Investment that it slows down the rate of expansion of the Heavy Industries, on the one hand, and the rate of growth of employment, on the other hand. The choice is between Heavy-Investment Strategy for Growth as well as Social Justice on the one hand, and the complete breakdown of the economy on the other hand, securing neither rapid growth nor social justice—which is what the Mechanised Light-Machinery Strategy is expected to provide. The choice is, therefore, only an apparent choice, in reality no choice exists for it is a case of either following a certain course or continuing to be underdeveloped in the long run.

IV. RESTRAINTS NECESSARY FOR THE U-SECTOR

The next point which the National Political parties have to decide as a national policy is regarding the restraint the Government will impose on the various sectors of the economy. The restraint which has to be imposed affects three disparity-creating sections of the community. Firstly, the unnecessarily high standard of living enjoyed by the members of the U-Sector (composed of management and large property-owning class in the economy) makes it imperative for its inessential expenditure to be severally curtailed, whether it is out of personal income or as fringe benefits given by the employers, or out of dividends. This class includes the company management, the professional executive and the block shareholder. It also includes the large landowner and the richer farmer, the independent businessman, (the professional experts) the senior civil servant and the higher salary earner (whether he is in a firm of rayon manufactures, the airlines or in an atomic research laboratory. It includes the better paid wage earners in organised industry).

The Standard of Living of this privileged class is many times the multiple of the country's median standard (which pertains to the representative individual who stands half way down the array of people ranked according to the 'height of" their quantum of consumption). Our industrial economy has basically tried to cater for this 10 per cent of the privileged class in relation to the neglect of the rest of the 90 per cent who live in circumstances of hardship.

The neo-classical economic theory justifies the production of the goods of luxury consumption on the ground that demand for them exists, and a high rate of profit is obtained by an investor who follows the rule of sovereignty of the consumer. From the point of view of the consumers, the higher capacity to purchase consumption luxuries is defended by the Neo-classical economists on the ground of the higher productivity of these people, or of their efficiency, or skills possessed by them because of higher educational investment in their training, etc. This is an altogether fallacious idea because the earnings of higher skills arise because of the scarcity of the persons possessing them rather than due to personal achievement. In the modern theory of economics (following von Neumann's model of 1932) the wage is not the reward of skills or efficiency of productivity, but is a maintenance payment for the needs of each type of operative. It is a compensation to an individual for cost of keeping his body and soul together rather than a reward or benefit for his qualities. In this situation, the further proposition of equalitarianism indicates that purely the technical needs would create disparities of standard of living only within a narrow band, and all the rest would be disparities stemming from social conventions (of maintaining a higher standard of living) which have little to do with functional needs for the efficiency of the operatives. Thus, the convention among social elites that a dinner party is not successful unless there is a choice of at least seven main dishes, has nothing whatever to do with the nutritional needs of the sedentary community which attends these parties. Under a system of equity, anyone outside the narrow band of functional consumption must be penalised for drawing away resources of the community from investment to consumption.

So also a penalty ought to fall in a graduated progressive scale upon an entrepreneur who invests in lines which further the functionally-unnecessary consumption, as also upon skilled workers who offer their services in industries where this consumption is being catered for. Thus, the persons spending upon inessential consumption (whether conspicuous or concealed), and the persons investing in these industries, and earning a living from working for them, all form a class of parasitical persons. From those who frequent the race courses and those who invest in refrigerators, or those who artificially increase the demand for superfine suiting through advertisements to those who earn their salaries or commissions in these industries and trades, the skilled personnel together form a community which is engaged in mis-allocating the resources of the economy through diverting them from purposes pertaining to long-term growth and production of necessaries of consumption, towards activities creating unnecessary disparities in the standard of living.

The fiscal instruments should be aimed at penalising all such persons to varying degrees. The present system of direct taxation hits at the addition to resources rather than at the wastage out of them through unnecessary consumption. The present system of direct taxation does not discriminate between the approved and unapproved trades from where the income is earned or between the forms in which the investments take place out of the earnings. It has, therefore, proved to be neither an incentive for growth of the product nor an instrument for reducing the disparities of consumption for ensuring social justice. On the contrary in corporate undertakings, the higher the level of funds disbursed as salaries and perquisites or non-taxable benefits at the firm's expense, the less is the net profit of the firm and the less is its tax base.

The Allocative-Tax system seeks to reverse the position and in such a system of direct taxation of the expenditure by a firm (or by a trust or by a public-sector undertaking, or even by a government department), on inessential consumption (from the maintenance of liveried peons to special trains for dignitaries or golden-cars for the festivals) would all be subject to severe panalties.

V. BURDEN ON THE RURAL POPULATION

The second section of the community which needs to be taxed are the agricultural farmers and landlords and peasants who consume the surplus above their necessary self-consumption at the subsistence level. As non-inflationary growth requires a plentiful supply of foodgrains in the industrial areas, after satisfying the consumption by agriculturists themselves (though at a restrained level) the highest degree of attention has to be devoted to the encouragement of agricultural production. But it is generally accepted that in these circumstances, the taxation of the agriculturist will act as a disincentive. Hence some other method would have to be found to evoke larger quantities of agricultural production and its delivery.

A higher floor price for foodgrain procurement is sometimes suggested, but it cannot provide an incentive that would be in keeping with the principles of non-inflationary growth, for the higher prices of food products cause money wages to be higher in organised production, and therewith the prices of industrial goods also would rise, which would not only affect the industrial worker but turn the terms of trade against agriculture through a higher cost of industrial inputs or consumption-goods of industrial origin demanded by the rural population.

The more useful way of dealing with the agricultural incentives is to establish a low procurement price, and along with it to supply inputs at really cheap rates. This would allow a high enough rate of profit to act as an incentive.

The encouragement is thus achieved through subsidising the infrastructure for agricultural development. This requires a much lower rate of interest for purchase of equipment, provision of cheaper equipment, cheaper rate for use of water, free training and advice, subsidised servicing centres for equipment, facilities for collection of inputs and raw materials, or for distribution and marketing of the products etc. These are the proper incentives, rather than consumption goods in the form of transistor sets, and stainless-steel utensils.

From the total produce the part which forms necessary consumption, or is invested for it should be exempted from all direct taxation. That part of the produce beyond the limit of necessary consumption can be taxed in such a way that it allows leaving a higher rate of net profit after tax with those who will part with more of the product and a lower net profit for those who consume it themselves. There is a level of the narrow band of disparity allowed by functional exigencies in professions for instance, intake of calories for the peasant must be higher than for a research professor in pure mathematics, and requirements of books higher for the latter. Beyond this level, the agriculturist must stint himself to provide foodgrain for the industrial expansion, and the tax which assists him in making the choice between eating more and selling, and then investing the proceeds in socially-useful channels is a Mis-expenditure Tax.

One of its schedules allows rebate for payment of tax in the form of essential assets, for instance, shares of monopoly firms or certificates of deliveries of essential grains, etc. This would be used as a further inducement for drawing out more marketable surplus over to the industrial sector.

It is fallacious to think of only taxation of the agriculturist as "exploitation of the peasantry". All development of an industrial character requires the agriculturist to keep his own consumption of the agricultural products restrained from rising beyond functional necessaries, as is to be insisted upon also for the industrial workers and entrepreneurs. It is only that in some forms the exaction is sugarcoated to cajole the unsuspecting farmer (or the industrial worker), to part with his product (or his services) for almost nothing, in return for selling him trinkets of industrial origin like what Columbus offered for the purchase of the privilege to lay claim to the territory of the new world on behalf of his Imperial Sovereign in Europe.

The fundamental problem is that workers in infrastructural industrial projects in an underdeveloped country require food which they do not themselves produce, not own the produce, and if the products of their projects are to go largely for further expansion of capital in the same sector, then there is little left as return to the rural sector, beyond the small input which H-conserving techniques in agro-industries require.

Thus an exaction in real terms upon the rural sector becomes a necessity in securing development. In one form of exaction, the Government takes the tax through agricultural procurements in physical terms without compensation in another form, it pays a money price for the procurement; but the money given ever to the peasant buys for him little in exchange, because the prices of industrial products tend to be high enough to be classed as exploitation of the agricultural consumer. Further, for the supply of industrial products which are supplied to the rural consumers, larger procurement becomes necessary for feeding the additional industrial workers, and this tends to raise the price of procurement of grain. The prices of industrial products further rise and in larger proportion than does the cost of procurements of foodgrains. The adverse terms of trade that this gives rise to is a form of taxation for the agriculturist, exacted through the open-market free-entreprise capitalist system.

In yet another form of exaction the peasant is sold pieces of paper called National Savings Certificates which, even though they bear interest, do not yield him consumption while he has them. In the long run, they get him no more than he would have got otherwise; for the moment he, or someone else, decides to cash the certificates and to spend them on consumption goods, the prices of these goods will rise and allow them to consume only that much which they would have consumed had they been taxed at the outset (rather than being induced to buy savings certificates). The savings certificates, like hoarded cash, represent extra purchasing power only so long as that power is not exercised.

We thus set forth different forms of exactions that are in vogue even now for the purposes of drawing out the producc of the agriculturist, whether they are called taxation or the price-mechanism. The burden of development is a bitter pill which has to be taken by the agricultural sector in some form or another. The choice to be made by the Government relates to how to get the corporation of the agriculturists with the odds of the development process heavily against them. But there is no choice between imposing the restraint and not imposing it, if development is to be achieved, which, furthermore, is necessary if the country is to survivc.

It may be observed that the peasantry will be willing to shoulder the burden, provided its implications are explained to its members well, and provided they are assured by visible signs that the fruits of their refrainment are going for national development and not the enrichment of only a few people in towns and villages, Hence, if others are also made to bear the burden in rural and urban areas, the cooperation of the agriculturist would be given more willingly. The burden will be still more easy to bear if the peasantry is made to realise that industrial development will raise the standard of living of the next generation rather than their own, and, but for this taxation the latter effect can never take place in future. It is futile to promise (within five years) a lot for the present generation—like a house for every household—and then be unable to fulfil that promise. The method has ceased to befool the electorate, and is now only a means of throwing dust into the politicians' own eyes.

VI. RESTRAINT UPON ORGANISED WORKERS

This takes us to the third class of interests from whom restraint is expected for development. This is in the organised working class. The socialist action developed in advanced countries stresses the conflict of interest between the entrepreneurs and the workers and the trade-union organisation serves to give a higher money wage to the workers, in concerted actions in which the organised workers are successful. In a near-full-employment advanced economy, this does provide the means of protection of the working class against exploitation. In an underdeveloped, overpopulated country, the strengthening of trade-union action, no doubt, serves to secure higher money wages, and sometimes higher real wages, for the highest tier of workers (arranged according to the income level) and protects their interest. It may also tend to narrow, but only marginally, the gap between the highest tier of the working class and the management-cum-entrepreneur. But it has three effects.

First, the expected fall in the standard of living of the entrepreneur does not take place—only his investments become lower than they would ordinarily have been, and this easily replenishes by recourse to agencies of public financial support to Industry.

Secondly, the rise of money wages is passed on, in a sellers' market created by a growing economy, to the consumer. This inflation which follows depresses the standard of living of the members of the middle tier (according to the income level of the workers) composed of unorganised worker. It thereby creates an intra-class disparity between these two sets of workers.

Thirdly, if the rise of money wages and prices in an industry which is not very important from the point of view of direct or indirect weightage of the cost of living index, the consequent general inflation in the economy is low, and there is a rise in the standard of living of the organised workers in that industry. Most of the industries of the U-sector or the luxury-sector fall in this category, because their products are consumed by the management within that sector of industries. The rise of the standard of living of the organised workers in these industries slows down the rate of investment. This brings down the rate of growth of employment, so that the third (and the lowest) tier in the income pyramid, composed of the non-employed worker, bears the burden of the increase in the standard of living of the higher tier of the workers (or for that matter, of the management class also).

This last tier is inarticulate politically, and does not have the wherewithal even to subsist, what to talk of exercising political authority through expensive electoral procedures. It would be the moral duty of the sincere and honest national political leaders to advocate the interests of these citizens of the country without any privileges, as the first priority in securing social justice. This is the duty of academics whose views do not have to be coloured by exigencies of support from vocal electoral quarters. Also the concept of social justice in a developing economy dictates in this case that there is no choice but to implement procedures whereby an increase in production of consumption goods should not be in the form of luxury goods which are then concentrated in the hands of the entrepreneurs and the organised workers, yielding thereby a low rate of growth of the economy. Consumption goods should be more widely distributed through a higher rate of accumulation of Heavy-Investment capital and employment-creating equipment for production of consumption necessaries. This should be secured through a constant standard of living and a falling-standard of living of the management* (compensated by a rising level of investment in production of consumption-necessaries with the approved techniques, and rising participation in Heavy-Investment).

The industrial workers, again, like their agricultural counterparts can be induced to make the sacrifices when the issues are explained to them, provided the machinery is brought into motion for this. This first step would have to be for the entrepreneurs to be required to share the burden of development through a fall of their consumption levels in the type, quantity and quality of goods. This would primarily

---

* It is to be noted that at this stage of the author's thought the Allocative Tax System was supposed to be supplemented perhaps by the direct controls. In later thought the suggestion of supplementation has been replaced by reliance almost entirely on Inducive Instruments.

be taken care of by fiscal policy geared at the discouragement of either consumption of or investment in the production of inessential consumption goods. The Disparity Tax is designed as an instrument of implementation of this structure. This is to be supplemented by the licensing procedures (if any would continue) but they would have to be conditioned to a more well-directed policy of priorities.

In an ideal situation, all profits should be reinvested and there should be no consumption out of profits. The income of the self-employed has to be notionally broken up into wages and profits, and consumption should take place only out of the former element which should also be kept constant. Correspondingly among the workers, during the period of rapid development (and at least for the austerity phase of it while non-employment is substantial) a general wage freeze is imperative not only in real terms but in money terms also. However, as a spur to Trade Union activity some form of benefit accruing to the workers should be allowed during a wage freeze. This should be in the form of opportunity and ability to invest and partake in management rather than opportunity to consume and create consumption disparities as well as inflationary pressures. The restoration of real wage should take place through pricing policy rather than money-wage rise. Only for intra-class adjustment of wage should money-wage be allowed to rise.

The second step to be taken is the fixation of a statutory percentage ceiling beyond which no wage award or settlement of a labour dispute for wages is to be taken in the form of rise of money wages, there being other forms for the rest of benefit. The ceiling would be high where the degree of depression of the wage in sweated-industries is high. In industries where wages are high already, the ceiling would be low (about zero for the very high-wage industries). This would be irrespective of the increase in productivity in that industry. Increase in productivity per unit of input in an industry may take place on account of the activities of invention, research and cheapening of inputs in other sectors of the economy. There is no clear demarcation whereby the workers of one industry can be identified as the sole claimants for any observed increase in productivity per unit of input in that industry. In any case the recent researches into, 'Theory of Human-Capital Valuation' show that the real wage is not a reward for effort or for productivity; therefore, in industries where productivity is low, this fact ought not to be used as argument for depressing the wage (and vice versa, where productivity is high). The causation is really the other way around in non-employment situations, namely; that where wages are low, techniques of low-capital intensity are found to be profit-maximising and they also happen to have though it may be higher per unit of capital, lower productivity per man, in relation to more capital-intensive equipment on the spectrum of mutually non-superior techniques.

The third step is to describe three parts of the benefit accruing on the settlement of a labour dispute for wage-rise. If the wage dispute has been settled at a wage-rise of Rs. 300 per year, then on the basis of, say, a percentage share of 33.3 per cent, one part (that is Rs. 100 should be directed towards current benefit to the workers, and this is the only part which benefits the worker as industrial labour. A second chunk of it would be for removal of intra-class disparities of wage. The third chunk should be given by issuing bonus shares by the firm in favour of workers, equivalent to capitalised values of the flow of income with provision for automatic reinvestment of the dividend in specified number of ten years.

The second part and the third part should be taken by the workers' movement and not by the individual worker. They should be in the form of transfer to workers of capital of the concern for which the settlement takes place. The quantum of this capital transfer should be equal to the capitalised values of that part of the settlement not taken in the form of benefit to the individual worker (that is, two-third of Rs. 300 or Rs. 200 per year in the above illustration). Say, half of it should be paid in the form of capitalised values of this income on the basis of current rate of dividend. This should be in the form of shares of that concern. Thus, if rate of dividend is 10 per cent, bonus shares worth Rs. 41,000 would be transferred to the working class in lieu of money wage foregone (Rs. 100) as second part of the settlement. This second part (in the form of bonus shares equivalent to capitalised value of this part of the benefit) should go to the local union which has organised the labour in that industry. The ownership of these shares would entitle the local union to a share in management of the concern. The proceeds of the dividends would be used for organising the labour movement in the other industries in that locality, and providing for reserves for payment of maintenance of workers during strike period.

The third part of the settlement, i.e. capitalised value of the balance of money wages foregone (Rs. 100 in the above illustration) ought to go a Statutory Central Corporation for Workers' Investments to be set up by an Act of Parliament. The funds will be obtained from the Life Insurance Corporation as a capital sum in lieu of the firms undertaking to pay Rs. 100 as a perpetual stream (through the mechanism of LIC buying this annuity from the firm). This Workers' Investments Corporation would get its fund replenished by settlement of each strike and the annual dividends of its investments after costs have been paid. The funds would be invested in the priority industries of the economy to supplement other government actions in ensuring a balanced allocation ratio in the overall economy, between the inflation- dampening activities and the inflation creating expenditures. This would control inflation and give benefit to organised and unorganised workers. The funds of the Workers' Investments Corporation could also be used for collaborating with private enterprise in management, or owning certain undertakings wholly, to be run by first-rate professional managers. In regard to the issue of licences the Workers' Investments Corporation may be given preferential treatment over the mammoth privately-owned corporations or companies, and its operations would be excluded from the purview of the Monopolies Act. This Corporation may become the largest single invester in the country in the course of the next fifteen years. It should be allowed to purchase stock for the purpose of acquiring controlling interest (majority if necessary, or minority, if sufficient) in existing enterprises.

This system will tend to check the disparities between entrepreneurs and organised workers in regard to control of management. It will check the disparities between organised and unorganised labour on account of the inbuilt mechanism of support to track-union movement among the latter and control of inflation through investments to secure a balanced allocation ratio between inflation-creating and inflation-dampening investments. It will tend to reduce at a fast pace the disparities between the employed and unemployed workers through an investment programme in the industries required under the Heavy-Investment Strategy which will rapidly create productive employment opportunities. It will serve to perform the functions of Disparity Tax at a level below the exemption limit of that tax by allowing the incentive to earn and possess, but restricting the rise of the standard of living. It will prevent the betterment of living of a privileged few workers at the expense of the rest of the workers. It will be supplemented at the higher consumption levels by the Disparity Tax which will certainly encompass the consumption group to which belong the non-gazetted officer—from civilian airlines pilots to bank cashiers. It will be a means of the gradual transition of the industrial society from the private enterprise of capitalists to enterprise of workers which is one of the prime objectives of the Age of a transition towards Socialism in a Mixed Economy.

The choice again is in details, but in the broad frame-work there is no choice, for the organised labour movement with wage rises does at present create crises of inflation which is making the working of a planned economy with social justice extremely difficult. The choice is again between survival, and the suggestions in furtherance of social equity recommended above.

VII. RESTRAINING THE INDUSTRIAL MALALLOCATOR

We turn now to the public control over the giant-sized houses which hold the private industrial sector in thrall, as also exert influence over the civil servants, politicians, government, and the press in various effective forms.

In the recent literature on Control of Monopoly, it appears that large degree of concentration of control over assets lies with barely a hundred and thirty industrial houses and large firms. A classification has been done in terms of size of assets controlled through multiple-tier subsidiary companies, and it appears therefrom that only two business houses controlling more than five thousand million rupees each, from the core of the industrial activity of the country. Their rate of growth has been phenomenal, because each of these firm had in the year 1951, assets in the range of five hundred million each. Their rate of growth works out at an annual exponential rate of about 13 per cent. This has been obtained during the total planning period with an avowed policy of drive towards an equalitarian society, and the differential growth of the Public Sector.

In respect of the liberality of our attitude towards monopolies in our theory of Capitalism, for the three planning periods, we seem to have departed even from the classical economic models of purc capitalist countries. In the theory of capitalism as presented in capitalist economies, it is well-known that perfect competition was ideal state and Monopoly Capitalism much to be feared as a condition which makes the allocation of resources distorted, the price level higher, the production lower, and the welfare of consumers and workers also lower. In classical theory of Capitalism, Monopoly Capitalism also freezes technical advancement till patent rights have become legally out-of-date.

However, in the Indian economic practice, these severe strictures in classical economic theory against monopoly elements in capitalism were pushed aside under various arguments. Thus the general ideas which we had, ran as follows in logical sequence. "Ours is a poor country which needs production. The Government does not have enough funds. It cannot tax people excessively because per capita income is low. The savings propensity of the lower 95 per cent of the population is also extremely low. The Government cannot increase the money supply without inflationary consequences. Under these conditions those who have the funds should be allowed to reinvest them anywhere they like; for they create production and employment, both vitally needed by the country. Thus if the large firms have got funds and wish to expand, they must be allowed to invest and produce and give employment. Produce, Produce. This must be our catchword."

Under this policy we did not mind if firms grew in size to become monopolies or giant concentrations of economic power, because priority was given to what was thought to be an increase of production, and as regards the distributional aspects, there always was the rider that once the product was there no difficulty would be posed for distributing it through fiscal means, for it was national asset in any case.

This argument was reinforced by the concentration of managerial skills within the same sectors. In addition, the entrepreneurial and risk taking capacity was with the same business houses. They also had the experience and the capacity to assure any Government official that they were capable of delivering the goods which they must have shown many a time in the past. They also had the power to block the work of another smaller competitor through various devices. The use of this power on a few occasions, demonstrated to many a civil servant that if smaller firms were given permission to produce in preference to larger ones, it would lead to disaster, if one is interested in production. They also had the advantage of economies of costs which firms of smaller size were not supposed to be able to possess, even if they were given assistance as regards finance and certain creation of infrastructure. They also had the capacity to pay taxes, and thereby to facilitate the administration for running the Government through the burden which they shouldered. They gave employment to the skilled and the unskilled, better salaries to the managerial staff than they could get in Government, and in some cases higher wages for the unskilled worker. In many cases, the costs of materials became low, because they were buying at concessional rates from a firm within the same organisation. They were able to guarantee a market to a large number of linked firms in this way. Lastly, they were able to attract foreign collaborations and other sources of finance.

Under these conditions, we departed from the classical model of perfect competition which decried monopoly practices and recommended curbs on monopolies. Hence an indigenous model of capitalism was adopted to encourage production. The Industrial Policy Resolution No. 2 (of 1956) was based upon stressing the role of public enterprise in a mixed economy to be guided towards socialism. Under this, further investment in the Heavy-Investment sector was reserved for the Public Sector to help in keeping the commanding heights in the hands of the Government. The Government was strong enough at that time to keep the private sector out of the share of Heavy Investments in the plans. But it was not strong enough to keep the private sector out altogether, and a Mixed Economy was enunciated.

Now the fields comprising necessaries of consumption were depressed industries yielding a low rate of profit. So the large ones among the private entrepreneurs having been kept away by the Government from the Heavy-Investment sector and being unwilling to go into production of the consumption necessaries, found their natural habitat in the light-machinery sector and in consumer luxuries. It was all right to say : "Produce, Produce:" But no one stopped to inquire, "Produce what?" The Planning Commission was interested in the growth of National Income. In aggregated figures 10 crores additional produce looks as good whether produced in the form of foodgrains, or rayon fabrics. All the luxury goods require substantial percentage of foreign aid, foreign technology, foreign expertise and when these were not available in the desired quantities, it called forth the complaint from the entrepreneurs that foreign capital is shy and although it is the bottleneck to production foreign know-how is denied to them. They tried to show how far we are from a self-reliant economy, and how much we need foreign assistance.

Under the name of import substitution all these were rectified and we gave permission and facilities to build a huge sector of foreign collaboration for manufacturing U-goods. The harassment of licensing procedure and import-trade control were used to discourage the units of medium and small sizes but allowed entry to the large houses who had resources to tackle the problem by short cuts in procedures. In particular the two firms in the core sector benefited exceedingly from the procedural restraints and controls imposed on business in general because they hit others more than these two.

The luxury consumption goods also required a high degree of mechanisation in their production, and a high content of the products of Heavy Investment. Along with some equipment for necessaries they draw away the major part of the resources of our Heavy-Investment into itself became a flood, leaving—it is found to our surprise—only between 18 to 25 per cent (and average of 20 per cent) of the product of Heavy Investment to be ploughed back within itself.

Not only did the U-goods cater far only 10 per cent of the population but they reduced the rate of growth of the Heavy-Investment sector and of the consumption necessaries. They created lower employment opportunities in relation to what was alternatively possible on the basis of production in the small scale from even lesser use of resources of the Heavy-Investment sector. The cry of "Produce, Produce; No matter what, but Produce:" increased production in elephantine proportions in the inessential sectors and affected it strongly in the essential sector in an adverse manner regarding relative growth rates. The costs of production were shown to be low in monetary terms in large-scale manufacture, but turned out to be very high in terms of social opportunity-cost, because we got biscuits at low cost and wheat at high cost; we got cosmetics at low cost and deprived ourselves of steel. We got rubber foam cushions at low cost, but at the expense of gear boxes for trucks. We got refrigerators, but lost cables for distribution of electricity. We used the argument of neo-classical thought applicable to individual firms regarding the lowering of the cost of production in large scale, when it suited the interests of the larger houses and firms, but departed from the basis of that very same model when it concerned monopolism in the industries, or where expansion of the size of a firm drew resources away from other essential sectors of the economy and raised the costs therein.

The above arguments prompted us to encourage the private sector in the mixed economy even if it were to lead to formation of Monopoly Capitalism and concentration of economic power. It was also thought that the existence of a growing public sector in an important segment of the economy was a protection against the ill-effects of Monopoly Capitalism in non-priority industries.

Some of the arguments are invalid from the point of view of economic theory of development, while others have proved wrong on account of expectations having been belied during the later experience of development of the Private Sector. Thus, the argument for low costs flowing from economies of large scale and large market demand are borrowed from micro-economics and do not necessarily apply at the level of national planning. Air conditioners will be made cheaper by larger scale of production and there is a lot of demand for this commodity from the growing number of people becoming rich. The climate of the country justifies the use of some cooling device from efficiency point of view also. But the lowering of costs of airconditioners through larger production increases the use of scarce materials and skills so that we get a thousand air conditioners at the expense of fifty turbines which are prevented from being produced alternatively. The cooling devices of a less-capital intensive character like straw curtains in towns full of shady trees might have served the purpose for another twenty years and not competed too much with the other more urgent needs of the scarcer sources of the basic industries.

It was thought that the industrial growth with the help of large-size firms will be self-financing, and will, to that extent, relieve the government of the responsibility to finance investment. This is an invalid argument from the very beginning, because it also is taken from micro-economics, and is applied to a macro-situation. It is the goods in which the investment takes place and the availability of inputs which is relevant, not the finances, at the national level. For a government, finances are not the bottleneck and for the government to be relieved of providing these seems to neo-classical financial advisers to be, but is not really a favour, for there is no burden to be relieved. The Government can always create the funds at no cost to itself or to the people, provided the goods being manufactured with the new investment are necessaries of consumption and their equipment, allongwith long-gestation investments in proper ratio for non-inflationary growth. Finances are a bottleneck for an individual unit, not at the government level.

The bottlenecks at the macro-level are the physical resources and the skills available at the consumption levels of human capital desired for efficiency. If a plan is feasible in physical terms then there must be a counterpart financial plan which is equally feasible whether the finances are raised from borrowing or from deficit financing. If a plan is not feasible because of physical constraints, then no amount of deposit mobilisation with a rising rate of interest can make it possible to convert it from a writing on a piece of paper to an actuality. Such action (at encouraging savings in money term through keeping interest rate high) only discourages investment in essential consumption goods like foodgrains and coarse cloth (where there is low profitability and low capacity to digest a rise in interest rate).

A savings drive is, therefore, a powerful instrument of reducing the proportion of inflation-dampening investments in the economy, for the inessential goods having a lot of cushion in the profits are not discouraged (to the same extent as necessaries) by a rise in interest rates. No plan formulation which does not seek to discard the notion of deposit mobilisation as a part of monetary policy for control of inflation or revenue raising as a part of fiscal policy, can cope with the real problems of development planning. This is so because it will always be based on fiscal measures which are misallocative (by blunting the edge of the type of taxation which could be allocative instrument), and which will encourage monetary policy which is anti-investment through raising rates of interest hitting against essential investments. It will also distort the attitude towards monopolies by reprieving them, because of an expectation that they lessen the national burden of investment. As a preliminary to action against monopolies we must clear the cobwebs in our minds and choose between classical public finance or development-oriented economic policy.

It fact, the large firms have, in general, acted in just the opposite direction to what the old financial doctrines expected of them for their expansion. They have used up substantially the meagre financial assistance from public financial institutions which could have been alternatively made available to the smaller firms (which could be H-conserving in techniques and capable of producing necessaries, and their equipment). They have used their own resources for consumption by management and the promoter or controlling agents, showing less profit base for taxation or for distributing as dividend to the shareholders (who are generally unorganised). They have invested in production of inessential consumption goods and in advertising their own products. All this increased consumption in the market and the so-called savings of resources for the Government was illusory.

The political dangers of man with corporations are large indeed—finance of elections and consequent influence over party policies, liaison with the civil service and the parliamentarians, maneuvering the appointments of their own men into key Government positions, hold over the media in private hands, control over higher education and creation of the privileged class of the educated with corresponding elite values, etc. But the economic case against monopolies has not, in general, been properly presented on account of the distinguished economists (who have attacked monopolism) being traditional economists in their general thought. The real case against monopolies is not the micro-argument of restricting production and increasing prices which classical economists feared. It is the increase in supply of certain goods and their increased demand through advertisement which is to be feared, for the type of production itself is to be questioned. When goods licensed are inessential, then cornering the license, not producing the commodity oneself, and preventing others also from producing the same, turns out to be a socially-useful activity (rectifying the initial policy mistake of the government in allowing such licenses to be issued at all).

In the last twenty years the government, the public financial institutions, the agencies of foreign exchange control, the licensing authorities, the Planning Commission, the Parliament and the large firms have substantially assisted one another in the establishment of the Economy favouring U-sector — manufacture of goods which are in plentiful supply for 10 per cent of the population, but which the rest 90 per cent of the economy see the privileged group purchasing thus creating (through demonstration effect) the desire which they are unable to quench, as the goods must remain in short supply vis-a-vis the huge population outside the organised sector of privilege. The glass curtain, as it has been described elsewhere, prevents anyone from stretching his hands because the card of entry in the form of purchasing power is denied to the bulk of the population.

The choice is between deliberately and consciously, following henceforth a policy of reversing trends which have created this economy by proclaiming a phase of austerity, while non-employment is substantial; or carrying on merely in the same way in the belief that consumer sovereignty is being satisfied, and finding one fine morning that the non-consumers have shown their sovereignty by smashing the glass curtain.

The choice between the public and private-sector production becomes very much less meaningful when the monopolies control the government policy and its implementation through a whole network of tentacles. That which is produced in the public sector and its management then also serves the interests of the large-sized houses in the private sector. Under these conditions nationalisation passes ownership from directly controlled firms in private auspices to corporations in government ownership which are still indirectly controlled by private hands through the tentacles of the Octopoid mammoth corporations among the core of the industrial sector gripping the economy, its institutions and government in a vice-like grip. In such an economy, the Government itself also earns the titles of an Industrial Malallocator.

If the goods chosen by the Government for public-sector production are going to belong to the Glass Curtain Economy, then public ownership is only an attribute without real content, for the large firms which orient the investment policy of subsidiary companies in the private sector also, indirectly, influence the investment in the public sector. In such a climate, nationalisation by itself is no cure, for the choice is not so much between public and private sector as between the type of goods to be produced. The basic choice is whether we shall have plentitude of necessaries or of luxuries, whether we shall try to reach blankets to those who die of cold in winter, or to provide small cars to 1 per cent of the population.

The growth economist for the mixed economy in the age of transition is not against large scale of production, but against largeness or smallness of scale in the production of wrong types of goods and he is against wrong types of techniques. The production of inessential consumption goods is inappropriate and of the essential or inessential consumer-goods with H-using techniques is also undesirable. The growth economist is not against large size of firm by itself, but exigencies of proper allocation dictate that large-sized firms should be in the public sector or better still a sector where social control of the channels of output is easy to manipulate, namely; Joint Sector with simple majority of government or Workers' Participation sector with a sizeable minority ownership of workers, say, 1/3rd (it being assumed that workers are a but more vigilant than the representatives of a government which is indirectly controlled by the private sector).

VIII. CONCLUSION

In implementing the various policies, various fiscal and monetary devices have been suggested. These are the basic instruments of running a mixed economy with public sector and private sector existing, but the latter having a widely different frame than it has shown in the past. The private sector will have to choose between the forms of directions given through inducements and disincentives suggested in the above essay, on the one hand, and the whole spectrum of physical controls as the alternative. The realization that Government always has the power to supplement the fiscal instrument by way of the physical checks like rationing, price control, direction of capital and labour, nationalization, capital levy etc., and the knowledge that in future they might not hesitate to use this power when necessary, should by itself be a support for the instruments of incentive and disincentives to work. The choice, therefore, for the Government is to reverse the processes of inequality and slow growth which twenty years of planning and twenty-five years of self-rule have given us, by immediate firm action on the finer instruments of economic action advocated above.

These are some issues which, though it has been found to be difficult to decide to take firm action upon, yet are believed to be fundamental for survival. The choices are restricted by the constraints in which only the details can now be open to choice, for the fundamental policy of economic development is also the policy for survival of the nation as a free country; and for that there is not much choice as regards what needs to be done. Deliberate decision is to be taken in a bold fashion on the implementation of the choices at national level; for the problem will not get solved by shelving it, or closing one's eyes upon seeing it. In case of delay would reap the fruit of our indecisions in the form of social and industrial unrest, of lower production of the essential goods, and consequent political instability.

2

THE REGIME OF THE LARGE CORPORATION

I. THE NEED FOR RE-EVALUATION

During the past year one can notice that certain tendencies are afoot which might result in effecting some major changes of national policy in the direction of allowing freer play of forces that will increase the concentration of economic power in private hands.

These tendencies are reinforced by the advice regarding the possibility of considering a change of policy towards the large corporations coming from a group of distinguished economists of the nation's capital town, as also independently from administrators of undoubted competence, and men of eminence in public affairs. They have been impressing upon the Government the desirability of attending to arguments which stress the great economic benefits which would be reaped for the sake of the country by allowing rapid expansion of the productive capacity of the large corporations within the country, and others of multinational nature to be invited from abroad to invest in the country.

This was augmented by some citizens of "credit and renown" belonging to the field of industry emphasising that the large houses within the country would themselves be able to finance development plans substantially, so as to reduce dependence of the government on deficit financing, and thus they would also be able to expand production to compact inflationary pressures. These attitudes on the whole tend to highlight the beneficial effects of the large corporation, be it multinational or indigenous. As the ostensible production record of some of these large houses in this country and abroad is impressive, the attitude favouring them will lend a certain degree of weight , and on its face, appear to be acceptable for the national good.

However, apart from the obvious political dangers involved

Published in *Young India*, Independence Day Issue,1974.

there are certain serious differences with this approach amongst economists themselves, as to the significance of the achievements of the larger corporations for a country committed to a policy of growth with social justice, and the detrimental economic consequences which this expansion might result in, for achieving the social and economic objectives outlined in our plans of development.

It is, therefore, not without reason that there is a deep sense of concern regarding these tendencies amongst a large section of economists spread all over the country. These economists may be having different political views; they may be belonging to different schools of economic thought; they are unorganised and uncoordinated, and do not have organisations supporting them by virtue of which their point of view, could have been expressed in unison in a quick manner. Nevertheless, it is undoubtedly true that there is a consensus of opinion amongst the economists of the country in general, including the more representative sections of the economists of the metropolis, that a change of direction of national policy in this major field would be of grave danger to the realisation of the hope of formation of an economic democracy dedicated to the principles of equality and social justice combined with growth. It is, therefore, the duty of economists who are sensitive to the dangers of a change of policy in an undesirable direction, to speak out at this juncture, and to apprise the members of the public, their representatives and the government (which, one is sure, is having an open mind on this issue) that there is need to be forewarned about the dangers inherent in accepting the advice of taking such government action which will strengthen the tendencies towards concentration without regulatory control over expenditure, and that there are some serious economic issues involved which span the whole sphere of economic policy. The arguments in support of the removal of restrictions on the expansion of the large corporations hide some of the features which would lead the economic life of the country away from the path of rapid development in addition to affecting social justice adversely.

II. COST-PUSH AVENUES OF FINANCE

In the first instance, because the large corporation, through its supply of finance, is supposed to combat inflation by removing the pressure on forces leading to increased deficit financing, we ought to remove from our minds the cobwebs regarding the causes of the present inflation, the origin of which is attributed to deficit financing or an increase in the quantity of money. It must be understood clearly that inflation is caused by the unbalanced allocation of expenditures by the Government, by the public sector enterprises and the private sector taken together, in lines which create inflation through diversion of resources from the production of necessaries and their equipment, to either long gestation projects or defence or to the field of semi-luxuries, luxuries, conspicuous consumption, and wasteful uses.

When blaming deficit financing for inflation, it is forgotten that for incurring the latter types of expenditures and with the consequent diversion of physical resources from the production of necessaries, the immediate inflationary impact would be equally great if they were to be financed by borrowing from the general public, or through the provision of finances from business houses. The effect of borrowing from the public would be worse in later periods when interest payments have to be doled out, because they would create income (and hence, consumption expenditure) without any mechanism of ensuring simultaneous production.

A policy of depending upon financing a plan of development mainly through borrowings from the public has two alternative direct consequences—either a high rate of interest without any restriction on the credit, or restrictions making funds available to only a few categories of uses, or persons, but at a cheap rate.

If a sufficient volume of funds are to be raised for utilising the physical resources of the economy till the limit of feasibility for their full utilisation during a time period is reached, this results in raising the rate of interest in the economy for loans. Such a phenomenon has three further effects. Firstly, it reduces the quantum of investment and hence, cuts down the rate of growth of production and employment opportunities, as well as reducing the utilisation possibility of physical resources, which are consequences which were sought to be avoided when one raised the rate of interest to attract enough funds to finance the development plan to the full.

Secondly, the high rate of interest shifts the physical allocations towards investments in luxuries from investments in necessaries, because the gross rate of profit is higher in producing the former. It also transpires that whereas the luxuries can absorb a small rise in the rate of interest, it hits the low profit investments in necessaries very severely. This not only militates against social justice, but also causes the inflationary situation to worsen, which is again what was sought to be avoided when the plan was financed from borrowings from the public rather than deficit spending through creation of cash (directly or through borrowing from the central banking system — both of them creating a base for further credit expansion).

Thirdly, a high rate of interest policy deals unevenly with the type of borrower. Whereas the large corporation as well as those who have access to unaccounted money, are capable of finding finance from their own sources and insulating their investment policy from the ill-effects of a high rate of interest, the small borrower who depends purely on assistance from financial institutions is unable to afford borrowing of funds for essential investment at the high rate quoted. This contravenes the principle of social justice which was the very thing which an anti-inflationary policy (through the supposed remedy of borrowing rather than deficit financing) seeks to avoid. Further, this has ramifications in regard to increase of monopolistic elements in the market, a greater skewness in the distribution of income, an effective demand pattern oriented more towards luxuries, and consequent diversion of physical resources away from necessaries of production leading to a high degree of further inflationary potential.

If the rates of interest are not raised, then sufficient funds are not made available from deposit mobilisation to finance the plan, and hence, employment opportunities are curtailed as well as physical resources remaining unutilised, while the rate of growth of the economy falls below its potential at a given rate of technical knowledge. There has also to be, in this case, a restriction on credit, because it is going to be scarce. In such a situation also the large borrower has a better deal than the smaller one, because from all the principles of so-called sound management on the basis of which the efficiency of the branch manager of a bank is to be judged, he must show favour to large parties as regards giving various facilities, including offering to give them loans at the minimum rate of interest allowed by the Reserve Bank, as well as making the largest practicable quantum of credit to be made available to them, lest they shift their current and deposit accounts to some other branch or another bank. The large borrower also is usually a part of greater ability to show security, and the possibility of liquidating the loan automatically because of the high rates of return expected from the transactions which he undertakes.

Hence, the smaller parties are denied credit in practice, even though all government pronouncements are in their favour. They are either forced to abandon investment projects or to finance them from private money-lending sources at high rates of interest. This not only oppresses them, but enriches the money-lending sources, causing a greater skewness in income distribution along with its accompanying effects of higher demand for luxuries diverting the resources from the anti-inflationary channels of production of necessaries. Hence, the high rate of interest which was originally sought to be avoided through a credit rationing policy, comes in through the backdoor and produces, in effect, similar consequences.

In an actual situation, the two alternatives of a high rate of interest policy and a credit-rationing policy are both put into operation to some extent by the Government at the same time, and, therefore, the effects of both of them are felt, and as they work in the same direction, they aggravate the situation. A policy of financing a plan of development by relying upon borrowing from the public is thus one of the most potent weapons which government can put into operation for inflicting inflation upon the economy, absolutely contrary to what the traditional theory as advocated by some eminent economists, and as used by the government, indicates.

The inflation thus created by malallocations of expenditure and aggravated by financing through borrowing from the public, is fed by consequent rise of money wages and costs, and under traditional economics, the further attempts to remedy it by financing higher expenditure of the government through more borrowings (or through the type of taxation which tends to raise revenue rather than being an effective instrument for shifting allocations) enhances the inflation. The government becomes a prisoner of the instruments which it uses; and the more the flames shoot up, the more the nozzle in the Government's hand spurts out oil (rather than water). Under these constraints the fire can never be contained.

III. COST-REDUCING ELEMENT

It is unfortunate that following some theories of money (which had long ago been formulated abroad under the assumption of a static unplanned economy and applied blindfoldedly to an economy where the primary feature is growth and that also under a planned system), attention of the public and the government has been systematically diverted by traditional economists from these real causes of inflation which attach importance to the unbalanced distribution of expenditures, and has been brought to focus on forms of finance, and isolation of deficit financing to be condemned in particular by making it a scapegoat. But no amount of curbing of deficit financing would cure inflation if the ratio between inflation creating and inflation-dampening expenditures remains lopsided — as it has hitherto been. Conversely, no amount of deficit financing for investments within the limit of the physical resources which the endowments of the economy allow (in the form of land, mineral resources, capital equipment, employed and unemployed manpower skills), could generate real inflation if expenditures in the two directions were in balanced proportion.

It ought to be clearly understood that expansion of money to any extent (for investments within the constraints of physical resources) cannot create an inflationary situation if the allocation ratio is made to be different and more weighted towards expenditures of a quick-yielding nature for the purposes of necessaries of consumption rather than against them. Not only is deficit financing to be exonerated from direct responsibility for inflation, but its judicious use is to be highly commended, for when used for the different types of expenditures in the correct ratio, to any extent feasible physically, for the two in complementarity, it is a powerful instrument for the control of inflation as well as for achieving the objectives of growth and social justice.

The achievement of a high rate of growth depends upon the expansion of investment which can be carried out only if, correspondingly, the necessaries of consumptions are increased, in order to supply the demands which are created by the incomes generated by the extra investments. This huge increase of supply of necessaries to support rapid development and a high rate of investment can come about only if the low profitability usually encountered in the field of the necessaries is countered by inducements to invest. This depends upon monetary and fiscal policy discouraging investment in non-essentials and encouraging them in the essential activities.

Because the production of necessaries of consumption requires massive programmes of widespread and diffused activities, they can be organised best through very small operatives dispersed over the countryside and small towns.

This policy requires a substantial creation of credit reducing the interest rate, for helping the production of necessaries through operatives who are not already in possession of wealth, like the small farmer and the small producer of necessary consumption goods and of their equipment. For this purpose, deficit financing can be the only source of provision of funds for the programme of investments—at low cost and as large as will be required in the country as a whole. This is so because we are faced with a situation in which, alternatively higher borrowings from the public would require higher and higher rates of interest, which would further bring down the profitability in the lines of necessaries of consumption, considerably more than in the fields producing luxuries.

We are also faced with the probability that the expansion of government revenue through the tax system would require putting such taxes which effect more and more the poorer sections of the public either directly (as with commodity taxes* on essentials) or through the burden of taxation passed down by the richer producers through higher prices, or reduction in investment as also a decline in the possibility of further creation of employment.

With such a state of affairs, if deficit financing is rejected as a valid avenue of providing finances, the economy is left with no instrument whereby the programme of increase of necessaries may be sustained in order that the rapid expansion of investment necessary for growth may take place. Along with this, there would be no instrument whereby the smaller operative could be supported, and hence the moment we decry deficit-financing and accuse it wrongly of causing inflation, we are depriving ourselves of the most important means of raising finance which we have got in our economic system of ensuring growth with social justice.

If the doctrine of non-inflationary finance (that cash created and expended in a manner generating a balance between inflationary and

---

* To note that from 1973-74 there exactions are referred to as imports, not as taxes, which term is reserved for an imposition with a specific social purpose, rather than raising general revenue.

non-inflationary activities is free from dangers of inflation) is to be rejected, then we would be attenuating the power of the only feasible method of planning in a mixed economy. We would also be virtually throwing overboard the attainment of growth and social justice along with it.

If, on the other hand, we accept method of selective deficit-financing for balanced allocation, then we do not have to rely upon the savings of large corporation to finance our development, for this finance is dearly bought by the economy.

IV. INAPPROPRIATE CHOICES OF GOODS AND OF TECHNIQUES

Having disposed of the argument that the large corporation is desirable for providing finances because the alternative of deficit financing is supposed to be inflationary, we go on from here to note that the argument against the large corporation flows from four basic angles.

Firstly, in an economy where self-reliance is a goal of short-term policy, the difficulties stem from the choice of goods which the large corporations make.

Secondly, there is the question of the choice of degree of mechanisation of the techniques which are used by the large corporations.

Thirdly, one should be aware of the distribution of income which is created by them.

Fourthly, there is the problem of the creation of concentration of economic power in a few hands with the possibility of affecting the already accepted national policies of the Government.

We shall take the first two in this section.

In the first instance, when it is said that the large corporation has got a fine record of production, the clarification is generally missed out as to what elements constitute the spectrum of production. In an economy oriented towards social justice, there is no meaning to be attached to the aggregate index of industrial production. This is because the composition of the production as to the types of goods in terms of social relevance is an all-important consideration. The large corporation no doubt produces goods in large quantities, but the goods it tends to produce are those which give high profitability rather than high social benefit.

With regard to the constituents of the Heavy-Investment Sector and the infrastructure, the social profitability of investment is exceedingly high but the profitability actually achieved tends to be low, particularly where the prices of the end-products ought to be kept at a reasonably low level, as in the case of electricity undertakings, or public transport.

In the sector for consumption-goods greater profits can be earned by producing goods which cater to the demand of the section of population which is capable of paying whatever prices are charged, and this comes to be the effective consumption for the top 5 to 10 per cent of the population constituting the 'Glass-curtain Economy', and pertains to goods which can be classified as semi-luxuries, or luxuries and their equipment. The large corporation does not usually undertake (nor does it normally have programmes and plans for undertaking) the investments in necessaries for the common man—unless the meaning of the term necessaries is distorted as to include products like stainless-steel utensils, transistor sets, breakfast foods, cosmetics, bottled soft drinks, etc. (which are sometimes paraded as the common-man's goods but which according to our distribution of consumption would substantially pertain to the inessential consumption by the top quartile of the population).

No doubt, the large corporation provides finances for production, but with those finances it buys resources which should have otherwise gone into necessaries, and invests them in highly profitable non-essentials. For instance, the large corporation may affect the activities producing foodgrains and their inputs by depriving them of physical resources and organisational and technical skills and it may use them for grape-gardening or production of intoxicants. It may take up the manufacture of refrigerators and jumbo-jets (for trains part of the most affluent) and the production records may be shown to be very impressive indeed, but the manufacturing skills and essential materials like aluminium would have been diverted from some proper use which would perhaps have been in power lines for the distribution of electricity to villages (through a national network which would have prevented droughts from affecting agricultural production in any part of the country).

It is the undiscerning economist who is impressed with the statistics of high production-achievements of the large corporation, and who misinterprets the production as one which is capable of increasing the supply of those goods which are really the key ones for controlling inflation. No doubt, the supply of certain types of luxury and semi-luxury commodities would increase rapidly under the regime of expansion of the large corporation. But it is not the increase of supply of these types of goods which are relevant for the control of inflation. The argument of the increased supply of finance by them to produce consumption goods, has been misapplied without bringing out clearly before the public what are the types of goods which the corporations are likely to seek to foster in the economy.

Secondly, the large corporation by the nature of its organisation goes in for a very high degree of mechanisation. When techniques of a high degree of mechanisation are used in the consumption sector, they draw heavily upon the resources of the Heavy-Investment Sector. But in an economy which is on the path of rapid development for becoming as self-reliant economy (as well as entering, within the foreseeable future, in the ranks of economically-advanced countries) it is imperative that the Heavy-Investment base must be exceedingly high and the growth of that sector should take place at the highest pace which technology allows. This makes it necessary for a high feedback of the products of the Heavy-Investments Sector for its own production and for the production of improved technology within that sector itself.

Any diversion from the production of Heavy-Investment here is a leakage of the valuable product of the Heavy-Investment sector for uses where alternative methods of production are available. Their processes are in the form of techniques with a low degree of mechanisation which conserve the use of the scarce resources like products of the Heavy-Investment Sector and foreign exchange.

The use of highly-mechanised techniques in the Consumption goods sector, not only reduces the growth of Heavy-Investment sector and jeopardises the present and future growth of the economy, but it reduces considerably the employment opportunities in the Heavy-Investment and Consumption-goods sectors and causes the continuance of the malaise which afflicts the economy in the form of a growing level of non-employment. Hence, the regime of the large corporation not only is incapable of evoking the production of goods which being necessaries are the key factor in the control of inflation, but it is also incapable of solving the problem of unemployment in the country through its choice of a degree of mechanisation in the Consumption-goods sector, which stultifies the growth of the Heavy-Investment sector and reduces employment opportunities in that sector and in the Consumption-goods Sector, both.

V. UNFAVOURABLE DISTRIBUTION

Now we come to the third main consequence of dependence upon a regime of large corporations which is regarding the distribution of income which such an economy generates. Not only from the point of view of the power which these corporations possess of charging prices which increase the element of surplus in relations to costs, the very nature of the techniques which they adopt is biased towards the ratio of profit to wages being exceedingly high in an economy with a wage near the subsistence level. Hence, in such a regime the distribution of income becomes more and more skewed in favour of the richer sections of the population.

The effect of this enhancement of inequality of wealth and income is felt in the consumption demand which it generates in favour of the luxury and semi-luxury commodities. In a regime whereby the planning authorities fix the target in response to demand for certain goods made by a section of the market backed by high purchasing power, these commodities get an unduly large proportion of finance allocated to them from Government financial agencies. Thereby, they divert physical resources from the production of necessaries which are unable to command the finance in a correspondingly liberal manner. In that manner also they aggravate the inflationary situation in the country and also create social tensions through wide disparities of consumption standards both in regard to amounts of consumption goods, and in the nature of the goods consumed.

If a country is economically advanced and its real wage at the threshold of employment is also considerably high, perhaps the distribution of income would not have been so unfavourable. But the real wage in the country existing at the moment for people who are on the verge of entering employment is very low compared to the wage level for which the highly mechanised forms of production were designed in the advanced countries. The highly-mechanised techniques aggravate the element of unfavourableness in the distribution of income which is attributed to the large houses even in advanced countries on accounts of restrictive practices. Hence, the highly mechanised techniques become totally inappropriate (for the wage rate prevalent) on grounds of low profitability in relation to what is attainable if the organisation of production with less-mechanised techniques was undertaken with substantial attention by the government (rather than with half-hearted condescension).

There is, further, the ground that the factor endowments in the country indicate a strategy for priority to Heavy-Investments which, in order to be successful must conserve the resources of the Heavy-Sector for its own expansion. Hence the strategy would allow only a small proportion of its product to be leaked out to the consumption sector, thereby compelling the latter to use H-conserving techniques which happen to be of low of income. Such techniques would create more employment and a more favourable distribution degree of mechanisation.

There is an argument advanced by many economists that because of the economies of scale, costs will be reduced, and hence prices will go down when large-scale industry is encouraged. This, it is implied, will cause the distribution of incomes to become more favourable to the workers.

These economies of large scale do tend to reduce costs and as a result prices, but this effect is applicable to an individual unit in a competitive market. It is not applicable to a monopolistic or semi-monopolistic situation; for the real costs to the economy may be exceedingly high, because the larger the scale of production in monopolistics or oligopolistic situations, the larger is the amount of diversion of resources from other essential uses. Hence, the average cost to the firm is lowered with respect to the size of the firm, but the average cost to the nation rises with respect to the size of a particular unit in imperfect competition. Taken together these firms raise the costs to each other, and hence the prices are not lowered; but, on the other hand, they raise the prices of other goods deprived of materials by the firms in the large-scale sector taken together. This affects the prices of necessaries of consumption produced by the small operator, and is the basis for wrongfully dubbing the miniature scale as uneconomic.

VI. CREATION OF WAGE DISPARITIES

Fourthly, the regime of dependence upon the large corporations (whether controlled from abroad, or from within the country) militates against the spirit of equality (which our Constitution enshrines from its Preamble onwards and which is the basis of the provisions implementing the rule of law). The regime, further, renders it impossible to secure in our body politic the formation of an economic democracy. The move to turn to the large corporation for fulfilling the functions which otherwise the medium, the small scale or miniature-scale producer should have performed, is an escape from the responsibilities of improving performance in the public and the joint sectors outside the sphere of the large corporate enterprise.

The moment we turn to the large corporation in private hands for providing the productive drive in the country, we virtually give up the responsibility of improving the methods of administration in the public sector, and in the Joint Sector. These two forms of enterprise can have systems of organisation wherein performance can be highly efficient and in the national interest, but it requires the promulgation of certain administrative formations which are quite alien to the system of bureaucracy as is prevalent at the present juncture. The system of regulation in the form of audit for running a Government department is completely different in character from the form of account-keeping and performance audit which is relevant to commercial organisations in a development context. The proper system of regulation is being glossed-over because of easy escape into inviting the large corporation (in private hands) to take up production in many sectors of the economy.

There is also no attempt made by the Government to solve the problem of wage differentials and creation of wage disparities by the large corporations. The pull on money wages in general is exerted by the high salaries and wages which are offered by the large scale private corporation. The average real wage depends upon the price level which, on the one hand, depends upon the allocations to necessaries and on the other hand, the real wage is governed by the average money wage (which cannot rise in the unorganised sector at the same rate as in the organised sector). Hence, we get wider disparities of money wages among different classes of workers. The larger the disparity, the average real wage of the non-organised worker in the bulk of the economy will be lower, because the higher-wage brackets will draw away physical resources from the production of necessaries to provide semi-luxuries for themselves.

Hence, it is an illusion to exonerate the large corporation regarding detrimental action in aspect of wage earners by pointing out that they pay higher wages, and hence asking the rhetorical question as to what is wrong with them from the viewpoint of workers. Upto the present time, the fiscal policy which our government has adopted has been quite ineffective in tackling the problems created by these disparities.

For all these ills in the public and joint sectors, remedies exist in the administrative and the economic fields. These remedies lie in the direction of controlling the supply of inessentials through cutting out investment in those fields and diverting present capacity towards exports or for common consumption (like free hospitals, technical schools, cheap public transport etc). They do not lie in mopping up some cash from the public either through its temporary immobilisation or deferred payments as the various ordinances recently promulgated, purport to do. Instead of trying to understand how these remedies affecting allocations would help in solving the problem of growth and social justice, it is extremely unwise to raise deposit rates and the loan rate. This action helps the large corporation and the luxury industries as against the small producer of the manufacture of necessaries. It favours the large saver as against the smaller saver, and it enriches the private moneylenders even more.

Apart from the other pressures in favour of the large corporations, the fiscal and monetary policy is based upon the superstition that it is expansion of supply of money which causes inflation rather than relative allocations. Such a policy will result in a guaranteed continuation of inflation and the prosperity of the large corporation, of its original shareholders, and its executives, along with the hoarders and receivers of income from unproductive activities. There are the only ones who would remain capable of affording the luxury commodities, even at high prices after a higher level of indirect taxation.

There could be place for private enterprise in general when guided under a strict planning system, but the above analysis indicates that there is no place (in the viable form of mixed economy called the Composite Economy) for the section of private enterprise which is based on the large corporation (except if it be under the aegis of the joint sector with Government ownership but private management, producing goods not according to market demands, existing or induced, but for social benefits).

The attention of the public is being diverted from these basic issues by the ineffective remedies for inflation based on traditional theories, and in the process the regime of the large corporation gets strengthened and encouraged to take up a larger share of production in the industrial sector in the utterly wrong belief that they will solve the difficulties pertaining to the present economic situation of lack of rapid growth and rising non-employment.

3

THE RULE OF ORDER

I. COBWEBS IN CAPITAL THEORY

I have firmly held the conviction that Capital Theory is the base of all Economic Theory and without an understanding of its methods of analysis, the economics which we get becomes divorced from reality. The whole theory of money, for instance, tends to disregard capital theory, and it is for this reason that the theorists in that field get entangled in the veil which money casts over the real transactions, and their prescriptions become applicable to the outer covering of the economy only, rather than to the core of reality which Money envelopes.

Since Mr. Sraffa started writing his monumental work on "Production of Commodities by Means of Commodities" fifty years ago, Capital Theory itself has become divided into two categories. The first one, the Aggregative Capital Theory adopted by writers of economic fiction treats capital as a homogeneous mass, as a jelly, a liquid or even as the imaginary ectoplasm. It can be easily seen that this is indistinguishable from treating capital like a fund, and, therefore, this part of capital theory (having its roots in Neo-classicism) is in fact merely dealing with the veil of money rather than with real entities. Unfortunately, many of the most brilliant minds of Europe and America, and of countless other countries both of the developed and the under-developed regions, who have been working in the field of Economics and Econometrics, have, in the aggregate, spent thousands of man-years in dealing with this type of capital theory and thinking that 'K' standing for capital meant something tangible, whereas it is not only as unreal and elusive, but also as evil-eyed as the Basilisk in the Winter's Tale (in Act I, Scene II, line 388).

Published in *Rule of Order,* Presidential Address to Diamond Jubilee session of the Indian Economic Association, reprinted in the *Indian Economic Journal,* Vol. 26, No. 4 and 5, April-June 1979, pp. 1-43.

Not accepting 'K' as one entity, in the second type of capital theory studied by economic realists, one disaggregates 'K' into the goods required for production, and 'L' into the various types of manpower skills required for the same purpose, and these, along with the natural endowments, are then treated as several different factors of production. In the Disaggregative Capital Theory, capital consists of a host of real entities, and their conversion into other entities requires the various productive processes; whereas in the aggregative capital theory one form of capital equipment is interchangeable with another or convertible into any of the others at no cost and instantaneously. Much of the wrong economic policy flows from the aggregative type of capital theory where homogeneity is lightly assumed, whereas in the disaggregative capital theory owing its origin to Sraffa and von Neumann a hundred wooden ploughs may be equal to a steel tractor in value, but cannot, by any simple process, be converted into one unit of the latter.

From the heterogeneous-capital model forming the Disaggregative Capital Theory, the realisation dawns on us that for a proper model of development, even for broad categorisation, the minimum types of capital taken should be two, namely higher-order capital, (H), which reproduces itself and makes the lower order form of equipment—the Mechanised Light Machinery (MLM), derived from H, which, in its turn, yields consumption goods. Higher-order capital also produces the machines required for complete change of capital structure to a new technology with H+, its higher-order equipment. Hither-order capital, which is the type of equipment necessary for changing the form of capital structure, usually requires a much more laborious process than merely adding to the volume of capital in the economy through reproduction of the same sort of lower-order capital equipment. Capital Theory pertinent to development ought to be based on models which have at least a higher and a lower-order type of capital, and must be capable of answering exactly the question as to how much of each sort is required for balanced growth, so that capital formation in higher-order equipment (steel, power, heavy transport, heavy engineering, machine tools etc.) does not produce a deficiency of the lower-order capital good and consequently of the consumption goods.

Neo-classical Capital Theory (with its aggregative nature of capital) is incapable of dealing with this dual capital investment, and though some of its protagonists use mathematical models which foster the illusion among the unwary that they are dealing with development as a change in the amount and quality of capital per man, the methodology which they employ is to call various types of capital K_1, K_2, K_3, etc., yet at the same time retaining the homogeneity assumption. This is incapable of preventing their falling into grave errors, because to think of a pool of liquid as if it were having separate compartments, when it is partitioned only by wire-nets into various segments, is no substitute for having different containers with solid walls containing different liquids. One is still dealing with a homogeneous material in the pool with wire-net partition.

One of the errors which is most commonly committed under the influence of Neo-classical Capital Theory is to consider that Saving is a factor of production, and that it is necessary for Investments. Even an elementary look at an economy with real goods shows that it is only real commodities and not savings embodied in pieces of paper which can be treated as means of production, and the deployment of these real commodities creates production, both of the consumption goods and of capital equipment. If the existence of these real goods is there, no lack of bonds or bills or national saving certificates should be considered as a bottleneck to growth; and if the Custodians of the Exchequer and the High Chamberlains of the Federal Reserve system fail to supply the funds of individuals capable enough to make proper use of them, it is the authorities who are bottlenecks to growth. If the goods are not there for being used as inputs for investment, no amount of sale of saving certificates (with whatever rate of interest the Federal Reserve Bank may favour the depositors) can add one iota to the investment capacity of the economy.

The causal sequence from Savings leading to Investment towards the dictum that Investment creates its corresponding Savings is the great contribution of Lord Keynes from the early thirties, and forms an essential element of modern economic theory. It is this message which we ought to retain to the exclusion of the mass of Keynesian paraphernalia of marginal efficiency schedules, the consumption functions and liquidity preference curves, with or without the Hicksian embellishments of the LM and IS tracks (which are rammed down the much-burdened brains of silently-suffering economic undergraduates in myriad universities and colleges all over the world).

However, great as is the achievement of Keynes, his model itself was a one-commodity model, and from the point of view of Capital Theory it stood in the neo-classical camp of aggregative analysis. A proper application of Heterogeneous Capital Theory would have immediately shown that not only does creation of fresh goods by Manpower by the use of real goods lead to an addition to stock of each good (which is termed the Investment of the system) but also that Real Savings are no different from this physical creation of stocks. It is not correct to think of National Savings as the difference between Income and Consumption. A nation saves by diverting real inputs from production of consumption goods to production of capital goods. It saves in the form of roads and bridges constructed, of smithies and forges for fabricating machine tools, of plants for tempering steel and manufactories of textiles; it saves in term of building of dams and digging of wells. In short, the vector denoting National Investment itself is the collection of goods (and equipment) denoting Real National Savings. Having so defined and visualized it in real terms, heterogeneous capital theory does not need the term National Savings at all when it has the concept of National Investment.

The continued use of the Keynesian term National Savings in economic theory and policy can only cause the obfuscation of the message derived from Keynes himself that it is Investment rather than Savings which matters, and how to get Investment augmented should be the concern of economic policy. The term National Savings and the image it invokes of exhortations to purchase bonds and certificates, hides the principle derived from post-Keynesian Capital Theory that what is required by the Nation is a deflection of resources from production of consumption goods of inessential kind to the production of necessaries to be currently consumed, and towards the production of equipment for further production including the kind of Higher-order investment which changes the character of equipment to those required by the economy for its long-term needs (H+).

The neo-classical elements in Keynesian thought are not confined to his lack of perception of the redundancy of the term National Savings. The character and composition of Investment also suffered because of the one-commodity aggregative model which he took for his analysis. The definition of Investment itself would possibly have been different if Mr. Sraffa had been successful in impressing upon his friend, Lord Keynes, the virtues of a proper heterogeneous capital-theory model right away in the period 1928-36 instead of keeping it a close secret for full thirty two years after its discovery.

Firstly, production of capital goods which have a zero value for the economy, on a social valuation, ought to be excluded from the term Investment. It ought to be included only in Investmentesque expenditure which provides employment and cause money incomes to grow, but does not necessarily add to the capacity of the economy to expand production. This type of investment could occur from two causes, one because the goods invested in, may be inessentials, and the other because some equipment is produced in a quantity out of balance with the other materials with which it can combine. To produce a heap of nails but hardly any wooden plants, does not lead to larger production of funiture. The excess nails are of zero value to the economy and in producing them any employment given does not differ materially from digging holes in the ground and filling them up again. Such expenditure, though leading to employment, calls for a reorganization of the structure of production to divert resources to making more of the bottleneck goods and less of the undesired ones, which process also would, with the appropriate technique, create equivalent employment.

Keynes himself had referred to employment for pyramid-building to house the dead, with great derision (as creating employment for chanting prayers for the souls of the dead when there were live human beings in need of real housing), and in the Kalesckian version of the Keynesian analysis there is imperative provision for investment to be socially useful. This appears in striking terms in the thinking of the foremost disciple of Keynes, Professor Joan Robinson in whose works social consciousness had been throughout exhibited to be of as high an order as her rigorous insistence on logic.

Secondly, with a proper capital theory, the Keynesian re-appraisal of Say's Law of Outlets that "Supply Creates its own Demand" would have been different. If haphazard expenditure were to take place, the products created need not find markets and, hence, gluts (whether of Malthusian over-production origin or of Keynesian Under-consumption type) may occur. But a proper allocation of expenditures between goods pertaining to immediate essential consumption and investments of a purposeful variety distributed over forms of equipment in a manner that avoids shortages or excesses may be called Effective Supply. When there is Effective Supply there cannot be deficiency of Effective Demand, for this type of supply includes Investment which creates the incomes, and the goods at the same time matched to cater for the demand created by those incomes. There can then be no under-consumption nor excess of it, no shortage nor over-production, no unplanned and transient rise of real wage nor any inflation cutting down the standard of living of the workers. What Keynes would have had in mind, has the proper Capital Theory to help him, would not be suppression of Say's Law but rather its translation into the dictum that "It is not Supply, but Effective Supply which would create its own Effective Demand". In that case, Keynes would have reached very near to the dynamisation of his model which we owe to the pioneering work of the Late Sir Roy Harrod forty years ago.

Following this line we can derive the essential substance of Harrod's model that steady growth would result from Investment creating supply and demand simultaneously. Again, if proper capital theory had been known and been used by Sir Roy in 1939 he would have stressed that this means that a total stock of equipment with balanced mix is required which gives, through an average output-capital ratio, a supply matching the demand (for output) created by the current accretion to that stock.

If I represents the column vector of investments, and K the column vector of stock of capital, σ_a the row vector of average output-capital ratios in respect of each type of capital goods in stock, Y is the column vector of outputs composed of investment vector and consumption vector, σ_m the row vector of increased output-investment ratio in respect of each type of fresh investment, k the scalar multiple of the volume of output generated by investment (post-multiplied by the sum vector of unity as elements), and p is a column vector of prices of goods, then taking care of the direction of causation by an arrow, we have

$$k \bullet I \bullet p \rightarrow Y \bullet p \quad (1)$$

or $$k \bullet \Delta I \bullet p \rightarrow \Delta Y \bullet p \quad (2)$$

and $$\sigma_a \bullet K \bullet p \rightarrow Y \bullet p \quad (3)$$

or $$\sigma_m \bullet I \bullet p \rightarrow \Delta Y \bullet p \quad (4)$$

In case of investment being so defined as to form a balanced vector having the same constituents as the stock of capital (as in von Neumann equilibrium-proportion-vector which is akin to Sraffa Standard-System), and logically speaking only in that case, I becomes Effective-Supply vector. In those circumstances

$$\sigma_a = \sigma_m = \sigma$$

Hence, from (1) and (3), with g standing for rate of growth, and assuming all processes to have same capital intensity,

$$g = I' \bullet p/k' \bullet p \rightarrow \sigma_a / k \quad (6)$$

and from (1) and (4)

$$g = \Delta Y' \bullet p/Y' \bullet p \rightarrow \sigma_m / k \quad (7)$$

and also from (2) and (4) in Domar form

$$g = \Delta I' \bullet p/I' \bullet p \rightarrow \sigma_m / k \quad (8)$$

From (5), (6), (7) and (8) we derive the result that in balanced, steady, growth with a neutral Wicksell-effect technology only is the principle of Harrod and Domar valid, whereby

$$g \rightarrow \sigma / k \quad (9)$$

which signifies that the output-capital ratio divided by the output-investment ratio will always get so adjusted that the resultant quotient will equal the autonomously determined rate of growth.

This is the correct form of the equation, as it indicates herein the direction of causation. The use of the Harrod-Domar formula for determining the rate of growth is entirely invalid, as it is the quantum of investment high or low which governs the growth rate for a given capital stock, and this depends under the assumption of efficient growth, on conditions of non-employment upon the real wage rate, technology and the propensity to consume of the entrepreneurs, and of full employment upon the rate of growth of labour and of technical advance. In neither condition, of full-employment or of non-employment, does the rate of growth depend upon the output-capital ratio or the multiplier (or its reciprocal, the aggregate rate of saving) as the Harrod-Domar formula purports to tell us. Capital Theory again shows this equation to be devoid of any utility for economics of development or of steady growth in advanced countries, and its being based upon the rate of savings can be recognised to be a neo-classical element in post-Keynesian thought.

We have now brushed some cobwebs off from our minds by use of Heterogeneous Capital Theory in eliminating neo-classical economics altogether, and also its unnecessary elements in Keynesian and post-Keynesian Economics, as alien and incompatible intruders. We now turn to the use of Capital Theory in economics of development.

II. THE ORGANIC ECONOMY

Early in history of economic thought, following Simon de Sismondi's dictum of 1803, it was well recognised that the subject matter of economics is not commodities and materials, but Man. But the capitalist system with the egocentric economic man has warped the system of values to give us the concept of individuals motivated solely by private gain. In fact, side by side with the egocentric economics there has been a strain of study of man as belonging to a species and of man as a biological organism. Apart from Adam Smith's concern for man, and Malthusian bio-economics from which was evolved Darwinian thought, Marshall had great insight into behaviour of man, and of organisations which he likened to tree as biological organisms. Side by side, Marxian and other socialist thought had put man's responsibilities to the community, and the use of wealth for human welfare, uppermost. But further researches in this line had awaited the development of theory of life in biological sciences itself.

A re-appraisal of work in biological theory upon living organisms was the work of an Australian Biologist, Dr. W. Agar, in 1951, who analysed the structure of a living organism and its hormic goals or objectives. We can notice that a living organism is a special kind of input-output system which bears to it the same relationship which a man bears to the mechanical system, called a Robot. But we do not find a Agar's Analysis the assumption that the hormic goal is survival of the organism. It was not difficult for us to introduce this to obtain a theory of living organisms which are activated by the will to perpetuate themselves.

With the aid of the biological advance there was derived in the middle fifties, the Theory of Living Organisms whereby a self-propelled system seeks survival to perpetuity. The living organism in developed forms has constituents which are themselves living cells imbibing matter and energy for the purpose of current maintenance. But these cells do not look for their own survival at the expense of the central organism. The constituents are, therefore, merged entirely for the social good of the larger organism to be realised in the form of long-term survival. There is the ingrained realisation of each constituent that if the central organism as a whole survives then the constituent also will, and if the whole entity perishes then the individual cells cannot long survive. In that case, the adaptation of structure for survival in a changing, and possibly hostile environment, follows the requirements of the larger organism, and not of the individual cells or members.

If a human organism is a collection of living cells as members so also the possibility exists of the human organisation, the Society itself, to be thought of as a Social Living Organism. Like its individual constituents, the human beings, a social organism has the characteristics of a living organism in as much as it has a continuity as a whole, although its members keep on being replaced. It does consume matter to convert it into energy for its maintenance and activity, and it seeks perpetuation of its existence, either through its own continuance or through replicas of itself which it generates, or through creation of a higher living organism of which it will become a member cell. Sigmund Freud in 1930 writing upon "Civilization and its Discontents" talked of the ego and the superego of a social community in a way which can only mean the attribution of life to the larger organism. He had made this suggestion even in "Group Psychology and the Analysis of the Ego" published nine years earlier.

The concept of a collection of persons forming an economy as a social organism has been in economic thought since Adam Smith. But this collection is the sum total of the individuals, and, as recently as thirty years back, the work of George Kingsley Zipf deals with ecology of a community of living organisms, the human beings, without itself being a living organism. In the sense in which it can be itself conceived as a Living Organism, it would be much more than the sum of its members, and the properties of the aggregate collection would be widely different, for the interlinking would yield an integrated structure whereby the survival of the whole becomes the prime objective. This is what is meant by thinking of the collection as having been infused with life. In Capital Theory we study merely the mechanics of the Input-Output system. But just as a Living Organism is more than a collection of its cells, Society is more than an economy organised as a system which uses material inputs to produce material outputs.

Following a different strand of thought, Zipf who was originally a specialist in semantics but later turned into a sociologist, showed in 1949, in his work on Human Behaviour, that the postulate of living organisms actuated by the Principle of Least Effort would explain actual human actions. It seems that this principle itself was based upon the Principle of Least Action which we owe to Maupertuis, the French physicist who, in 1744, enunciated it in the course of a philosophical discourse upon the existencc of God. The Principle of Least Action in the form given by Hamilton in 1834, along with the Law of Conservation of Mass and Energy are basic laws of classical physics, and when applied to human organisms they will imply that self-interest is not achieved by profit maximisation or utility maximisation, but by minimisation of average rate of expenditure of human energy per unit of time, to achieve the objective of the organism. The course of history of civilizations as Professor Arnold Toynbee had depicted, can be interpreted by us as showing the search for capital forms through responses to challenges in ways which achieve the continuance of the ecological communities as a whole with Least Effort.

It were these various strands of physics, biology and social psychology which, it was realised in 1955, could be interwoven by looking at an economy as sustaining a Society as a Lining Organism working as an input-output system. The possibility of the extension of the Principle of Least Action to society as a Social Living organism seeking perpetuation was then postulated, and a system of input-output of energy was evolved to conduct the analysis and presented for the first time in Allahabad University Lectures delivered by me in December, 1955. The tract Organic Economics (of which a summary was published in Science and Culture, in 1959 under the title "Economics of the Living Organisms"), seeks to derive modes of behaviour and social formations which will help and hinder the task of survival.

Further work of mine in Capital Theory is a search for patterns of growth towards the same end. Equilibrium leads to the economy of repetitions and habit formation which, in an unchanging environment would find its standard illustration in Gold-Age Economics of steady expansion with unchanging allocations described by Professor Joan Robinson in 1954-56. This can be interpreted, in the above terms, as an expression of the Law of Least Action. But in a changing environment, unless the organism is resilient and ready for adaptation and change of modes of behaviour and structure, it is likely to get concealed in its faculties, or to become petrified in its channels of information and sensing, and to harden its arteries. To keep itself adaptable and resilient, Society must keep on a path of Dynamic Balance wherein Equilibrium and Disequilibrium are deliberately mixed in its course of existence, a theme further explained in a paper presented by me to the Ciba Foundation Seminar in London on Civilization and Science and published in 1972.

In Living Organism which have reached a degree of evolution which is efficient for the purposes of survival, the degree of integration of the individual member with the larger organism is very high. In these organisms, centripetal forces operate and central coordination is high, and each member-cell performs its own functions according to the best interests of the organism as a whole. It is in the interest of the central organism that each member cell be treated with equal solicitude as any other, for the health of the total depends upon the efficient working of each part. No question of distribution enters in this structure, for whatever is necessary is supplied to the best ability of the whole.

When there are centrifugal or fissiparous forces, then the degree of integration with the central organism becomes low. The questions of whether there is fair or unjust distribution becomes a matter of concern, because certain cells or group of cells consistently extract more materials or energy from the rest as ransoms.

A Ransom is a payment obtained by a powerful agent taking advantage of the helplessness of any victim. In a highly-integrated society where centripetal or unitary tendencies are strong, this exaction would not be possible, for the individual entity (or the whole social class from which a ransom is sought to be exacted) would not be unprotected and helpless, because the whole might of Society would be diverted towards preventing the exploitation of helplessness.

In any economy pertaining to low level of integration of the cells of the Social Organism, a situation of exaction of ransom may occur on account of charging of prices higher than that what essential costs dictate and thus cause many to be deprived of the goods for lack of purchasing power. Alternatively it may arise out of membership of a supposedly inferior caste from the constituents of which unpleasant work is taken without their sharing in civic privileges. It may perhaps appear in the form of the landless cultivators hungering for land to till when it is concentrated in the hands of others demanding an increasing rent as population grows. It may occur when operatives look for work which is made available by those who hold the means of production but only at wages below subsistence for them and their families. Ransoms may take the shape of civil officers asking for gratification from the public to do that for which they are in any case paid by the Government (like issuing a permit in a system of physical controls when goods are scarce and the people demanding them many with some at least affluent enough to offer the illegally-demanded fee without experiencing a burden).

In the same manner, demanding or taking from the economic system any payment which allows one to maintain a standard of living higher than what is required for subsistence according to the equalitarian norm, whether it be by organised wage earners or executives or by dividend earners, or recipients of rents or money lenders, is a ransom. The extortion of payments leading some to exist at a sub-maintenance standard of consumption is also classified as ransoms inflicted upon the rest of the economy. They arise (as Marxian exploitation by capitalists does) on account of the economic power possessed by a few privileged individuals whose so-called rights thereto are given legal sanction by our laws, and the temporal power of the State brought to their aid is superimposed upon the oppressive economic power of the individuals or classes.

A well-knit anthropological-community exhibits the attributes of a highly-integrated social living organism with human being as its cells or constituents. It is centrally directed, however democratic may be the means of choosing its commanding authority. It is the high degree of integration which these tribes possess which has allowed the survival of such organisms over thousands of years of onslaughts of alien civilizations or natural calamities. A well-knit country (with spirit which gets exhibited during defence against external aggression) gives vivid indication of the underlying unity of a social living-organism. But it would be a very sick organism if it exhibits the signs found in a country broken up into federal states which look for the interests of their own sub-constituents regardless of the social good of the country as a whole. It makes matters worse if it is stratified into social and economic classes which look to their own benefit and extracts ransoms from the rest. Such an organism is far away from the conditions which will give an efficient structure for survival.

When certain elements of the mass want to feed upon the rest without consideration for the health of the economy as a whole, they sometimes form subordinate organisms of the nature of cancerous growths. The flow of ransoms and goods received by them are to be classed as subsidies to a dependent process (without return of benefit to the main economy) and are in the nature of parasitic consumption. The flow of benefits goes out of the economy, for consumption of the parasites and for capital to produce their consumable goods, rather than going into investment for the social goods which will increase the capacity of the central social organism to survive. Through the latter, adequate support to the functioning of the constituent in an efficient manner would be ensured. The cancerous growth, through looking for the survival of the colony of centrifugal cells rather than survival of the whole, are liable to destroy the whole, and consequently the cancerous cells themselves will not survive, for they are parasites upon the central organism.

The community as a living organism, then requires the interest of the next generation to be as important as of this generation, because the latter is not only the continuation of the former but also because the only way in which it physically survives beyond the physical life span of its present constituents is through the continuity given to the community by the next generation replacing the present. It is important to realise that the democratic system casts upon the elected representatives not only the burden of benefiting the present generation, but an obligation to act for the unrepresented members of the next generation. Too often the electoral system tends to conceal this from the eyes of the elected body, but the difference between Politicians and Statesmen is that the wider obligations and the vision are not forgotten by the latter for immediate gains.

III. THE GLASS CURTAIN

The insistence upon capital theory in relation to the theory of Living Organisms makes us realise that in the economic process money and funds are only a means towards the provision of real goods which are necessary to make the long-term survival of the social living organism possible.

Economists have, for long, based their analyses on the motivation of profit or of utility or enjoyment of gain. What is required is a means towards making the economic action of individuals on the above motivation coincident with that required for creating a structure whereby the survival of the social entity as a living organism is ensured. For instance, the motive to build capital for the future is not merely for the purposes of increasing the material enjoyments at a future date which capital accumulation makes possible, nor merely for providing justice through intergenerational equity, but because the accumulation of some basic forms of capital goods makes for a greater probability of the survival of the community as a living organism over the long run, with least action required from its human members per unit of time for ever after the capital projects are completed and are currently maintained.

In the context of Organic Economics, the function of Capital Theory becomes to unfold the inner working of the economy, so that the structure of capital formation may be adapted to serve the needs of social survival. During the last quarter of a century, techniques have been invented, or earlier tools of analysis perfected, by which the accumulation of capital can be made to follow the pattern required for various long-term objectives. These long-term objectives have, alternatively, included a stable increase in the standard of living at full employment, on the one hand, and a stable non-increasing standard of living, on the other hand, according as the underlying ethic has been to cater for a world of ever-increasing wants or to move towards wantlessness. These objectives have been given on *a priori* considerations. However, it is possible to show that both these are special cases of a more general theory of capital development which emanates from two alternative applications of Organic Economics.

The minimisation of human effort for survival from an individual's point of view creates demand for effort-saving gadgetry whether in the household or the plant. This, demand in its turn, creates the quest for equipment of a capital-investment nature which, further, makes it necessary for investment in Basic Industries to be done. There has then to be a massive attempt, requiring the expenditure of human effort intensively during a short period of industrial revolution, to get a smaller human effort per unit time thereafter. To decrease the number of men who will provide for the food requirements of a hundred people from eighty to a mere five need not cause unemployment, as the others will not only make the equipment for these, but will cater for the other wants which are not as basic as food. At the personal consumption level, an economy of household gadgetry is inescapable if the principle of minimisation of effort operates; and, hence, wantlessness cannot be permanently enforced.

The place of wantlessness or austerity is on the path towards a high standard of living while capital is being built. The greater is the level of austerity which can be enforced, compatible with provision of basic needs for all the working population, the greater is the possibility of deflecting the resources towards the production of equipment. This is one essential aspect of long-term growth in which Gandhian economics of austerity has a definite place.

The other aspect of Gandhian policy of austerity flows from the need for equality. To provide for a plentitude of effort-saving consumption durables is not possible for all households. A policy which gives these benefits initially only to a small proportion of persons who can afford these (in the hope that, in time, these goods will percolate to the rest) is a proposition which not only contravenes the need for equality, but also perpetuates inequality; for the privileged few receive (by virtue of the exercise of their effective demand) a huge portion of the nation's investible resources into production of greater and greater capital-intensive consumer goods for themselves, and little percolation takes place.

The techniques of production for these kinds of consumer goods are also capital intensive, and create a high Profit to Wage ratio. This accentuates inequalities which aggravates the demand for the same type of luxuries the production of which uses techniques which, in a vicious circle, strengthen the inequalities. With inequalities of consumption, the continuance of the social organism without schism is jeopardised. The resentment of privilege by the under-privileged is not because of the power over investible resources, for it is not the power to give employment which is offensive (whether possessed by the public servant or by an industrialist), but the power to command limousines for the family members of the management staff and the owners of capital, while the workers are denied enough wages to afford even bus transport for their children.

In the long-run also there is place for Gándhian austerity explained by Organic Economics. The ossification of the economy which is likely to result from the sole pursuit of effort-saving gadgetry will, of course, give it Golden-age equilibrium. This would continue as long as the environment, both as regards natural causes, or depletion of the earth's non-reproducible endowments (by continuous acceleration in human crunching into them), would require adaptation in the social organism from time to time. A social organism composed of members used to little human effort would not find them adaptable and capable of bearing the burdens for an absolute restructuring of capital when required, and the organism would break under the strain. A state of Dynamic Balance described in the Economics of Living Organisms (referred to earlier), requires periods of deliberately imposed austerity to alternate with states of comfort, in each case distributed equally among the population. The state of dynamic balance in which steady-growth equilibrium and purposive disequilibrium co-exist, prevents the modes of production of the social organism from petrifaction.

With the obligation for continuity which the theory of society as a living entails, the conflict between the present and the future gets resolved through a balance. Too much stress on the future without providing for the basic amenities for the living members of the community would certainly be undesirable, and hence a policy of emphasis on Basic Investments must not be at the expense of the standard of living of the subsistence-level workers.

On the other hand, the denial of the importance of Basic Investments by an elected Government on the ground that the electorate looks for present benefits is entirely misplaced. If it wishes to secure short-terms gains without programmes of Higher-order investments, it would be forgetting the fact that the level of industrial and agricultural activity generated by autonomous investment in the sector of Higher-order equipment and in the infrastructure, as well as the employment created by these investments, are not insubstantial gains for the present generation itself.

Some economists wishing to act as arbitrators between two extreme views upon Basic Investments take an ostensibly middle view that Higher-Order Investments would not be stopped entirely but will concentrate on providing the mechanised equipment for the production of consumption goods for the present generation. Laudable as this desire seems to be, the way this is necessarily going to be implemented is misconceived and capable of being dangerous on two grounds.

Firstly, this is another variant of the stress upon the requirements of the present generation which is presented by the group which can be called Economic Existentialists. Its superiority over the views of the somewhat more simple-minded Economic Existentialists suggesting no Heavy-Investments at all, lies only in considering Higher-order equipment to produce mechanised equipment for consumption goods required at present, as an essential element for success of the present consumption drive in a manner preventing bottlenecks. The vision is still short-sighted and confined to the existing generation. It does not do justice to the economy as a continuum as per what the theory of living organism requires as an obligation to the next generation.

Secondly, it has the danger of leading to a Strategy of Development whereby the products of the Higher-order Investment sector are increasingly used for the consumption sector.

In the traditional community the deprived seldom aspired to be affluent except in fantasy, as this was not a part of the prevailing culture of real possibilities. In a democratic community with equality of opportunity guaranteed by the Constitution, the aspirations which are generated, and frustrated by non-fulfilment, create a perpetual state of social tensions. As mentioned earlier while discussing the need for Gandhian austerity conditions, the goods demanded by the top five per cent of the population are of the modernised variety manufactured with the help of highly-mechanised equipment. The policy of low plough-back within the Heavy-Investment sector encourages large content of Higher-order investments in the consumption sector, and supply is thereby increased for catering to the demand for modernised luxury goods which the extremely unequal income-distribution of the Glass Curtain Economy generates. Instead of a system of Effective Supply of consumption necessaries to cater to the needs of the low-income groups in rural and urban environments, there is danger of the policy of priority for consumption goods slipping towards the satisfaction of wants of the more affluent urban and rural interests.

The policy of permitting Heavy Investments only to the extent required by the current consumption needs, ostensibly sets out to accord social justice to the deprived members of the present generation, but will end up with doing the reverse. The satisfaction of the wants by the only technique available for the modernised consumption goods (which is highly capital-intensive in nature) will further create a high Profit to Wage ratio and will reinforce inequality resulting in the generation of fresh demands for luxury products. It was on account of a policy for catering to consumption demands that the Glass Curtain organism gets sprouted as a cancerous growth with parasitical hold on the Social Policy, and it will get further entrenched with the new policy of apparent priority for the present generation. Just as no priority can be given to one particular industry in preference to others when each industry depends upon inputs of the others, no priority can be given, meaningfully, to the requirements of the present generation, for it will defeat the requirements of current social justice.

IV. ON MULTI-GENERATIONAL SURVIVAL

Contrary to the fallacious view being much canvassed by a section of men of public affairs who are votaries of economic existentialism, it is herein asserted that instead of the policy of low ploughback of Higher-order Industries (as has been practised in our country during the past twenty-two years, and is being surreptitiously and unwittingly continued now under the banner of priority for consumer goods), it would be a policy of high ploughback of Higher-order investments leading to a rapid expansion of the Heavy-Investment sector which would give employment and social justice, not only to the next generation but to the present generation also. The philosophical treatise of Professor Johan Rawls entitled *A Theory of Justice* (1972) gives (on pp. 302-3) at least one of the essential creteria for assessing the furtherance of social justice as the enhancement of the interest of the constituents which are least-advantaged. But the learned philosopher not having had opportunity to be introduced to the works of economists (at least of under-developed countries who choose to reside in these unfruitful climes at a vast distance from the centres of learning familiar to him) could not know about strategies of long-term development which reconcile growth and social justice as for instance, to be found in "Investment Criteria in a Platinum Age", published in the Oxford Economic Papers, in 1967. He has, therefore, little to say about the manner of organising planned growth in which the welfare of the least-advantaged can be secured as a part of economics of development, and how inter-generational interests are to be balanced.

In the strategy for multi-generational survival, outlined here, the Consumption-goods sector uses techniques with low content of Higher-order investment, and thus a very much lower degree of mechanisation results, a miniature scale is preferred, and it generates larger employment both among the wage earners and the self-employed. For the next and subsequent generations, it will give the Higher-order equipment for future production according to the capital structure it will require in a state of dynamic balance with constant restructuring of forms of capital.

As it will allow only a trickle of the products of the Higher-order Investment sector towards the Consumption-goods sector, the use of techniques conserving Heavy-Investment products will enforce the use of other substitutes for products originating from Higher-order Investments as regards materials and fuels. Because it will encourage the miniature scale of production, it will not lead to monopolism. Its distribution will be created in less unequal fashion, in the consumption-goods sector, at the source of production itself

— thereby permitting the State to cease to rely upon the instrument of taxation (which endeavours to exercise a responsibility of redistribution which it has not been able to discharge to any substantive effect till now).

The stress upon Higher-order will thus be anti-inflationary in character, as it caters to the massive supply of necessaries of consumption and their simple type of equipment. It diffuses industry into the countryside rather than concentrating it in large towns, and thereby it avoids metropolitan growth. This type of growth of the consumption sector and the foot-loose Heavy Industries can be expanded easily in backward districts. Because of the anti-inflationary character of the investments they can be financed without fear of price rises. For this purpose expansion of credit and currency would be the most appropriate source of financing because in that case one would not have to rely upon Imposts or Borrowings from public at high interest-rates (both of which generate cost push inflation in the economy).

Above all, the strategy of multigenerational survival creates employment as an aspect of social justice, but in such a way that the growth potential of the economy instead of being dwarfed, is increased (through the rapid growth of Higher-order Investments which is made possible only with this strategy of low leakage of its products towards the consumption sector). It thus holds the balance between present and future consumption. It renders justice to the present generation and to the future it gives assurance of economic strength and large quantum of basic investments with which a vast quantity of consumption goods may be drawn at that time. It yields Inter-generational equity which Society (as a living organism) requires for its long terms survival. It is this strategy which will secure a high count in terms of the Rawls Criteria of Justice.

It is this strategy which uses a large amount of human effort of idle manpower now (for production in the consumption sector) to permit the rapid expansion of the Heavy Investments, so that the accumulation of equipment of basic and light nature that it will make possible for all the workers at full employment and the housewives in the future, will eliminate back-breaking effort and drudgery altogether; and will thus, thereafter require per unit time little human action for survival of the Social Living Organism to perpetuity. On the average, over the long period, human effort is thus minimised, as required by the Principle of Least Action.

It is this strategy which we ought to follow after the failure of the previous one, rather than turning away from Heavy Investments under the misconceived and false expectation that social justice will follow thereby. To give priority to the present generation one should start by giving it to the future generation; just as for seeking happiness for oneself one has to start by giving it to others who are less fortunate.

In terms of the terminology regarding long-term strategies based upon Sraffa-von-Neumann matrices, used in the book *Planning for Steady Growth* (published by Blackwell, Oxford, in 1965) wherein they were first discussed, and in other papers later, the Mahalanobis strategy and the one for priority for consumption-goods with equipment using Heavy-Investments largely, both belong to the same genus "Strategy Steeldams-Tractors-Corn", or "Mechanised Light Machinery Strategy" of its variants. The "Strategy of Inter-generational Equity and Long-term Survival" belongs, on the other hand, to the category "Strategy Steeldam-Ploughaxe-Corn" based on non-mechanised light machinery. It is worlds apart in its effects from the previous type, even now continued in effect, though under a new banner.

Having described the profile of the optimum strategy, we now turn to the means of implementation of the required allocations for it.

V. THE VISIBLE HAND

Social Justice is often measured by the distribution of income after taxation. However, the end-product of purchasing power, apart from the capacity to invest further, is consumption. An economy which yields social justice in the form of equality of income, of wealth and of consumption is very much to be lauded, but it is futile to expect that an economic system based on the principle of the co-existence of the private and public sectors will be able to achieve it. Freedom to run private enterprise is concomitant with freedom to make at least normal profit. Normal profits with pure competition (but without the further attributes of perfect competition, like absolute mobility of factors and perfect knowledge) are themselves sufficient to create substantial disparities in gross income and wealth, where the scale of enterprise is above the miniature scale. If entrepreneurs are taxed at rates which reduce the income and wealth disparities substantially, the motive of accumulation of assets is affected.

To permit the private sector to be continued as a partner in the economic system adopted, and then to expect that disparities of income and wealth, as also of consumption, will be levelled all three, is to bury one's head in the sand. This the policy-making agencies in many countries with mixed economies did some decades back, and they have not yet taken it out of that safe place. It is one of the contradictions of Capitalist Planning with Socialist Objectives; and it cannot be resolved except by retaining only those aspects of each system which are functionally necessary and compatible with the vital aspects of the other system. What can, therefore, be achieved is to get the system of private enterprise to perform the primary function for which it was invented and which is its basic and essential aspect to build up the capital stock of the country, but to do it in the essential fields only.

The essential functions which the private sector performs are not provision of funds or so-called savings, nor the provision of certain managerial skills, but methods of organisation which ordinarily are neither available (in mixed economy) to the Government with a hierarchy of antedeluvian administrative procedures, nor to the public sector with non-commercial and bureaucratic modes of operation. Hence, as long as the mixed economic-system remains as a part of the political structure of the country, the utmost has to be extracted from private enterprise as regards its entrepreneurial skills, its capacity to give scope for such managerial and technical expertise which finds government service irksome, and its methods of organisation which permit quick execution of plans of production and of investment. But clear understanding has to be given to the entrepreneurs that the resources belong to the nation forming a Social Living Organism and the direction of their flow and allocation will be governed by the Central Guiding Agency of this organism and for the benefit of the nation. This follows straightaway from the necessity of survival which each person is subject to, and which is only possible if Society itself survives as a Living Organism.

In order to achieve this, the various members of the social organism must perform their tasks only for the public good, and in case they manifest a dominance of personal benefit or of any subordinate group, then the Central Guiding Agency must use inducements and disinducements so that the process of following private gain may iead to the public good. In laissez-faire economics this is supposed to happen on its own (on the prompting of the Invisible Hand), although it is possible that Adam Smith may not have believed in it with any degree of conviction when he knew that on account of self-interest (when given the opportunity, and in a situation lacking external supervision) some categories of the privileged could misallocate the nation's resources. Thus, he had thought that production and consumption could be carried out by the privileged to the extent that the common men "were provoked and disgusted by the variety, luxury and expense" of their richer echelons "who appeared to spend upon their own pleasures the patrimony of the poor". He further pointed out that "the vices of levity are always ruinous to the common people", in *Wealth of Nations*, Book V, Chapter I, Part III, Article III when discussing the enforcement of morals among the agents of the supreme Invisible Hand on the earth, namely the ecclesiastics.

We know that in an economy devoid of perfect competition proper allocation can come about only by deliberate guidance (by the Firm State) of economic affairs of public and private sectors so that both contribute to the social good. The Central Guiding Agency of the Social Living Organism is thus the Visible Hand which will ensure a proper allocation of resources which an egalitarian economy would have exhibited and which the Invisible Hand cannot do, because the conditions of perfect competition do not prevail which would have made the vector of production therein coincide with that of the egalitarian economy.

As a result, private enterprise will become an agent of social production in a mixed economy; for social considerations must determine the type of goods which it will produce — whether catering for the mass of population and permeating the economy, or attuned to the luxury demand of a severally inegalitarian income-distribution in the vain hope of those goods percolating downwards, while others are deprived of even necessaries and other amenities of subsistence. The Visible Hand must give guidelines for the type of techniques private enterprise will use — whether H-using or H-conserving. It must, on behalf of Society, lay down the policy for location of foot-loose industry — whether to be attracted to metropolitan towns or diffused in the rural contryside. The Firm State as a manifestation of the Visible Hand must decide the policy regarding the degree of diffusion of ownership measured by density of ownership of assets of households — whether it will allow it to be, as at present, concentrated hard in the hands of a few, while as regards the mass of population it is rarefied thin, or it will take steps to have a production spectrum and techniques of production which do not permit these extremes to be created.

Many of these attributes for which, in unrestrained capitalism, an unrestricted choice is exercised by the entrepreneur, will be subject, in a proper type of mixed economy — the Composite Economy — to the Social Will. This Social Will exercised by the Central Guiding Agency (on behalf of the Social Living Organism) for the benefit of Society as a whole, will actuate the resources to be used in an optimum manner. The entrepreneur in a Composite Economy will be free to manage his enterprise under the policy represented by the Social Will, but he will not, as in a capitalistic or a mixed economy, manage society itself. The Visible Hand of the Social Organism will condition the entrepreneurial choice in the private and public sectors both. Further the democratically elected representatives of the people will (while keeping in view the desired continuity of the organism beyond the present generation) decide the pattern of allocations and the profile of Society which we want to build. This would be in place of a short horizon of vision merely looking forward over a span even less than that of a generation across, perhaps only to the end of the present electoral period.

Statesmen who will run a Composite Economy will be trustees of the nation as a continuing entity. It is the function of academic economists constantly to remind the statesmen of their duty to change the production spectrum so that the rulers may fulfil the responsibilities to the future generation as well as to the under-privileged members of the present one. If consumption disparities and the Strategy of Low Ploughback of the Higher-order Investments continue, it is difficult for either of these responsibilities to be fulfilled, except in speeches.

The conversion of a mixed economy into its particular form of Composite Economy will ensure growth and social justice together.

It will allow accumulation by private enterprise, but in the socially-correct lines. It will allow incentive for production, but not of the goods which an inegalitarian income-distribution demands. It will use private enterprise to be an agent for permeation of necessaries for all sections of the population; and before all these needs are satisfied, it will not cater to the requirements of the affluent. It will not start with goods for the upper-income groups being produced with the hope that they will percolate down to the lower and lower income classes. One of the essential steps for the survival of the Social Organism is to break the artificial dualism in society which is created by the structure of the Glass-Curtain Economy described earlier.

As long as the Glass-Curtain barrier exists there can be no harmony of class interests of capitalists and workers as co-partners in production. To break this segregation of classes is possible only by an equalitarian pattern of consumption. The exercise of excess purchasing power has, therefore, to be prevented from coming to the luxury consumption market, if planning is to be successfully implemented through the aegis of a mixed economy.

There are various other types of centrifugal elements in society who sometimes act in a way which may well result in being impediments to the survival of the social organism and which will attract the action of the Visible Hand. They were described in my article "Growth under Parasitic Conditions" published in the Seminar, Delhi, in 1966. Apart from profiteers, and the idle landlords and receivers of dividends, one category is the Executive Managers who draw salaries much higher than the functional requirements of discharging the duties of the office which they hold. Their income is often defended on account of differential ability.

In the United States the highest salary (cum bonus) is 200 times the median earnings in their lowest paid occupation, namely helpers in private households. In underdeveloped countries this ratio of top earnings to median earning in lowest-paid occupations may come out to be as high as 500. Even after implementation of regulatory rules recently formulated in this country, this salary differential may still be possible for specially-qualified personnel. There is no system of economic valuation free from logical flaws which can justify this differential on the ground of moral desert, or functional necessity, or efficiency or productivity or free market price. It is clearly discernible to be of the nature which Mr. Maurice Dobb described in 1923 as rent of institutionally-created scarcity, being a particular form of the general species described here as ransoms. It may be noted that it would make no difference to its being still described by the term 'ransom' if the scarcity were not artificially created by restriction of entry or class configuration, but were natural like superior intelligence or talents, or if the amount were willingly offered by employers and not demanded by the employees.

It is said that because managerial talent is scarce, it will be withdrawn from the firm if the remuneration offered to it were lower. This position is like Corn-Law supporters arguing in times of Ricardo that land will be withdrawn from use if the rent of land is decreased. It is only to cloak the nature of the managerial income as a ransom that the apologists for high salaries in business flaunt the illusory scarcity of the managerial skills. The capacity to withdraw rests upon the market in the country. If in all the Industries the policy were framed by the State that salary norms would depend upon maintenance requirements and facilities for functions performed (without excepting the rare skills or talents), then the top remuneration level will go down considerably and this will happen throughout industry. If they are attempted to be withdrawn they will not then have another place to go to where they will be able to extort the ransom of their skills. As a matter of fact, in the cases of most managers the skills themselves are not more than what can be learnt by anyone else (with moderately-good intelligence and abilities) who may be placed in the same happy position as these executives who were snugly ensconsed in their cadres at the inception of their careers because of the abilities or connections of their ascendants. It is, hence, not very fruitful to maintain that if the salary were reduced throughout in the private sector as a mater of general policy, then work will suffer.

The State Government also sometimes act as centrifugal elements. For instance, the inhabitants of one province which is rich in mineral endowment are often heard to be saying that they supply so much material to the whole country and that the rest of the country does not give the people of that state a fair recompense. No economy can work on the basis of maintaining a balance of payments among all states constituting a country. The resources of the economy all belong to the National Social Organism. The organism exploits its own resources, wherever they may be located, for the use of its economy. If the poor belonging to a state which is rich in minerals, deserve to be helped, it is because they are less-advantaged not because they live in a region which is richly endowed. The poor in another region where there are no valuable natural endowments are equally deserving of the transfer of resources. It is not a tenable proposition to hold that because their contribution to the social organism is perforce low, hence lower standards of living must prevail there.

If the basis of natural endowments being used for inhabitants of that region were taken to be correct, the states which have good natural endowments would have consistently higher rates of growth, and would be getting to be richer and giving their constituents higher and higher standards of living, while other members of the same social organism unfortunate enough to be living in territories of ill-endowed states will lack necessaries. This is not a tendency towards social justice which will act as a centripetal force to strengthen the Social Living Organism., and its emergence in the country visible to all who go beyond statistical figures, needs to be urgently reversed.

The Trade Unions in organised industry are another form of centrifugal group which acts in a manner which may not always be most conducive to the social goods. They form a nucleus which itself acquires the character of a living organism. The Trade-Union action is a countervailing power to the exploitation by monopolistic and monopolistic organisations among the employers. However, Trade Unions are most successful in industries where the people from whom ransoms are extracted are not executives in firms but consumers in general. The action of Unions themselves enhances this extortion from the consumer, for it is well known that their action in pračtice, unlike the theoretical intention behind it, does not lead so much to diminution of profits as to price increases through adding to the cost of production. The increases of prices which are engendered, hit the workers in unorganised industry. If the ransom leads to increase of standard of living of workers in the highly-organised industry, it affects the investment capacity of the economy as a whole, and through that hits the creation of employment for the non-employed.

The working class thus breaks up into three distinct income-groups and interests—those in highly-organised industry at the top, then workers in unorganised industry, and lastly the non-employed. Trade Union action instead of integrating the working class to be able to counter capitalist power, makes these organisations co-sharers of the spoils of the capitalist system through exacting a ransom from the firms as entities who further extort substantial investible and consumable materials from the economy for their own ends and not for the public good. These subordinate living organisms, the Firms and the Trade Unions then act contrary to the interest of the social organism of which they form part.

To mitigate this, it was recommended in my article on "Economic Policies", published in the Republic-Day Issue of the *Young India*, in 1971, that one should divide the fruits of settlement of a labour dispute into three parts. One part would go to the workers to be paid not in the form of a wage increase but its capitalised value as bonus shares. Another would go to the Trade-Union movement for expansion in unorganised industry to better the bargaining power of the workers there to share the ransoms of their respective employers. A third part, again in capitalised form, would be handed over to a Workers' Investment Trust to be set up by Parliament to be managed by them, which would invest on their behalf and thus provide more employment according to plan allocations. The three tiers of the working class will then all benefit, and the Workers' Investment Trust (earning dividends and reinvesting them entirely, as also fed by the settlement of each labour dispute in the country) would, within a decade, become the single-largest investor in the country. Each industry would also move towards a larger share of workers' ownership in capital, which would make the firms therein less of cancerous growths in the social organism.

If the growth of the self-centered sub-organisms continues or they get duplicated in large numbers, it will ultimately wreck the Central Organism. It is for this reason that the growth or continuance of these sub-organism is to be permitted only if they are to be highly integrated with the Central Organism. It may conceivably come about by the individual sub-organism itself recognising that its interest is best served in the long run if it can be assured of survival, which can only take place through the survival of the Central Organisms; for it that collapses, so will each of the sub-organisms which are either its members, or parasites upon it.

But this is like preaching Christianity to the maggots upon a carcass. This integration can come about only if the action of these organisms is to be directed towards the social good rather than of the individual benefit; and action of the Central Organism is clearly invited to be directed towards giving more support to the least-advantaged rather than to the well-protected constituents of the social organism. The proposition of Adam Smith regarding self-interest, by, itself, leading to the social good is denied by the Theory of Living Organisms in cases where a high level of integration is absent — because there is no mechanism whereby self-interest left to itself would lead to the public good. On the contrary, there are mechanisms which positively prevent the Central Organism from looking after the interests of the less-privileged constituents because of the ransoms which the parasitic living-organisms extract from the economy — leaving little as residue for the benefit of the least-advantaged. Even out of social-welfare programmes and projects the mixed economy allows a substantial proportion to be cornered so that it does not reach the poor.

In a Glass-Curtain Economy the burdens imposed upon the top percolate the stones, downwards while the benefits are retained by the affluent. On the other hand, burdens imposed upon the poor remain with them, while the benefits meant for them rise like cream to the top. Even schemes of direct distribution of benefits (like blankets and milk) run into difficulties of proper implementation, for the top organisers belong to a more affluent class and they, sometimes, resent why such fine materials and goods should be 'wasted upon the idle poor', while they themselves (by dint, presumably, of their hard work in maintaining their air-conditioners in working order) consider themselves to be more deserving candidates for the bounty. The whole group of organisers of welfare for the poor has a different class interest than that of the least-advantaged. Many of them informally, get orgnised into parasitic organisms and collude with each other to prevent the Central Organism helping the unprotected, and then they draw away its cream leaving little evidence whereby the Central Organism can punish the guilty through its disciplinary processes.

In the absence of an inbuilt mechanism of the Invisible Hand to make self-interest coincide with the social good, and the presence of obstructions to the Central Organism in protecting the least advantaged, the efforts of each of the sub-organism has to be guided towards actions which are for the public good, through some powerful instruments. Without Central coordination (by the Visible Hand) guiding individual output, the actions for self-interest cannot be made to coincide with the public good. But a strong Central Organisation like a Commission of Economic Co-ordination in a Firm State, using more powerful inducive instruments and having a much greater grasp ove the social function which it is called upon to perform than a traditional planning body exhibits, can ensure by various devices that the actions of the individuals or entrepreneurs regarding utilisation of the physical resources of the economy following self-interest, are nevertheless guided towards the social good by making the pursuit of the lines dictated by social benefit to be profitable and of other lines unprofitable, unlike the present. The Visible Hand ought to be created to take the reins of economic command where the Invisible one never had its grip.

This is achieved by reproducing the conditions of production which would rule under a hypothetical concept called the system of perfect competition. A system of perfect competition would be inconsistent with any assumption but of perfect mobility of resources, and hence it would, if it ruled, contain no individuals with access to resources or skills or talents which others are not equally well capable of possessing. It would tend, therefore, to have equal division of property, and of income derived from work (which includes the capacity to work, or to render labour services). The demand for goods generated in any notional economy by this type of perfect competition will coincide with the demand vector dictated by a socialist state for socially-necessary consumption and expansion of its capital structure as well as transformation of its energy-converting apparatus to forms requiring less expenditure of effort per unit time for each of its human constituents.

Following Vilfredo Pareto since 1897, allocations under perfect competition (in a capitalist economic system) have been usually used as the standard to define ideal allocations in a socialist society. But eight years earlier, Friedrich von Wieser had found it appropriate to use the reverse form of this procedure, and to define natural values according to what would be ruled in a socialist economic system.

We would be inclined to follow von Wieser by giving a definition of perfect competition to be that form of a capatilists economies which reproduces conditions of production and demand which would coincide with the allocations over time in an egalitarian society. An efficient programme of capital accumulation in perfect competition would then be the same as inter-temporal allocations in an egalitarian economy with real wage at subsistence level whatever the technology chosen.

Arising from the above, it would be against the interest of the Society to give choice of what is to be produced in the hands of individuals (whether consumers or producers) when there is neither perfect competition, nor possibility of it, as is the situation in present-day economies of most countries. We know that exercise of unrestricted free choice in an economy where inequalities are prevalent, is not in keeping with establishment of an economic democracy wherein each person would exercise on the market one and only one vote unweighted by the mass of his affluence. Hence, one cannot expect the spectrum of goods (produced even under condition of a fair degree of pure competition) to coincide with the goods which perfect competition (leading to equality of assets) would have generated, had it existed.

Uniformity in exercise of purchasing power is of such fundamental importance for our democratic commitment, for Equality is enshrined in the Constitution, that if no other method is available to implement it but to abolish the hybrid form of structure of enterprise, our socially-conscious economists would have no hesitation in recommending it. But one may observe that before taking such a drastic step one would exhaust all possibilities of reform and rectification within the existing system and it is known that all efforts have not been made to re-create the conditions of an equalitarian society. For instance, it can be accomplished by converting the concept of the mixed economy into a more socially-useful form within the framework of a mix of public and private sectors. It is a blue-print of this restructuring which is, therefore, a matter of immediate concern.

The Composite Economy which is meant to create these equalitarian conditions will reproduce the production vector, or the basket of goods, of an egalitarian society, and will therefore, yield a consumption basket accordingly. It will establish an Equalitarian society yielding consumption benefits equally for all, these being the utilities which, ultimately, are the important ones. It does not, by itself, seek to create equality of income or of wealth, nor can it abolish ransoms, but it does prevent higher income or wealth derived from ransoms to generate unequal consumption. The present form of Mixed Economy wherein socialist objectives aim at equality of income, of wealth, and of consumption, all three on the one hand, and rapid accumulation on the other, succeeds in achieving not even one of these. The economic device to be sought in a Composite Economy is one which, though it allows the right of free choice in entirety, makes its exercise with incentive and disincentive system built into the economy sucessfully—lead to the result required by social considerations as regards at least one out of the three constituents of an equalitarian economy, namely; the Consumption basket—which is all that it endeavours to do.

VI. THE STERILISATION OF RANSOMS

The objective for which the Visible Hand is to be created, is achievable by two complementary devices; one rooted in Public Administration and the other in Economics. The administrative device is the Firm State which has neither a lack of supervision as in the Soft State, nor dictatorial regimentation as in the Hard State. The Firm State concentrates upon ensuring the complete integrity of a relatively small number of key people, the public servants (whether belonging to the civil service or the political field). It does not necessarily require, nor does it expect, that the people as a whole would, suddenly, become more honest or moral than what circumstances have hitherto required them to be. With the key people's integrity assured, the rest would be able to be deflected to the path of rectitude within a span of a few years. The basic device of Magnifier Instruments first appeared in my article in Gandhi Centenary Issue of Interdiscipline in 1970. A further study was invited by the Union Finance Ministry thereupon and submitted in 1971. It was published in 1975 under the title "Disparity Tax in a Composite Economy". The question was fully discussed in a separate Minutes of Supplementation to the Report of the Central Committee on Unemployment which had been appointed on a Resolution of Parliament, and was published many years back (in 1973). The basic principles are simple and may by now be known, hopefully, to some at least among the economists in authority.

The instruments pertaining to a Composite Economy entail recognition of the nature of Income-Impost as an instrument encouraging corporate mis-expenditure and acting as a disincentive to adding to the produce of the economy even in the desired channels. They require replacement of Income Tax by a regime of Mis-expenditure Tax wherein each investment is weighted by a factor of approval depending upon the social necessity of the investment and then deducted from income to yield the quantum of notional mis-expenditure (which represents the misconsumption element in expenditure). This notional mis-consumption would then be taxed on the basis of a schedule of progressively-progressive marginal rates, crossing the hundred per cent level. Thus, the marginal rate being 400 per cent for an assessee, then if a sum of Rs. 1000, instead being consumed were invested in a line of social approbation with 1.20 as approval factor, it would lead to 1,200 as notional decrease of tax base and, hence, it would save Rs. 4,800 as Misexpenditure Tax. This also would have to be invested in lines at least having unit approval factor. The additional Investment in the Economy is then Rs. 5,800 and it is directed into the right channels.

The special variant of Misexpenditure Tax, called Disparity Tax, requires income also to be weighted upward or downwards by Disapproval factors respecting the source of income being socially undesirable or otherwise. Income earned through extortion of ransoms or earned by raising prices to pay a high quantum of Disparity Tax would be treated as a disapproved source of income. This latter aspect of Disparity Tax prevents the incidence from being shifted (as happens in the present Indirect and Direct Impost-System) through various rounds (by charging higher price to consumers, till it falls on those who belong to the alienated mass of persons outside the Glass-Curtain economy). The power with individuals to misspend resources belonging to the Social Living Organism for inessential consumption is discouraged even in a Kaldorian Expenditure Tax. But what is more important, for undesirable investments also, which is the source of supply of inessentials, the opportunity would be taken away from the individuals and firms through this powerful disincentive device where marginal rates would run to several hundred per cent (as they already do in Indirect Tax). Wealth in private hands will then become a servant of the public good. On the other hand, an individual or a juridical person who treads the right economic path, who does not misconsume by spending on it beyond the median consumption of the members of the Social Organism, and who does not misinvest, will be liable to pay no tax at all. The Tax is a penalty for misallocation, not a means of sustaining the "Expenses of the Sovereign of Commonwealth" as Adam Smith incorrectly thought taxes to be.

In this fashion the differential of direct-tax payment between unapproved and approved activities would become so large as to make the rate of profit in luxuries lower and in the production of necessaries higher (so that physical resources are actuated to shift from the former to the latter field). This is accomplished by using this allocative tax-device purely by inducements and disinducements, without any fiatory instruments being used at all.

Side by side, for reasons of preventing the formation of dangerous cancerous growths in society of the type of octopoid corporations (which grip the economy through their tantacles spread into many diversified fields, say from tobacco to hotel keeping, and which are outside the pale of the Monopolies Acts, a Concentration Tax would have to be levied.

The Disparity Tax forms a system which (through permitting inequality of wealth and income to remain, and even to grow) would convert the character of ownership of capital and property immediately by taking away the pcwer to mis-spend. It does not act like a capital levy taking a part only of the property and leaving the rest in private hands, unfettered and sufficient in quantum to cause huge disparities in consumption spending. Nor does Disparity Tax, like the Estate duty, wait for the accident or death, to be levied on a large holder of assets. Consequently, the Central Guiding Agency takes control of disposition of the entire assets of individuals for social purposes immediately.

As has been shown, beyond a certain limit all incomes are of the nature of ransoms obtained by the powerful and the influential by exactions upon the helpless, and all private property properly belongs to the Social Living Organism from whom it is leased to individuals for functional purposes. Hence, one cannot justify the unhindered enjoyment of the ransoms during one's life time. The Disparity Tax system would affect the whole property, not a part. But it would not, on the other hand, dispossess to the whole extent or part of it, any holder who is willing to avoid it by keeping his course of action upon paths approved for the social good. It would rather make him deal with private property in such a manner that the social requirements are met. To do so it would neither order, nor compel, nor prohibit, nor restrict directly. It would do so through the mechanism of following of signals of the market (as amended by the Disparity-Tax system) by virtue of which the operative while following self-interest would find it most profitable to change his behaviour pattern to reduce the deviation between the actual and the optimal one (which the public good dictates).

The reduction of the disparity between actual and desired behaviour from the point of view of the social living organism as a whole, would be the prime target of implementing agencies. The Fiscal and Monetary Instruments would be used only for this purpose — and in concert. The proper one among these instruments are Inducive Instrument in the armoury of the Guided Economy working under the administrative system of a Firm State, as distinguished from the direct controls and the physical compulsions which pertain to a Fiatory Economy, and which require a Hard State to implement. The fiatory instruments even in a Soft State become powerful engines of oppression of the mass of alienated people outside the Glass-Curtain Economy.

For a Firm State to use the fiatory methods would require administrative machinery many times more powerful and incorruptible than what a disordered country (used to governance as a Soft State) is capable of organising. Further, it would be liable to be much more dictatorial than what the members of the community can tolerate particularly as the opportunities for those in authority (to extract ransoms and to oppress by arbitrary action) are going to be in abundance; and purchasing power sufficient with some to afford the condonation of any misdeed, even if the standard fee for it were set at a high level. The disparity Tax in a Guided Economy under a Firm State would act immediately in converting a Mixed Economy into a Composite Economy (where private sector co-exists with the public sector, but both are meant to subserve the social good — though the former would still use the incentive of private profit to expand its investments). It would convert the economy from the present structure of being socialistic in outward form and capitalist in substance, to being capitalist in appearance, and socialist as well as Austerity capitalist in the desired result whereby the actions (of private-sector firms and of individuals as also of the public corporations) would reproduce the production spectrum of an egalitarian economy which would be expected to rule under true socialism as also under perfectly competitive capitalism.

As the structure of a mixed economy is accepted even though perfect competition does not prevail, it would be futile to expect an equalised income-distribution to follow. One cannot also expect that income-after-tax will be very much less unequal, because the taxes are usually paid out of profits, and prices are set high enough to especially pay the dues to the government out of the pockets of the consumers. The poor suffer from this inflation caused by taxation, while the profit earners benefit from it. It is no use expecting that legislation to impose ceilings on incomes can be carried through without altering the character of the economy from the mixed to a collective-enterprise structure. Socialist radicalism which takes the form of calling for ceilings on income and property in a capitalist structure of economy without expecting that it will require complete socialisation of ownership, is like throwing balloons made of lead into the air and expecting that they will fly. If the occasion so demands, the Social Organism would certainly be well-advised to secure the resumption of all its property into its own direct control from that of its members; but let it not be thought that taking away bits here and there, while leaving the rest with them (subject only to the marginal influence of Imposts) will reproduce the conditions of either socialism or of perfect competition (with equal income-distribution), or would bring the economy much further away from unrestrained capitalism.

Power lies in ability to spend, not in the fact of ownership. The rentiers or lenders of funds may have huge ownership but they have little power over the enterprises or the government which invests the funds they lend. So also, the ordinary holder of equity has little power except the right to be voted down at a meeting once a year where the Board of Directors of his joint-stock company can manoeuvre to muster much larger support than can the odd shareholders who are dissatisfied with the working of the firm. An Under Secretary for Finance in a State Ministry has much more power than the richest individual, but not because of ownership. Disparity Tax dichotomises the power of spending from rights of ownership, The Income-Impost or Wealth Exaction or Estate Duty take away only a part of stock of assets or their flow, but leave the rest for free exercise of the power derived from spending or misspending in an economy which has no effective mechanism of curbing expenditure. The balance which is always left with the assessee in impositions falling short of wholesale confiscation is always enough to distort the pattern of demand, and to purchase the goodwill of men in administration towards performing actions which are contrary to their social duty.

The Mixed Economy puts the private sector under control of individuals, and the public sector under the control of the State. But it is observed in many under-developed countries that private enterprise finances political parties in elections, and subsidises the expenses of many elected representatives. It provides employment for the relations of the latter at salaries with large ransom elements. It has direct links with the civil authorities through liaison officers paid or aided. It has control over the main press media, and over the Boards of banks. It supplies the list of goods demanded by the affluent public, and materials needed by private enterprise (for their profitable production) are then required to be targeted in the economic plan. The Planning organisation then uses Input-output yardsticks to target the further inputs of inputs and secures their inclusion in the Plan. Instead of a list of the goods to be produced given by the Visible Hand of the Central Guiding Agency, private sector decides these and the planners merely calculate the input requirements in the aggregate, with some priority items strewn here and there. Instead of taking the helm in chalking out the production pattern for essential goods and eliminating the rest (which is what planning implies), the Planning Commission of such a country merely follows the causation emanating from the market demands and thus it may, more aptly, be described as a "Planned" Commission.

The private sector even invades the educational sector, for it is mainly controlled by the private sector even when finance is provided by the Government. Even at the university stage, some publishers affect decisions in the Boards of Studies. The high-pressure salesmanship is used in the defence sector also. The public sector purchases from the private sector the materials for producing their goods and sells to them their products. Their staff and managers themselves are in many cases drawn from the private sector. Their supervision comes from the public authorities themselves influenced by the private sector. In short, one finds the private sector's invisible hand so all-pervading that one may say that a mixed economy is run by the private sector — partly directly and partly through the state sector. The mixed economy is then subject to a regime of Capitalist Planning and is mainly capitalist in tenor and temper.

When we come to the special type of octopoid firms, the Multinational Corporations, we find that they are immensely large organisations which have resources by virtue of which each of these forms of control over the public authorities and organisations is fortified manifold times. These corporations are firms which have acquired the characteristics of living organisms. They do not owe allegiance to the countries in which they operate and it is sometimes doubtful whether they owe allegiance to their country of incorporation. They act for their own survival, and for that purpose carry on investments which yield constant stream of benefits for the sponsors of these corporations who draw huge ransoms from their activities in order to use lesser and lesser human effort of their own for ensuring a living, for countless generations of their descendants. No feasible amount of Imposts through Income and Profit exactions can curb the purchasing power of these corporations. Only a direct tax on misexpenditure can channel their expenditures in the right activities, for the progressive progressiveness of the Disparity Tax makes the penalty for wrong expenditure larger, the larger is the corporation's size of misactivity.

It is deterrent to spending itself, discriminated according to type of spending and source of earning which will be an effective check on misallocations by the individuals or by the State or by small and large corporations It is for this reason that the paradox arises that a measure which shifts emphasis from egalitarianism to equalitarianism—from equality of wealth, income and consumption all three together, towards greater equality in consumption alone—a measure which effects guidance of investments and other expenditures to cater to essential social needs as well as to techniques with high wage to profit ratio in the consumption sector but leaves income and wealth untaxed directly, and hence which appears to increase inequality in distribution of assets; such a measure is a more substantial device of establishing the sovereignty of the social organism over the resources of society than exactional and imposts of the present fiscal system which purports to be redistributive and confiscatory. The Disparity Tax changes the production pattern, while the present Imposts merely transfer paper assets from private hands to the government.

It is also for this reason that the subordinate organisms within the social polity who look for the survival of their own class with least action per unit time through progressive reduction in effort to benefit ratio, would find it hard to accept a shift to Allocative Fiscal system rather than one based simply on exactions and imposts. These sub-organisms are the Management and the Bureaucracy. The limitation on effective choice of avenue of spending by managements also limits the private subsidies to the Bureaucracy, as also to such men in politics (unfortunately not very rare in many under-developed countries) who make it their business to further the causes of the private-sector donors with the political and bureaucratic authorities concerned.

We note that from the subject of Organic Economics we derive not only the propositions of Intergenerational equity and survival, of economies of effort through equilibrium of repetitive actions along with high adaptability following from purposive disequilibrium, but also the realisation that large proportion of distributive payments or surpluses of economic interaction, for which economic justifications are given as being costs, disguise the true nature thereof as ransoms. The application of Organic Economics also shows that whatever the distribution (in terms of money or assets), created by the vagaries of a Mixed Economy in which ransoms are rampant, the process of converting it into its special form, the Composite Economy, and using Magnifier Inducive Instrument of Disparity Taxation, would set the allocations all aright which unequal incomes do constantly turn awry. The fiscal system explained here cannot stop ransoms being earned, though they can be discouraged. But it can sterilise them once earned, to yield greater growth, optimum allocations and more equality in consumption.

VII. ON THE KINGS' TREASURIES

A hundred and ten years back John Ruskin announced at Dublin a lecture entitled; "Of Kings' Treasuries". When the audience came avidly expecting to hear about crowns and half-crowns, they were regaled with the disclosure of the secret whereby one may open up, for one's benefit, the wealth which is to be found hidden in books. To-day you all would be less fortunate, for I now intend to talk about the true role of the State Treasury, of the literally, without any welcome euphemism; for therefrom one would like to derive the attendant Monetary Policy.

Disparity Tax being allocational in character makes the use of proper Monetary Policy feasible. It is well known that real inflation is caused by lack of supply of essential goods in relation to the demand. The expenditures of the government and the private sector create the demand while that part only of expenditures creates supply which is in quick-yielding projects for the production of necessary consumption goods. A balance between these investments and the rest, yields sufficient supply to cope with the demand. With the Balanced Allocation Ratio, any size of plan would be non-inflationay and the size would depend upon physical availability of resources and equipment, especially that which capital theory would indicate as bottleneck entities (manpower or materials).

One of the advantages of this physical approach to inflation is that it exonerates the Expansion of Quantity of Money of the charge of contributing to the increase of prices, which was not correct even in the neo-classical system wherein it was developed on account of its proponents forgetting the first lesson which Marshall had taught them that prices depend upon two factors, namely Supply and Demand, both of which, like blades of a pair of scissors, must be held equally responsible.

The exoneration of Monetary Expansion in general (and deficit financing in particular) of the grave charge of causing inflation, releases Monetary Theory from the bandage which classical economics had shackled it with. If physical resources permit of the balanced allocation in a non-inflationary manner, then lack of financial resources need henceforth never be pleaded by any Chancellor of the Exchequer, or High Chamberlain Custodian of a Federal Reserve Balances in any country. If physical resources are lacking or out of balance, real inflation is bound to arise and no creation of additional money can be of any use, nor for that matter can we delude ourselves that Taxation, or Borrowing from the public, will do the trick of saving us from the grip of inflation. The imposition of exactions for raising revenue (properly called Imposts rather than Taxes) would, instead of curing inflation, raise the prices because the parasitic elements of the social organism follow the mechanics of paying the additional tax liabilities or their dependants (that is the executives employed by them) as also their own corporate taxes, out of the pockets of the consumers.

Reliance on continued borrowing from the public is also highly inflationary because not only, in the absence of a Disparity Tax system, huge interest-payments received by individuals annually are liable to be spent in a way upsetting the Balance of Allocation between Quick-yielding production of neccssaries and Inflationary expenditures, but also because high rate of interest increases the costs at all stages of production and cumulatively the prices escalate upwards.

Expenditure of the Government from profits of public enterprises also comes usually from increase of prices of their products; and if the enterprises are for production of necessaries (like electricity undertaking or steel plants, or the railways) the price rise is diffused rapidly through the economy. It is no achievement deserving the gratitude and approbation of society for a public enterprise to exact ransoms from the public to make profits to subsidise expenditure of the government, and this act of public piracy is even more reprehensible when it is known that not the whole of the expenditure would be for public benefit as dictated by the needs of the alienated mass.

If the services of the public sector contribute to the field of luxury (like Jumbo Jets, Refrigerators and Multi-starred Hotels), they are also engendering inflation throughout the economy, for no master of the art of executive management would spend from his own pocket for purchasing the amenities or goods offered by these organisations, nor do his masters usually have any difficulty in passing the burden of his enjoyment on to the public at large, through the prices of the products which his firm manufactures.

All the traditional modes of raising resources in a non-inflationary manner are, in fact, highly inflationary and only deficit financing or expansion of currency does not suffer from the proclivity to cause autonomous rise of prices. In fact, it is even anti-inflationary in its predisposition because of the lowering of interest element in cost which it entails, and the tendency to make viable, as a result, the activities with relatively low profitability (of which the most important are production of necessaries, and that also by the weaker operatives, whether on the farm or in industry). Deficit financing is the ally of the weaker sections in production, whereas the incidence of imposts and the high rate of interest which borrowing entails, burdens the smaller producer more than the large firm (especially those in high-profit inessentials).

With traditional Public Finance, we burden the poor and make the allocation-ratio unbalanced. We break with our own clumsy hands the two weapons of pro-growth and anti-inflationary nature (which modern economic theory provides for any form of mixed economy in a Liberal Democracy), namely Monetary and Fiscal Policy. With these blunted instruments we have been trying to fight poverty, and having been, naturally unsuccessful, have blunted the edge of our instruments still further. The more has revenue-oriented taxation been inflationary, the more have our authorities asked for more of it; and the more has high rate of interest proved disastrous to our cost-structure, the more has the public asked for higher interest-rates to give to the economy paper savings at the cost of throttling its real investment. To an economist who looks only at real effects in terms of real Investment, it have seemed a suicidal economic ritual in which the academics advising the government have been engaged for countless years; and even when the governments have been replaced by the will of the electorate, the new governments have been holding the promise of reorientation of basic policies, have been induced by the same academics to proclaim their intentions even more resolutely to pursue the same type of counter-productive financial policies.

The Visible Hand in the Firm State which should rather be protecting the social organism against onslaughts by cancerous growths, which should be quelling fissiparous tendencies, countering centrifugal forces and curbing the parasitic elements, has itself been announcing a traditional financial policy which is equivalent to wielding a hatchet against its own community. The spell of continuing in the same mistaken notions of economic theory, is one long period which has been putting increasing burdens on the alienated mass of people.

As in the days of decline of Rome, the voices of philosophers like Seneca and Epictetus, imploring the successive Emperors to follow the dictates of reason and temperance, were drowned amidst the cries of gladiators whom the latter fostered, so also those who show reason and throw light on the ills of our body politic, are seldom listened to upon the unpalatable truths which they recite. But the invitation of a fearless democracy to utter what is right, prompts me today, to share with you all the misgivings which many of us have long had about basic flaws in economic policy emanating from faults in traditional economic theory for which our own brethren have been responsible. Hence, he who has died of under-nourishment when scarce capital has been unutilised; he who has dies of non-employment when resources have lain idle (yearning to be used for giving him productive work), has ceased to be because some of our own community among the economists following hoary tradition, have signed his death-warrant with their pens dipped in orthodoxy.

VIII. A RESUME

I have held you all in this audience captive long enough exacting a ransom of your time by virtue of my placement as President of your Association, and I must now draw to the end of my peregrination.

The strategy of multigenerational survival outlined in this system and based on previous studies in Capital Theory, gives promise of yielding growth and social justice together, by maximizing the rate of growth of Higher-order investments necessary for future survival of the Social Organism with least effort per unit time.

It combines social justice to the present generation with justice for the future generations through high ploughback ratio of the Higher-order Investments (leading to techniques in the consumption sector conserving the products of the heavy industries). The techniques conserving the products of Heavy Industries' Sector, incidentally, provide more employment through use of a lower degree of mechanisation which also leads to more favourable distribution of income because these techniques exhibit higher Wage to Profit ratios.

It avoids real inflation through plentiful production of consumption necessaries. The mass of people alienated from the Glass-Curtain Economy are rapidly brought into the fold of the growing economy as equal members of an economic democracy.

It makes the miniature, small and medium scale the only source of production in the consumption sector, and gives justification to Gandhian Economics for the span of development strategy at least, on the basis of economic analysis derived from modern researches in Capital Theory. It prevents monopolism through avoiding the large scale which is the natural starting point for concentration of economic power or avoidance of the concentration tax by conversion of assets into the frame of the conjoint sector. It diffuses industry over the rural countryside and avoids aggravation of concentration in metropolitan towns which comes about because of large-scale consumption-oriented industries also thronging there.

The interest of the future and the present having been shown to be in balance, Growth and Social Justice are also shown to be achievable together. The conversion of the Mixed Economy to its purposeful form — the Composite Economy with its instruments of inducive nature rather than of fiatory form — makes maximum growth possible to be achieved while retaining liberty. Finally, the Magnifier Instrument of Disparity Taxation and allied policies achieve the type of equality which is material, because the production and investment specturm in an Equalitarian Economy (with only consumption disparities removed) would be identical with the vector of consumption goods and equipment which would be produced if there were an Egalitarian Economy (with wealth, income and consumption all equalised).

This material form of Equality along with Growth, is possible to be achieved with use of the market system and liberty of choice without physical prohibitions or compulsions, through use of Fiscal and Monetary devices which make it compatible with the pursuit of private profit and self-interest to produce all the commodities which, and only the commodities which, the social good requires. The Firm State (armed with these Instruments of Inducement), represents the Visible Hand, by virtue of which the ransoms and private exactions of cancerous growths are nullified and the health of society as a Living Organism is restored.

The proposals set forth here, and elsewhere, by me are not ostensibly radical, but have the germ which will make it possible for redicalism to be implemented in substance. They do not abolish the economic classes but make them functional, removing the disparity in inessential privileges. They do encourage entrepreneurial growth but in the proper lines and with proper scale of production, and they take the sting out of ownership of capital by considering it to be, what in fact it is, a lease of resources from Society to its agents of production. They are measures of reform necesary if Society is to survive as a Social Living Organism.

Without harmony of interest of all constituents, the social organism cannot continue as a living entity; because an economy of class conflict is the antithesis of an Organic Economy which requires a high degree of integration. The Socialist Economy achieves this harmony by abolishing class; the composite economy achieves it by operation as per prescripts of equity in lexical ordering — that is by simultaneous implementation or pre-attainment of some in favour of the less privileged classes. If harmony of aims is to be achieved, it cannot be by the subordination of social aims by the parasites within the system, but by the establishment of paramountcy of social aims and social guidance over activities of its constituents, whether they be individual or classes. This is the true nature of the conditions under which industrialists or management or bureaucracy or larger farmers or the privileged labour organisation perform their respective tasks. If they accept its dictates on the basis of logic and discussion, the system will survive and develop. If this is rejected, then the economy will continue as a Glass-Curtain economy and the accentuation of class conflict is inevitable.

Sophocles writing the play Antigone in Athens twenty-four centuries and twenty years back asks for the "Rule of Order" to be upheld (in line 677). However, it was not obedience to the pre-emptory and impetuous authorities of the State, but subordination of all — the citizenry and the imperious forces of command to the Moral Law which the play is about. It is the Social Will (acting to prevent inequity to its constituents) which dictates the Moral Law; and makes Man and State like subject to its thrall. But where the entrenchment of privilege has suppressed the Moral Law and the State itself upholds the unequal privileges of the transgressors as rights, where settlement of the conflict by argument and by reasoning has failed, where intellectuals presenting their views in orderly conferences have been ignored, and citizens in conventions asking for legislations for the social good have become hoarse to no avail, then emotional upsurges must irretrievably take over.

But in that eventuality it must be clearly recognised that when logic will have failed to settle the conflict, its resolution will be through smashing the Glass Curtain of privilege by the tide of resentment which economic deprivation and its social consciousness will propel. It is not unknown for the temporal power of States (Soft or Hard) to crumble before such onslaughts; and all of us who belong to the decision-making classes owe it as a democratic duty to reshape the course of events by economic re-orientation while it is still time to reform the system; before the unrestrainable forces of armed resistance get unleashed and overwhelm the body politic.

4

THE TANGLED SKEIN
Planning for a Mixed Economy

I. THE SOCIALIST COMMITMENT

Learned Chairman, Director of the Nehru Memorial Library and distinguished scholars of public affairs, it is with a sense of great sadness and humility that I rise today to pay my homage to the great personage on the eve of whose 18th death anniversary we are meeting here this evening; humility, because of my being too inadequate to comprehend the full extent of his achievement; sadness because of the non-fulfilment of the vision of that statesman, — a vision that had for the first time made us, as youngmen, proud to be citizens of a free country which held moral leadership of the world. To belong to Nehru's India, in those days, was a passport to treatment with respect when abroad.

My mind goes back to a time thirtythree years ago when, in a world benumbed by the cold war, the Cambridge Union Society debated upon the topic of Peace (but at the cost of freedom) versus War (and possible annihilation). As an Indian, I had the privilege of being called upon to lead the House, and they listened with rapt attention because they discovered that in Gandhian analysis peace did not mean acceptance of subjugation but non-violent, mass, passive resistance, and the dangers of a world war could themselves be decreased by the Nehruvian Prescription of the "Temper of Peace". It was as a token of respect for these ideals that prompted the Cambridge under-graduates belonging to the Union Society (even though most members were ex-servicemen of the second world war, and belonged to the Conservative groups) to acclaim, by an extra-ordinary resolution, the move to nominate the Right Honourable the Prime Minister of India as Chancellor of the Cambridge University in succession to, and in clear contrast to, General Smuts of the Union of South Africa.

Published in *State Enterprises Journal*, vol.1, No. 4, Oct.-Dec. 1982, pp. 339-55.

There was an aura of reverence which the vision of Mr. Nehru cast over the young minds throughout the world, and India attained prominent position in the comity of nations. But during his own lifetime the dream had turned into a nightmare, and on the international scene in 1963 we had reached the lowest ebb in terms of prestige. We have, during the last ten years, regained a part of the lost status, though in intermittent fashion, and thanks to the rapid growth of our scientific and technical manpower, and our balanced approach in international politics, India's voice has once again a tone commanding attention.

Yet, it is the state of the internal economy that is the basis of continued support for international prestige to be retained and it is this which is the basis of a few anxieties which I wish to share, Sir, with the learned members of this group. The situation today is the outcome of economic forces set in motion in the pre-war period. These have been recounted by historians at various places but some salient points of relevance to our analysis may be noted. It is known that the deep socialist concern of J. Nehru, of Trinity College and the Inner Temple, Esquire, did not originate out of his association with progressive thought at Cambridge, in Edwardian years, but two decades later during his contact with Marxists in an International Conference (of Oppressed Nationalities) at Brussels and later on, during his visit to the Soviet Union.

The socialist commitment of Mr. Nehru was, thus, not Fabian in origin; but it was not Leninist either. He permitted and even encouraged a set of followers to express Bolshevik propensities, but out of regard for unity of all elements within the Congress party, he was not able to envisage a dominant position for this group in policy making. In 1933 on the eve of the setting up of the Congress Socialist Party Mr. Nehru wrote in "*Whither India ?*".

> "In my own mind it is clear that if an indigenous government took the place of a foreign government, and kept all the vested interests intact, this would not even be the shadow of freedom."

The statement is leftist in tone, but mildly so, and certainly not Marxist-Leninist in its content. In vain did the socialists within the ruling party hope for an immediate implementation of what their Meerut Conference in 1936 had described as "the technique of revolution, the theory and practice of class struggle; . . . and processes leading to the socialist society". During the tenure of the first Congress Governments in the Provinces in the late thirties, the struggle for agrarian rights of the peasantry as against the large landowners gained little support from the Governments in power. The complexion of the ruling party at the time of the withdrawal of the foreign armed forces from India (which is euphemistically described as "Independence") was predominantly towards the Right and the composition of the Consitituent Assembly itself reflected this. I was brought up to render the highest respect to the founding fathers, for the doyen among them was my late uncle, Dr. Sachchidanand Sinha, the first President of the Constituent Assembly. The Inaugural Address he delivered on the 9th December, 1946 represented the tenor of that body as being concerned primarily with balances between federal and unitary types of constitutions, and withdrawing up a charter concerned with the checks which the people themselves would exercise upon the public councils to ensure their integrity. He called for judicious compromises to be made as far as possible.

As events stood, the compromise took the form of the constitution-makers concerning themselves with protecting the fundamental rights of the propertied classes, alongwith the special interests of the socially-deprived scheduled classes. But even the directive principles of State Policy did not indicate a path towards socialism. At best, our country was to be under the regime of a Welfare State.

The wishes of Mr. Nehru for a socialist economy (expressed through "means of production, distribution and exchange in the hands of the community") did find expression in the report of the Committee on objectives and economic progress in the Delhi session of the AICC in November 1947, but only as an ultimate goal. However, this did not find even an echo in the Constitution. There is a constitutional mechanism of sharing central revenues between the centre and the states, through the Finance Commission, but there was no planning mechanism which the Constitution set up to implement the Directive Principles.

The peasantry wanted abolition of the rights of large landowners, but it did not want abolition of private rights to land altogether, and their transference to the State. Of the organisational machinery of the ruling party in the rural areas depending upon the middle-scale landowners, the command was held by rightist and semi-feudal forces. This organisational machinery also had the support of the industrialists. These combined rural-urban interests held the key to the ruling power, and Mr. Nehru was realistic enough to get the maximum which he could wrest by consensus, in a situation where comfrontation would have obtained little representations of socialist views.

The Jaipur Session of the Congress of December 1948 while endorsing the report of the Economic Programmes Committee, referred to the establishment of a Mixed Economy, but it assured the industrialists that their interests would not be injured. The proposal to set up a Planning Commission for eliminating inequalities, exploitation and private profit, was vehemently opposed in November 1949, and in the resolution which was finally adopted on the eve of the promulgation of the Republic, its functions did not include the phrase which Mr. Nehru had earnestly wanted regarding "the elimination of motive of private gain in economic activity".

Under these adverse circumstances, the mere setting up of the Planning Commission was an act of high triumph for Mr. Nehru. Though it got started with a mandate much less than it was expected to get, the mechanism was set in motion to make possible meaningful allocation of resources for equity and growth to be delivered which many economically advanced countries even now do not have. The Cabinet resolution which set up the Planning Commission in 1950 on the ominous day of the Ides of March was not socialistic in tenor; but in keeping with the philosophy of a liberal welfare economy, it confined itself merely to providing conditions for livelihood and making concentration non-detrimental to the common good.

But this was rightly taken to be good enough for a start. The situation was not linked up purely to the influence of Mr. Vallabhbhai Patel, but to the attitude of forces of political conservation as whole. Even after the death of Mr. Patel in December, 1950, it was not till full four years afterwards that in December 1954, the Lok Sabha adopted the policy of a socialistic pattern of Society. In that also there is some confusion as to what it connoted. In Mr. Nehru's views expressed to the National Development Council on the 9th of November, 1954 "the socialistic picture of society" referred to means of production to be "socially owned and controlled". The Avadi Session of the Congress, two months later, passed the resolution establishing a socialistic pattern of society" in terms of choice among alternatives of "social ownership or control," which is widely different from the earlier expectation of social ownership as well as control. The same document at another place declared the objective to be "socialist" which is different from "socialistic". It also expected that in such a structure, full employment may be achieved within a period of ten years, although there is not even a prima facie economic analysis as to how such a tremendous task was to be achieved in such a short time, just as in the Constitution itself there was no indication how economic resources were to be found whereby universal primary education would be imparted within a similar period. All this indicates that documents which contain pronouncements are evidences of faith, and not of government policy.

It is the endeavour in this presentation to show that the compromise in political objective created a situation in which irreconcilable elements of opposing policies were sought to be combined. A similar confusion occurred in the economic policies which went into the hands of non-economist plan modellers, on the one hand, and neo-classical economists, on the other hand. Various other policies together formed the amalgam known as the "socialistic pattern of society". These may be seen to be as follows:

(a) High ratio of investments of the Public to the Private sector
(b) Redistributive taxation
(c) Support to organised labour
(d) Physical controls of allocations.

All four of these flowed from Fabian Socialism as developed later on and assimilated into the theory of the welfare state

II. EGALITARIAN FABIANISM

Even the attempt at introducing the Fabian socialistic elements in a country, like India, with a semi-feudalistic base and a capitalist economic framework superimposed thereon, resulted in creating a mixture of conflicting tendencies.

The framework of a planned mixed economy of a predominantly capitalist milieu requires special instruments pertaining to its character. The proper instruments wherever introduced by the decision makers in the field of economic policy, who either relied on theories developed for unplanned free-market economies, or economies of physical controls requiring highly-developed administrative skills. Nor were the instruments applicable to fully-planned states (which are capable of human regimentation) relevant for this country's economic conditions.

It was thought that merely a higher ratio of public sector to private sector investments would, in time, usher in the socialistic pattern through the door of state capitalism. However, the public sector is surrounded by the private sector as suppliers of essential materials for production, of equipment and even of skills. It depends upon private enterprise to provide consumer goods for its workers and operatives; and for the sale of its products, once again, it depends upon the private sector as purchasers. Lastly, the public sector is managed by persons with cultural values of the private sector.

True that the private sector in many matters is governed by men of public affairs. But they, in turn, derive electoral support on the basis of financial help from the private sector. This produces a situation where the private sector governs itself directly, as well as indirectly the policy for the public sector (through the complexion of the State itself being oriented towards the wishes of the private sector). Even the criterion of efficiency applied to a government enterprise by the public at large gets shifted from the original purpose of the social good to showing accounting profits, as a part of the cultural values of the private sector. The ratio of public to private sector investments, thus, does not denote the index of convergence to socialism, but merely of direct to indirect form of governance of private capital over the country's resources.

The second main policy instrument of Fabian socialism depends upon redistributive taxation meant to produce equity in the system. When worked in the setting of a capitalist framework and classical public finance, it allows the inequalities to grow, for it results in price rises and consequently depresses the economic status of the least-advantaged worker. The burden of the taxes whether indirect or direct, whether on necessaries, upon luxuries, can be passed on by the affluent corporations upon the richer consumers, and by them, further, upon the poorer set of consumers (through a series of subsequent rounds of price rises); and this is what, in fact, has also taken place.

Further, the demand exerted for luxury goods remains at a high level with a system of direct income impost which puts the tax-liability upon the corporations in such a manner that the higher is their expenditure the lesser is the tax base. Unaccounted money is certainly a factor for exerting demand upon inessentials, but many times more is the demand for the same goods exercised by purchasing power emanating from legitimate channels providing a high standard of living to the industrialist, the executives, the owners of urban and rural property, and the professionals whom the above engage for their affairs.

The other fiscal instruments which are relied upon by neoclassical economists can be equally detrimental in their effects. Borrowing from the public (with a savings drive among the lower income groups) is a standard instrument for raising revenue for capital expenditures of the State. If the borrowing is done at a low interest rate, it exploits the small saver in comparison to the entrepreneur who makes high profits from his investments. When the instruments of borrowing bear a high interest-rate, the rates of interest are raised throughout the economy. This causes a high-cost economy to be formed, and consequently an inflationary environment which, again, hits the least-advantaged workers.

The profits of the public sector are another source for revenue relied upon by Fabian socialists and endorsed by paleo-economic modes of thought. To obtain these profits the units use their monopoly powers to keep prices of their products high. These types of price rises can, thus, be attributed to public sector efforts to show higher profits and higher public-sector savings, when they are unable to do so through the hard measures of introducing greater discipline, efficiency, and integrity or better management for reduction of costs. But these cause inflationary tendencies to be transmitted rapidly throughout the economy. This is especially so in industries wherein the public sector produces goods and materials of a Heavy-Investment nature (which are at the base of the industrial system).

Revenue-oriented or redistributive taxation, borrowing from the public, and profits of public enterprises are all favourites of classical public-finance experts as sources of revenue, and derive support from Fabian political economy. All these have the potential of becoming highly dangerous instruments in the hands of the State in a Mixed Economy, capable of generating an inflation which otherwise would not exist, and alternatively, of aggravating it where it has organised from other causes, say, imbalances in investments for production of necessaries in relation to other expenditures of the government and the public.

The Glass-Curtain Economy with results from the consumption pattern of the type of system which was adopted, gives (to about one tenth of the population within it) access to all the goods which the people in advanced countries enjoy, whereas those without purchasing power watch the consumption being made by the privileged people, but the fancy goods are sold in markets where the mass of the population has no right of entry. This is the single largest cause of social tension and industrial unrest.

Whereas the egalitarian policy adopted, aims at reducing disparities in income, wealth and consumption — all three together — it has not, by the nature of the economic framework of a mixed economy, succeeded in achieving any one of these. On the other hand, it has diminished the incentives to the private sector to make further investments in the essential channels, and has shifted investments to the more profitable avenues of luxury goods. Equitable growth which signifies that it must be in the fields of the socially-relevant and essential goods, and preferably also creates high degree of employment, has been the casualty. It has not been realised that egalitarianism, the continuance of the private sector, and equitable growth cannot all three be achieved simultaneously. The policy was internally contradictory as an attempt to combine the irreconcilables.

In a Glass-curtain Economy the benefits meant for the common man rise up, as cream does, to the top. For instance, the low-interest loans for the marginal farmers considerably benefited those who stood surety for the former. But in that type of structure the burdens sink to the bottom, like lead. For instance, the burden of redistributive taxes and other imposts was passed down through higher prices, as has been mentioned earlier. The remedies of classical public finance cannot help under these circumstances, and equity cannot simply be established by Fabian instruments alone. The socialist compromises with capitalism have not been able to achieve results, because it has not been realised that egalitarian action against the continuance of the private sector (which socialism requires) and the uncontrolled growth of the private sector as part of the mixed economy (which capitalist entrepreneurs and affluent public demand) are incompatible.

One of the effective methods of redistribution of wealth if the policy-makers were serious about it, would have been a wealth tax upon the corporations, but this was not introduced, though once considered. The wealth tax or capital levy induces a higher immediate consumption, and consequently it tends to increase consumption disparities but lowers employment prospects which come about through higher investments. Egalitarianism aims at compression of disparities of consumption, income and wealth; and the mode of reducing the first is the result of, and conditional upon, success in achieving the latter two types of disparities. Equalitarianism, on the other hand, concentrates only on reducing consumption disparities and does so directly, without affecting income or wealth disparities. In so doing it neither hurts investment and accumulation nor promotes a spending spree.

Where there is a predominant private sector, partial measures to achieve an egalitarian state are not only anti-investment (and hence anti-employment in nature), in the short-run, and anti-development in the long-run, but they are also anti-equalitarian. Fabian attempts at achieving egalitarianism gradually, when worked in the setting of a Glass-Curtain Economy defeat their objective of curbing consumption disparities (via the reduction of inequalities in wealth). If wealth is to be equalised, only a nationalisation of the whole economy or abolition of the private sector undertaken wholesale (and without prior announcement), would prevent consumption of capital. In that case we would not be dealing with a mixed economy, but one in which decision has already been taken to have a socialist state (and with immediate effect), and there is political will as well as the power to implement the decision. This can hardly take place in a social democracy through use of legislative procedures and peaceful means, unless the polity has reached a stage of predominance of workers' management of industry and has achieved a high level of organisational strength of the proletariat (both employed and unemployed committed to advancing the common interest of the working class as a whole, and subordinating the intra-class conflicts).

The economic system of egalitarian capitalism established in our country, has not broken down precisely because its effective aspects of wealth-equality have been kept subdued, but this element has been sufficiently strong to have resulted on its being an important coutributory factor in low performance. However, this has neither been good enough for yielding growth for purposes of taking the country into a state of industrial advancement, nor for providing social justice and equity to the least-advantaged of the present generation.

The Glass-Curtain Economy has an effect upon the functioning of the Trade Unions also. The labour movement is the basis of protection of the rights of workers as against management. It is also meant to be the means of decreasing the share of profits in income, and in mature capitalism it is supposed to build the proletarian strength whereby the workers will take ultimate control of the economy. In the Glass-Curtain Economy, workers in highly-organised industries look up to the executives who enjoy a high standard of living and wish to emulate at least a part of that, and are able to make the fulfilment of the wish possible. They cannot be expected to be content with what they have, as long as the demonstration effect of the standard of living of the executives and the industrialists is before them. One cannot give them sermons on "wage restraints for the working class", when one at the same time, advocates the necessity of private electric-generators to run the air-conditioners for the industrialist's household when there is interruption in the general power-supply.

The action of trade unions at getting higher money wages of members, increases the standard of living of those workers. This is so whether it is accompanied by or is without rise of productivity. The higher money wage lowers the investment capacity in relation to the state which would rule with the previous (lower) money wage. It does not decrease the consumption of the richer classes, which is governed by the social environment of the Glass-Curtain Economy. The burden is felt by those among the labour force who were waiting to get employed, and a lower rate of investment does not fulfil that expectation. The price rise resulting from money wages going up, causes an inflation which hits the unorganised workers in employment.

The only aspect of socialistic pattern which was given concrete shape in our planning process was the Two-sector model worked out by Professor Mahalanobis in 1953, and used later for the Second

Five Year Plan. By virtue of this, the commanding heights of the technological pyramid (the self-reproducing complex of parent machines and supporting inputs) were to be given priority. The priority to Heavy Investments and the only element in which Mr. Nehru had his way according to his wishes. It is also the most precious part of the planning theory in the Indian context, although the priority was fixed at no more than the modest figure of 1/3rd to be reploughed into the Heavy Industry Sector.

The two sector model is theoretically defensible, but under pressure of demand for social justice, two more sectors were added without changing the rate of ploughback of the Heavy Investment sector, which implies that the average degree of mechanisation was meant to be kept at a high level. The model was thereby made theoretically confused by adding another two sectors (ostensibly to yield employment). But it was innate in the model that this effect would not take place, because of the average degree of mechanisation having been kept constant (and at a high level), and enough employment opportunities could not be created.

The Plan-frame of the Second Five Year Plan gave importance to advancement of public sector and the development of Heavy Industry, but this priority got implemented only in the first few years of the second plan.

Within the second plan itself, the Planning Commission's policy of priority for the Heavy-Industry sector remained under successful attacks, mainly from the protagonists of agricultural sector (which, in fact, gains a lot from growth of Heavy Industry). In later plans, the pace of growth of heavy-investments was not maintained, and instead of making the sector grow, excess capacities were allowed to be built up. It was wrongly alleged that agriculture suffered as a result of investment in heavy industries, an argument which has been repeated since 1957 by men of public affairs (in high decisions-making positions), who if they had applied the theory of economic growth, would have known the consumption necessaries of workers in that sector, and the agricultural sector before it can be entirely modernised, needs the prior existence of a strong Heavy Investment base.

What was not envisaged in the Mahalanobis model was the demand created by the affluent of the economy. They demanded a basket of modernised consumer-durables and other fancy-goods (from the common man's point of view). The Glass-Curtain Economy's demand was catered for by a sector of modernised consumption-goods with highly-mechanised advanced-technology machinery. This produced a high profit to wage ratio, and was also responsible for an aggravation of the unfavourable personal income distribution including juridical persons in the population of consumers. This further created a demand for luxury goods and highly-mechanised equipment. This demand could be met only by diverting investments from consumption necessaries and heavy-investments both. It is not Heavy-Investments which have drawn away resources from agriculture, but mechanised luxury-good production and machinery for the richer farmer which has kept the growth of both heavy-investments and consumption necessaries (especially by the poorer producers), at a low level.

The other aspect of the commanding heights programme was aimed at public ownership of the financial institutions. Through this policy (which could get implemented not less than fifteen years after the first aspect was announced) priority sectors were to get greater attention in lending operations. However, in the manner it is implemented, priority is so defined that luxury consumption goods get great financial attention on one count or another — profitability, productive technology, greater repaying capacity, credit-worthiness of the borrower, opportunities to the self-employed, encouragement to young entrepreneurship, utilisation of local materials, transfer of advanced technology from abroad, export drive etc. The Glass-curtain Economy has, therefore, further flourished on the shoulders of the state-owned financial and banking institutions.

In the field of commanding heights of the economy also the socialistic measures followed did not bring us nearer to socialism, and in the total context we have secured a lower benefit in terms of growth, as well as of social justice, in comparison to what was technologically possible.

Over the wide field of the economy, we have seen above that Fabian and democratic socialistic policies undertaken in a system of mixed economy with dominance of the values of the private-sector have failed to achieve the objectives which Mr. Nehru had desired, and the cause of that was the adoption of irreconcilable aspects of the two constituents of the mixed economy.

The system of planned allocations is an aspect of economics of control under conditions of scarcity. It is not specific to socialist policies, for it can be implemented by a pro-capitalist government also, as was done in War-time Britain.

The two types of regulatory mechanisms which the State can use are the Vertical-Control System with its insistence on direct controls, decrees, fiats, orders, mandaments, and rules requiring permission to be taken by people to act in all matters circumscribed by permits, licenses, warrants and approvals. This may be suited to the conditions of a country with a large member of highly-skilled administrative-manpower units with the necessary qualification of possession of complete integrity.

However, in a Glass-Curtain Economy the bureaucracy feels impelled by social compulsions to levy a private impost upon the applicants for permits, so that the operatives in charge of implementing controls may be able to gather purchasing power to enjoy a higher standard of living. Such income of the bureaucrat or expenditure of the applicant cannot be declared to authorities and it creates a parallel economy. The allocations, on the other hand, do not come nearer to what has been set as the desired target by the planning agency keeping in view the priorities. The physical result tends to approximate what a non-planned economy might itself have obtained through the market system, but the prices are higher because of the element of private exactions by public servants and men of public affairs which enter into the costs of production.

There is a certain class of public servants, though small in number, who try to work in this system with integrity, but the Vertical Control System requires such a large army of government servants to run the machinery that the men of integrity are overwhelmed in numbers by those with other proclivities. The regulation of the economy in an underdeveloped country with a lack of administrative skills based upon integrity, would avoid the Vertical Control System as it does not achieve the regulation desired on grounds of allocations of resources according to national priority, and creates misallocations through demands generated out of ransoms extracted by those in authority, or possessing influence. The larger firm benefits from the system of vertical control, because it has more purchasing power for liaison work to be done by experts and consultants (many of them retired government officials knowing the way the procedural hoops can be jumped through). The smaller producer is at a disadvantage. It is for this reason that the larger houses have not found the system of controls too unwelcome, though it has throttled the growth of the smaller producer.

III. EQUALITARIAN SOCIALISM

However, there is an alternative form of socialistic planning which has been specially desired for working in the context of a mixed economy of the type existing in under-developed countries in general, and in our country in particular. In this form of planning, equity is sought to be achieved through egalitarianism, but through a spectrum of production which is relevant for intergenerational and intragenerational equity.

The dictates of intergenerational equity require considerably greater emphasis upon the sector of Heavy-industries, than was envisaged (or was possible) in the Mahalanobis model. The priority to Heavy-Industries requires the ploughing back of their products within that sector. This entails minimisation of the leakage of their products to the consumption-oriented sectors and indicates product of consumption necessaries only by techniques which conserve the use of products of the Heavy-Industries' sector (and of the non-reproducible deposits of the earth). These techniques happen, incidentally, to be of low degree of mechanisation, and can create greater employment, as well as a high Wage to Profit ratio. The plants using this type of machinery can be diffused throughout the countryside, and can be utilised through units of the miniature scale. Equity both for the future and present generations is obtained through the composition of the spectrum of production, and it is the equity for the future periods which leads to the equity for the current period.

The production policy for the consumption sector is dictated by the pursuit of equalitarianism. It implies the achievement of equity through a production spectrum which enforces reduction of consumption disparities. In this the consumption disparities alone are reduced, and directly, so, while not touching the income and wealth disparities, which the present system of egalitarianism wishes to reduce and which is treated as an essential pre-requisite for reduction of consumption in equalities. In this type of mixed economy the private sector can exist if it follows the production spectrum of social relevance firstly for producing necessaries of consumption, secondly their equipment of low degree of mechanisation, and thirdly the H-sector machinery. In this equalitarian consumption is achieved along with long-term benefits of growth. Such an economy is called the Composite Economy, and therein the continuance and growth of the private sector would not be attacked. Having been retained as part of a compromise political settlement, it would be accepted as a rightful constituent of the composite economy, but efforts would be made to gear it to social relevance and to that alone.

Where equalitarianism would be the immediate aim, and only consumption standards would be sought to be made more equal, higher accumulation would be permitted and encouraged without penalties, but only as long as the channels for earning and spending are attuned to goods of social relevance in an austerity economy. Luxuries would not be invested in, and thus, would not be produced; and hence, they would be unobtainable. The accumulated wealth would, therefore, exist, but unlike the present egalitarian system wherein the wealth which is left with the private sector after payment of taxes can be used in any manner that the owner wants, in the proposed system whether it be in the nature of accounted funds or unaccounted forms of the parallel economy, all wealth would become sterilized and would be prevented from distorting the spectrum of optimum allocations, (of physical and manpower resources) by diverting them towards undesirable ends. It is this sterilization of all wealth in the hands of the private sector and converting its nature from that of purchasing power to be exercised as one wishes, to a system of guiding it to be used for the common good which gives this system the attribute of a socialistic pattern.

The composite economy can achieve its objective of combining socialism and capitalism, as a form of socialistic pattern in a mixed-economy but would be of a sort different from the frame of the un-easy compromise historically entered into, and its socialist as well as capitalist components would have to be different in tenor. Above all, the Composite Economy will not be achieved by liberalisation of the economy and giving free rein to untrammelled market forces emanating from huge disparities in purchasing power. As a matter of fact, it will require greater regulation than has been imposed hitherto upon the private and the public sectors, though this regulation would not be through means of Vertical Control System entailing physical controls, of licenses or permits (which have been tried hitherto), but by a Horizontal Control System using powerful instruments of fiscal action.

The Horizontal Control System uses powerful monetary and fiscal instruments of guidance. It works through rewards for approved actions and penalties for unapproved ones, but the decisions regarding policy are entirely centralised, and for decisions to act, the power is entirely decentralised and dispersed among individual units. There is never any Government permission required for any reasonable action in this system, and the stranglehold of the licensing procedures is absent. The cost and ransoms which bureaucracy is capable of charging for running the Vertical Control System (and through which men of public affairs can show their patronage) are entirely eliminated. It is the Horizontal Control System which is suited for a country wherein the administrative manpower skills are limited, and their supervision to maintain efficiency and rectitude can be effectively done only when the total number of operatives engaged in administration is small.

The Horizontal Control System in a Composite Economy depends upon fiscal devices which have been known to Indian economic theory for the past thirteen years or more, and which were fashioned especially to deal with the structure of the Composite Economy. The Misexpenditure Tax (and its more generalised form the Disparity Tax) are the main allocative mechanism which can be used to channel the investments and manpower resources away from production of luxuries into manufacture of necessaries in employment-creating techniques. But neither knowledge about them nor an understanding of their significance has been able to penetrate even into the outer shell of the awareness of the academic or the governmental establishment imprisoned by paleo-economic thought.

In the Composite Economy private profit would continue and would grow, but the surplus would be utilised only for the socially-relevant production which would be in the fields of Heavy-Investment for intergenerational equity and consumer necessaries for the present generation. Hence, not merely the public sector, but also the whole of the private sector would become the vehicle of furthering the social good. It will keep the incentive to invest and to accumulate at a high public sector who could then safely seek profit maximisation (provided it is net of Disparity-Tax payment made for misallocations effected by the public enterprise). Such a society will have no need to emphasise the dominance of the public sector in relation to the private sector, as is enjoined by Fabian thought, for the private sector itself will also serve the common good, and only that. Thus, this particular principle of Fabian socialism shoulders the private sector in full measure.

The Composite Economy will not have any imposts designed to redistribute income or wealth or to sponge purchasing power as part of the egalitarian policy (which, if it had been properly implemented, would have been found to be incompatible with growth and continuance of the private sector, and when implemented in partial measure, as it has been, it has been found to have hampered growth in right lines, but has been unable to prevent the private sector flourishing in the unapproved fields). Hence, the other important principle of Fabian socialism based on redistributive taxation would be set aside, and substituted by the prescript of allocative taxation for channelling resources into investments of the relevant category to provide the production spectrum yielding equity.

The Disparity Tax would replace entirely the Income and Wealth Imposts, the Gift Tax and the Estate Duty among the direct exactions, and the whole Indirect-Impost system based upon excise and sales taxes and the various cesses imposed upon specific commodities, all of which are inflationary in nature. It would severely limit inessential consumption through providing powerful disincentives for undertaking any investments for production of luxury goods, and would encourage production of essential goods for curbing inflation through equally powerful incentives to invest in avenue of social necessity. This would be the means of transforming the production of necessaries into a profitable activity, and manufacturer of luxuries into an unprofitable activity.

For stabilising the economy the composite socialistic pattern will not depend upon revenue-earning imposts, or upon borrowings from the public, or savings of the public sector to balance the budget (all of which have proven to be inflationary). It will, on the other hand, control inflation through increasing budget deficits, lowering the interest rate, the profit rate and prices consequently, and channelling (through the allocative-tax system) the physical and manpower resources, so that necessaries of consumption with the aid of less mechanised equipment may grow rapidly along with long term basic investments, at the expense of modernised luxuries, and the highly capital-intensive equipment engaged in their production. The system would depend upon the planning organisation laying down the spectrum of production, rather than having its targets dovetailed to market demands originating from affluence. The managers of enterprises (public and private) would be guided into making the right choices through the device of the Disparity Tax. The profit rate criterion and market system would indeed continue, but the system, thus, retains the market structure, but tutors the prices, so that although profit motive is used, the levels of profits are changed and emit the signals for channelling of resources into lines of social relevance as being more profitable.

The socialistic pattern of society for its proper implementation in a Glass-curtain Economy, requires not only a change in the economic system from a mixed economy to a composite economy, but also a change in political framework from Egalitarian Fabianism to Equalitarian Socialism. The system will be an instrument for controlling inflation, and offering greater employment; it will build capital of the Heavy-Investment sector for the future generation, and shall provide consumption necessaries to the least-advantaged workers for the current generation. It will provide the basic minimum for the weakest sections to permit them to withstand repression and exploitation. It will make infructuous the white as well as black wealth (except for use in approved activities) by not providing opportunities for it to be misspent; for if it were so misused, it would then be attracting penalties to an extent inviting financial disaster upon the mal-allocating investor (whether an individual or a corporation or a religious trust or public-sector unit or a government department).

The system of horizontal control which is required, will have to make the State more powerful and capable of taking hard decisions. It would implement its adoption through a highly-centralised policy-making authority prescribing an austerity economy. The Constitution would have to be more centralised and unitary as regards policy decisions affecting national uniformity. But its implementation would be through decentralised autonomous corporations taking decisions regarding choice of manner of management to escape penalties and to earn rewards for the organisation. The firm of the State requisite for the Composite Economy will stand in between the Soft and the Hard States of Professor Gunnar Myrdal, and may be described by the term, "The Firm State".

This restructuring of our attitudes and instruments of implementation is what is required to be done for the objectives of Mr. Nehru to be achieved, rather than the withdrawal of regulatory mechanisms, or increase of liberalisations which is likely to be canvassed with the Government at the present juncture, as it has been done many a time in the past thirtyfive years. Because classical modes of thought have made traditional planning somewhat ineffective, there is no reason to joining the chorus for denigration of Planning which is basically a system of decision-making on rational grounds. The planning process needs to be reformed, in fact, towards its greater strengthening, rather than being reduced in importance. Income and Wealth egalitarianism needs to be substituted by a more effective form of Consumption equalitarianism, rather than the advocacy of abandonment altogether of the policy of establishing equality as a policy objective of the Government. The concept of the Composite Economy permits a fusion of the reconcilable aspects of socialist and capitalist systems in the framework of the Glass-Curtain Economy which exists today, and it requires the discarding of only the irreconcilable aspects.

In the light of the propositions discussed above, the orthodox economists, the traditional socialists, the pragmatic capitalists and the standard political philosophers all need to re-examine their premises and analytical frameworks with respect to the Glass-Curtain Economy in which the politico-economic system operates in an under-developed country like India.

With a redefinition of the aims and re-specification of the instruments of implementation, growth and equity would be achieved simultaneously as essential components of a planned socialistic society in an economy with public and private sectors both with roles as socially-meaningful constituents. No greater tribute can be paid to the memory of Mr. Nehru than suggesting a system which can, on the one hand, salvage his objectives from the danger of our side tracking them, and, on the other hand, implement his socialist commitment in essential spirit. No more opportune a time there is for us to do this rethinking when there is a danger of forces of great weight and influence (from abroad as well as from within) trying to overturn the basic premise of the economy from planned regulation to a system of freedom to follow the unbridled market forces. No greater faith in democracy, as introduced by Mr. Nehru, can be shown than by asserting that in the present political structure, the Government has the power and the capacity of leadership of the people, to be able to obtain their approval for making the required changes in the economic and constitutional structure.

5

CAPITAL THEORY AND POLITICAL ECONOMY

I. INTERNATIONAL EQUITY

It is known that the supremacy of the ancient but economically less-developed countries in terms of richness of their civilisations, or purity of ideals, is shown utter disregard in foreign economic affairs by economically-advanced countries. The attitude of the affluent nations offers convincing proof that in order to be successful in holding an independent foreign policy, we must possess, in a demonstrable manner, economic equality with them.

One can see that economic equality cannot depend wholly on the historical records of our past intellectual efforts or upon cultivation of soul force. It requires the capacity to eliminate fundamental disequilibrium so that firstly one can resolve the balance of a trade problems in the long-run, and secondly one can bridge the Under-development Gap. The latter task will have been accomplished when we have secured for our people a standard of living no worse than that of employed manpower units in an average advanced country, and that too at full employment of the polulation which will be existing at that time.

This is an aim which all underdeveloped countries must relentlessly pursue to be able to become members of the comity of nations on terms of equality based upon solidity of economic structure.

These twin aims of self-reliance and full development straight away puts the subject of Strategy of Development into the category of planning of long-run growth comprising many Perspective-Plan periods. The tentative projections on the basis of our capacity to attain Full Development under a proper planning mechanism were once worked out by me in 1971 for the late Pitamber Pant, a man

Published in *The Manpower Journal,* vol. XIX, No. 3, Oct.-Dec. 1983.

of dedication to the cause of planning. These indicated the time span to be a long one, going up to the year 2025 A.D. This incidentally, was not supposed to be a date in the remote future, but a point of time within sight, for the children born that year would still be in their productive years at the target date.

This degree of achievement necessarily requires the fastest rate of accumulation of capital which technology allows, and implies that we have the manpower management to take advantage of the capacities of the economy. The requirement is not for amassing savings certificates. The accumulation would have to be carried out in physical terms and would be comprised of the basic machines produced, manpower skills expanded and social infrastructure created. All these together would form a complex which could deliver sufficient mechanised light machinery to produce the huge volume of consumption goods which will be needed at the target year. One cannot escape the policy of build-up of the self-regenerating basic-machinery sector if our country has to achieve not only self-reliance, but the command of respect in the sphere of international policy.

II. SHIFTS IN EMPHASIS

The long-term policy of building up the basic industries, called Heavy-Investment or H for short, was outlined by Professor P.C. Mahalanobis, in economic translation of the vision of our first Prime Minister. But it gave way to a cry for priority for agriculture, which soon yielded to necessity for Defence. Somewhat later the focus was shifted to distribution, and from thence to removal of poverty, and later, to basic needs and still later to employment. Lately, it has been self-employment, and after that foreign exchange which is thought to be most worthy of being maximised, and very recently the transfer of most modern foreign technology is the prime concern of some advisors upon policy. But all these are short-term facets of a broader integrated approach which needs to be spelt out, to prevent the sectoral improvisations and makeshift arrangements of parts of the economy from masquerading as substitutes for a co-ordinated long-term policy for the economy as a whole. The models of planning officially recognised have also been framed with limited horizon and partial targets in sight.

The succession of acts seeming to change priorities is the result of two confusions. The first one is on account of the overall interlinking of parts of the economic machinery having been overlooked. One cannot give priority to one industry without, at the same time giving priority to the linked industries which directly or indirectly act as inputs to the priority sector. This confusion ought to have disappeared after the concept of "the sub-economy" had been used for steady-growth planning using the idea contained in Piero Sraffa's book published in 1960 that production of all commodities is by means of direct and indirect inputs of the same commodities themselves. The declaration of priority to the leading sector implies the allotment of the same degree of importance to the whole set of interlinked activities forming a sub-economy, this stress being higher in relation to the goods outside the priority sub-economy.

The second confusion emanates from not looking at priority as a sequence of operations, each operation getting emphasis in a phase of the Optimum Strategy of Development. The concept of sequence is fundamental to development, and is independent of the economic system. Even Professor Hirschman while advocating a fully-competitive and free-market economy, accepted the need of defining sequence of operations. In any socially-purposeful strategy, the luxuries, for instance must wait for their turn in the sequence, and necessaries must get prior attention.

There has been, in Economic Theory, choice between the present and the future from the time of Ricardo, whereby corn used as seed is investment for the future, and corn eaten up is consumption for the present. In neo-classical economics the inter-temporal conflict was manifested through the invention of concepts like social rates of time preference, or discount of the future. In modern development economics, following the pioneering work of Dr. Maurice Dobb, it was made over-through the problem of choice of techniques. Following it, Professor Amartya Kumar Sen in his famous Stevenson Prize Essay of 1957 demonstrated that employment-creating techniques cater to short-run interests, and surplus-creating ones to long-term benefits, while he further postulated the criterion of time-horizon to select one or the other degree of mechanisation. According to this formulation, for sights fixed at a distant point in the future, the more mechanised technique would be indicated, and this proposition has ruled as the economic orthodoxy of the sophisticated development theory for the last twenty-five years.

III. UNEMPLOYMENT AND MECHANISATION

The keynote of the philosophy of the learned Inaugural Lecture has been on the need to achieve growth with satisfaction of basic needs. Howsoever correct this approach may be in the context of his own set of aims, the submission of economists belonging to alternative schools within the country has differed from it. One set of economists held that growth by itself can generate employment, but they did not realise that growth through investment in higher degrees of mechanisation does not create efficient employment.

Some of them still adhere to their bias in favour of higher degrees of mechanisation in production of consumption goods, by producing statistics that employment does not suffer when degree of mechanisation increases. They maintain that mechanisation does not displace manpower, for, according to them, it re-deploys it in ancillary occupations. But they do not take account of the fact that higher mechanisation is efficient only if it saves labour. If five hundred people are to be employed to level a piece of ground when they use spades, and even the same number are required for the same task when one has a hundred times more capital-intensive earthmover, then one cannot claim superiority for this latter. Yet a high degree of mechanisation is tried to be justified on grounds of the employment it creates in repair shops and ancillary operations, and with a lower yield of the final product per unit of investment as well as per man. The cast of the mind and conclusion in favour of mechanisation have remained the same for this group of economists; the criteria have changed according to the fashion of the times, from justification on basis of growth, to that on grounds of employment.

There are others who consider the growth objective not worth pursuing and look for payoff only in terms of current social justice. A high degree of current social justice would be indicated firstly by the extent of removal of poverty, and secondly, by the low dispersion of consumption levels both within the classes at one place, and over various regions.

IV. MALEMPLOYMENT AND POVERTY

The remedies for poverty are interlinked with the analysis of its source and causes. One of the important causes of the state whereby a large mass of people (who are capable of being better off) are afflicted by poverty through real inflation is traceable to the large degree of Malemployment. This stems from the demands of the affluent and of the anti-social elements which attract away the skilled labour and physical resources both, from the task of producing necessaries with the optimum techniques towards inessential goods.

The affluent group can be stratified by consumption levels which may be represented by concentric rings each with a higher consumption in relation to the ring adjacent to it on the outer side, the persons in the next inner ring. Some of those who have been in outer ring are now enjoying a position in an inner ring and it is this which causes social tensions among persons in the outer ring. The consumption of the person in an inner ring is visible to those outside, and the goods possessed by him are also arrayed in alluring perspectives in showrooms of the various markets for the elite. But entry to the inner ring is possible only with a higher purchasing power. This acts as a barrier to improving one's status. The whole set of these rings is, therefore, called the Glass-Curtain Economy.

The psychological pressures of availability of goods and equality with the group of people just above any person's consumption standard, competes with the desire to save, but the force of consumption is stronger in many cases. In other cases, the consumers outside the inner consumption rings seize the opportunities of making extra incomes, through fair or unfair means. It leads to skilled manpower either weakening its moral fibre or changing the character of their interests from their own professional work to subsidiary money-spinning activities.

The demands created by the members of the Glass-Curtain Economy are for the luxury goods, and malemployment is caused by that demand. Equity suffers on account of the very existence of consumption disparities, and by the diversion of resources from employment-creating investments to current consumption of the affluent. The key to the poverty of the masses is thus the consumption of the affluent.

The well-tried prescriptions regarding Basic-Needs Programmes, Guaranteed-Employment Schemes, and Distribution of Goods among the poor can only offer palliatives but cannot cure the ailment, because they attack the symptoms of poverty while they refrain from tackling the real cause which lies in the continuance of the Glass-Curtain Economy. No methodology exists in a mixed economy by which poverty can be removed quickly without first of all attempting to channel the resources of the economy to uses more purposive than the consumption of the affluent within the country. Employment offered in providing luxury consumption is at the expense of larger true employment which may be obtained through providing optimal equipment for long-term growth and for providing the necessaries of consumption.

V. MECHANISED TECHNIQUES AND EQUITY

The average degree of mechanisation in the economy depends upon the ratio of Basic Investment Sector to the Consumption-good Sector. The self-regenerating basic machinery and infrastructural sector would largely be highly capital-intensive (in spite of some possibility of labour-intensive methods of production). The potentiality of only the consumption sector can be utilised to keep low the average degree of mechanisation of the economy. To the extent that this is made use of, it furthers the degree of current social justice.

But it is important to remember that current social justice is obtained through employment created by investments. Investment and growth are synonymous and identical in nature. There cannot be growth without investment and vice versa. But what we have shown is that if investment is in techniques of low degree of mechanisation, the volume of employment created is larger for a particular growth rate. If it is in techniques of high degree of mechanisation in which investment takes place, then employment created for a particular growth rate is smaller. Both types of techniques can be organised for non-inflationary growth and real wage need not decrease if there is a balance between productive investment and unproductive expenditures.

Employment (to a larger or smaller degree) and Investment rise in the same direction, and this has, to a certain extent, been achieved together during the past thirty years. But it is in the volume of each that insufficiency has become apparent due to a socially-incorrect choice of high degree of mechanisation in the consumption sector, aggravated by appearance of long-lasting industrial inactivity in the public and private sectors. The size of actual investment has been based upon either imagined financial constraints or inadequacy of our public and private management to deal with some basic issues of industrial relations and restructuring of managerial administration. The biased choice of techniques, and the insufficiency of activity in relation to potential physical and manpower resources, rather than real resource constraint, have been responsible for lack of creation of employment opportunities. The manner in which we have implemented the strategy of priority to Heavy Investment and the classical modes of public finance have together been the cause of the insufficiency both of social justice and of growth.

VI. LOW PLOUGHBACK IN THE H-SECTOR

Contrary to a general uniformed opinion, the error has not been in too much Investment in the basic-machinery sector, but in too little expansion of this Heavy-Investment Sector. Its expansion (dependent upon the ploughback of its products within the H-sector itself) has been kept low by the high degree of mechanisation in the consumption sector draining away products of the Basic-Machinery sector. This has caused not only a low rate of ploughback of the products of Heavy Industries within that self-expanding sector, but also a low volume of purposive employment. It has nullified the policy of priority for Heavy-Investment Sector.

At the time of framing of the Second Plan, thirty years ago, Professor Mahalanobis was vehemently opposed when he originally proposed the modest allocation of one-third for ploughback within the capital-goods sector. The research work of Professor Yadava Reddy at the Osmania University showed that this figure was firstly less than even in present day situation of advanced countries, and in fact according to the way we implemented the strategy of priority for H-Investment, we achieved only one-fifth allocation to it which represent the benefit for the future, while four-fifths was drained off by mechanised light machinery for production of consumption goods, which supposedly represents the interests of the current generation. But even the benefit to the present generation was not achieved because of the very fact that it was sought to be achieved by greater allocation to the C-sector rather than to the H-Sector.

The desire to allocate more to the consumption sector for attempting to achieve current social justice was implemented through the high degree of mechanisation in the consumption sector. It produced the twofold effect of low employment and low ploughback in the H-sector. It made an inroad upon growth and social justice simultaneously and we failed in achieving enough of either.

VII. HIGH SAVINGS AND MISCONSUMPTION

The effect of higher mechanisation was not confined to lack of creation of employment opportunities. It produced high profit to wage ratio and encouraged the scale of production to be on the larger side for an underdeveloped country. These together led to monopolism and metropolitanism — both aspects of Political Economy and Sociology of Development. This phenomenon added to the already existing skewness in income-distribution, and created a demand for modernised skewness in income-distribution, and created a demand for modernised luxury commodities. These were required to be produced by modern equipment with latest technology imported from abroad or invented in our indigenous laboratories. This further increased the degree of mechanisation and added to the capital requirement. Much of it being in foreign exchange, it aggravated the balance of payments problem, on the one hand, and on the other, it tended to decrease the output-capital ratio. This explains also the so-called paradox as to why a high rate of monetary savings has been associated with a low growth rate.

The increased capital intensity resulted in a still higher profit to Wage ratio. Hence, the skewness of income distribution increased and demand for luxury consumption went up. It is this high Profit-to-Wage ratio which is responsible for the Illusion of a High Rate of Savings, for what it hides is the fact that a search for it tilts the choice of technique to more capital-intensive forms; which, through a higher share of profits in income, increases the rate of savings, but at the same time increased the volume of national misconsumption also. Thus, both in statistical association as well as in logical causation, action to increase savings increases consumption disparities rather than reducing them.

The high rate of savings following a high Profit to wage ratio was, therefore, at the expense of a lower real wage for the worker.

If a low rate of financial savings were sought, and alternative action to lower the degree of misconsumption were to be taken, the degree of mechanisation in the C-sector would be lower and the output-capital ratio higher. With a Low degree of mechanisation in the consumption sector there would be no aggravation of skewness in income distribution, no further creation of consumption disparities, nor misconsumption leading to malallocation of physical and manpower resources causing inflation and low employment, as well as low ploughback in the Heavy-Investment sector. Contrary to what has been often alleged (sometimes at the highest political quarters at the national government), the fact is that it was not Heavy-Investment which has thwarted agricultural growth, but the search for a high growth rate through the aegis of a high rate of savings (rather than the alternative of limiting misconsumption directly, and adopting simultaneously, a high output-capital ratio. It is the search for high rate of savings which is associated with the consumption of the rich, and it is this rather than the priority to the H-sector, which has hampered growth both of the H-sector, and of the sector for consumption necessaries (which, of course, includes much of agriculture).

VIII. FOREIGN TECHNOLOGY

Machinery of high degree of mechanisation has also been fostered by adoption of foreign technology euphemistically called "Transfer of Advanced Technology". Due to an educational system which teaches technology and science without giving an understanding of social issues, the modern industrial and agricultural engineer is indoctrinated and biased in favour of technology appropriate to advanced countries from his degree course itself. The affluent public likes the goods manufactured, as they are usually luxury consumer items, like tri-acetate texturized fabrics. The management executive prefers the mechanised machinery because such equipment, and even robots and micro-processors, have not yet learned to form labour unions. The trader derives a handsome profit for selling it, and the marketing experts derive huge commissions for putting high pressure salesmanship into play to sell them. The banker considers them good security.

The large-scale firm likes the import of modernised equipment for the sake of its productivity to the corporation and because it gives opportunity for the firm to collaborate with multinational corporations which earn profits for the company, and for its sponsors the occasions to go abroad and be supplied with latest consumer goods of foreign origin. The small-scale entrepreneur likes the small and beautiful but capital-intensive machinery, for he can get license and financial aid to set up a unit to produce ancillaries, but he does not mind if he thereby becomes a dependent of the large corporations which act as monopsonists. The licensing officers think it worthwhile to put in effort to justify the use of such advanced machinery to secure permission for its import from highpowered watchdog authorities. The Finance Ministry advisers welcome such techniques which cause the savings rate to be high, and which consequently permit them to keep to a low level of the alternative sources of receipts.

The growth economists, if they are rightists, consider it in keeping with Schumpeterian innovative capitalism to foster the improved more capital-intensive machinery, and if they are leftists, they find it in keeping with trends of industrialisation in advanced socialist countries. There is thus a whole consortium of interests with various backgrounds in favour of high mechanisation in the consumption sector, and the proper growth strategist finds himself only in the company of protagonists of employment-creating inferior primitive technology who do not wish to have anything to do with advocacy of priority to Heavy Investment as being the logical reason for fostering low degree of mechanisation in the consumption sector.

IX. EQUITY AND GROWTH

If the component of high mechanisation were to be eliminated from the Consumption sector where this can be done, and a lower degree of mechanisation is substituted, it would have a dual effect. In one direction, it would, firstly, reserve the use of non-reproducible deposits of the earth for the H-sector where the use is indispensable. It would, further, conserve the products of H-sector, allowing basic machinery industries to grow faster. This is because of the happy but natural association of low degree of mechanisation with less roundabout methods of production, and thus with H-conserving characteristics.

On the other hand, techniques of low degree of mechanisation yield high employment per unit of investment, and through that dispersal of consumption is effected. The system restructured is capable of yielding long-run and short-term growth as well as current and intergenerational social justice, all together. Priority to the Heavy-industries sector is quite compatible with current social justice, and in order to achieve equity it is necessary to reduce emphasis on basic infrastructure. On the contrary, it is because of priority to Heavy Investment that low leakage to the consumption sector of its product is to be enjoined, and would enforce a low degree of mechanisation in that sector.

The justification of low degree of mechanisation in the production of consumption goods, then no longer remains its capacity to yield social justice. But one would have to stress its essentiality for rapid expansion of basic equipment and infrastructure for long-run growth. The justification through human elements (which carry little weight with the Economic Men who frame the doctrines for planning policy), is replaced by justification on account of long-run and short-run efficient growth (which the productivity minded planner and the benefit-cost calculator would not easily ignore). The conscientious objections of production economists against non-economic creteria in support of a low degree of mechanisation in the consumption sector ought to disappear with this realisation, and opposition to low capital intensity, even though demonstrated as above to be efficient, if it remains, would only be based on bias, and not on logic.

Professor Amartya Sen's proposition favouring the higher degree of mechanisation for growth with a long time horizon is then to be substituted by the opposite hypothesis of a low degree of mechanisation in the consumption sector to yield long-run growth as well as employment.

The conclusion to be drawn from this demonstration is that if attention is concentrated upon short-run growth (which excluded emphasis upon the H-sector) then higher degree of mechanisation would be indicated to be optimum, and neither growth would be achieved nor current social justice. If, on the other hand, one attends to long-term growth which necessitates priority for the Heavy-Investment sector, then both growth and social justice in the long-run as well as current period could be simultaneously achieved. Conversely, if one looks only for short-run equity, then one gets no long-run growth and little current social justice. But, if one looks for long-term equity or intergenerational equity, then also one will get both growth and social justice.

The optimum Strategy of Development would integrate the physical and financial aspects together through an integration of Effective Demand and Effective Supply. The strategy requires a production plan whereby the real wage of the least-advantaged worker is not to be reduced and luxury goods would not be produced. Austerity is its keynote, and would be reflected through the production spectrum being according to social relevance. It does not make for economic consistency to include in the Plan materials and goods for luxury manufacture to implement the same through the ministry of industries, and then to try to use fiscal disincentives to curb the consumption of the goods produced. It is not merely the imposition or withdrawal of taxes on occupancy of luxury hotels, but a fiscal device (like the Disparity Tax) which dissuades such hotels being set up which is the requirement of iong-run growth.

It is a production plan based on Austerity which alone can find physical resources for long-run investments and to fulfil basic needs of the employed. It alone is consistent with fiscal measures for curbing inessential demand. The function of fiscal policy should primarily be to curb supply and demand of inessential goods and to encourage socially-relevant commodities rather than to raise revenue irrespective of the contents of the spectrum of production. This is what ought to have been the principle of the Supply-side Economics. But the brand of it which is being encouraged abroad and is in the process of being exported to less developed countries, gives prescriptions which are the opposite to the principle of Effective Supply derived here.

The optimum strategy giving priority to the self regenerating H-sector would yield intergenerational equity, as also current social justice. Its feasibility and its properties have been well examined in various papers and reports (carefully folded and stacked in the archives of the various ministries and departments of Governments, and in the universities). The economist in each organisation governed by the traditional dominant modes of thought, ensure that they are kept well covered, lest some curious research officer set eyes on them. For the many bottlenecks to implementation of technological, scientific, sociological, political, educational, psychological, administrative and managerial nature, the answers exist in these disciplines. It is not lack of development of these subjects of the nature of sciences or the social sciences which offers a barrier to the implementation of the strategies. It is lack of methodology to secure for the new formulations, acceptability by the orthodoxy in the field of economic planning which now forms the barrier. The social scientists collected here are invited with their combined wisdom to address themselves to this and other problems of production relationships, so that the national objectives may be achieved and the system of planning of long-term strategies of development undergoes a radical restructuring.

6

PRECEPTS OF TRADITIONALISM FOR AIMS OF MODERNITY

I. ECONOMIC JUSTICE

The Relevant Constituents of Planning

The stimulus of interaction among social scientists should have a closer look at our plan framework, to assess the extent to which there is, in it, a mixture of ideas from abroad with our own indigenous economic thought. One of these interactions would take as a symbol the tenets of Gandhism to represent Traditionality and the Nehruvian aims to represent Modernity one could then try to ascertain the contribution made by the social philosopher Gandhi as an economist, and how far it is compatible with Theory of Planning developed mainly in India under the impetus of the aspirations of its first Prime Minister, for our country. Following from that, one would wish to see how far it would be of use to the economy to have this mixture.

For representing Traditionalism I shall select a few salient features of the vast philosophy which goes under the title of Gandhian Economics.

According to my reckoning, the basic pillars of Gandhian philosophy relevant to economic planning can be categorised into three.

The first tenet is to achieve Social Justice (whether through diffusion of production in many hands, or in many small land-holdings; or through attainment of a high degree of employment).

The second precept is to require of all citizens Austerity in living standards.

Text of Silver Jubilee Lecture at the Gandhian Institute of Studies, Varanasi on 28 Aug. 1987.

The third principle lies in considering the assets and the surplus of the capitalist to be, in his hands, property in Trust for the Benefit of Society as a whole.

There are many other contributions of the learned economic philosopher to economic thought. But these three basic economic doctrines of Gandhian thought we may select and concentrate upon. For the purpose of my presentation, it is these from which the economic planning systems can, at present, benefit most. But it does not preclude other scholars who are learned Gandhian specialists or consummate experts in planning to find many more Gandhian Precepts for showing their compatability with modern Growth Economics. In the frame set by the above three propositions, let us try to find out the place which Gandhian economics occupies in our times (which is constituted of an Age of Planning and of Advanced Technology).

When development planning was introduced to be worked in a political set-up of Parliamentary Democracy, it was the first time in the world for such a step to be taken. It was also decided to be operated through a mixed economy. It was guided and supervised closely by one of the greatest practitioners of Gandhian political philosophy in the nationalist statesmanship, the late Prime Minister Nehru. He brought together the opposing strands of the indigenous economy and modern technology, by visualising the country at a future date as having engendered an advanced Economy and a progressive state; but at the same time, it must be, in the intern as well as in the final state, under a plan regime which gives social justice to all its members. Therefore, in Nehruvian thought there was a fusion of ideas of equity (as in Gandhian Economics) with the transfer of achievements of advanced countries and our indigenous research in the field of technology. In accordance with this view, various growth-oriented projects were initiated which increase the production of the country in the long run, and which would bring it into line with advanced countries.

At the same time, the idea was that development must be subject to the achievement of social goals. Of these, the primary one was sharing of the national product more equitably amongst our people as a whole (which was interpreted as a less-skewed Personal Income and Wealth Distributions). Another component-set of social goals was the creation of greater employment opportunities and their dispersion over the countryside (and amidst the backward regions), along with the containment of Real Inflation for the least-advantaged employed workers.

If we assess the functions of planning properly, then we must recognise that the right sort of planning must yield both the constituents of development — growth and social justice together. Conversely, if it does not give growth and social justice simultaneously, it would not be the proper type of planning. Planning in that case would not be an efficient instrument either of welfare or of growth.

Let us try to find out whether our country's policy actually followed these guidelines. Apart from the fact that, backed by a correct perspective, Prime Minister Nehru put certain policies into orbit, one may try to ascertain whether the modalities actually followed for achieving them were capable of meeting the challenges with success, and whether the actual policies implemented have given us both growth and social justice.

High Mechanisation in Consumption Sector

If we really want growth to take place, the best way of getting it for a lasting benefit would be to build up, first of all, the industrial infrastructure of the economy — to build up reservoirs of energy, fuel and power, to manufacture the equipment which will help us, in later years, to produce the further equipment which will give to the next generation the consumption goods relevant to advanced countries. These industries comprise what is called the Heavy-Investment Sector — steel, non-ferrous metals, machine tools, mineral oils, fuel and power, heavy chemicals, heavy engineering, network of roads and water-ways for the industrial traffic, heavy transport (including railways shipping), etc.

All these come under the category of Heavy-Investment, (or H-Sector) along with the skills of a professional nature which are to be imparted to operate these units — like knowledge pertaining to professions of Engineering, Technology, Chartered Accountancy, and of Management, and the skills of being purposefully productive in the Heavy-Investment Sector in later life. These skills, some of the members of our educational system are supposed to be learning or imparting. The generation of all these skills forms part of the

Heavy-Investment sector, because only on the basis of these long-term human-capital investments will our future production reach a standard equivalent to technologically-advanced countries.

Now, if it is imperative that we must expand the Heavy-Investment sector, then we cannot allow its products to be wasted (or to leak out of the sector into other uses where they are not essential). For production of consumption goods if we take mechanised techniques (which are relevant to Britain or Germany or U.S.A. or U.S.S.R. or to the other advanced countries with shortage of labour and excess capacity of capital) and we adopt these techniques straightaway into our economy, then we shall observe that these methods of production would be out of tune with our factor endowments — there being in the case of our country a large degree of surplus labour and a general shortage of capital (in relation firstly, to the working population, and secondly, to the norms regarding capital per man-employed peartaining to our objective of becoming a developed country).

As Professor Amartya Sen had taught us (a third of a century back) this by itself, should not worry a growth economist with a long-term perspective, for he might expect (out of the surplus) more accumulation, with possibility for the economy to grow faster. Therefore, one could envisage a high employment level achievable at some date in the future. But we might also observe aspects which were not taken account of in Professor Sen's brilliant pioneering analysis of choice of techniques presented during the early part of the Second Five-Year Plan which rightly won him the Stevenson Prize at Cambridge.

These mechanised techniques use large amounts of foreign exchange. They have high Steel-content; and they use the sorts of fuels which do not now appear to have unlimited supply within our country and which should, therefore, be considered as permanently scarce. Therefore, the mechanised techniques (when used in the consumption sector) give rise to the observation that they take away the physical resources which could, alternatively, have gone into the further production within the Heavy-Investment sector itself, and this would have helped in fostering more rapid growth of that sector.

Instead of putting scarce resources in the Heavy Sector, instead of making the mileage of our railway tracks grow rapidly, instead of laying our electricity cables at a quicker pace we proceeded to use up the scarce resources of the Heavy Sector in production of sophisticated equipment for production of consumption goods. We had put these H-products into mechanised looms and mechanised agricultural machinery and these took away some part of the physical resources of the Heavy-Investment sector. We thus used up our basic sector's productive capacity in activities which were not for its own rapid expansion, but diverted it for the purpose of activities which assisted production of consumption goods.

Hence, we succeeded in decreasing the rate of ploughback of Heavy Investment by this process much below its envisaged limit, and consequently slowed down the development of railways, of telecommunications, of machine tools, of power generating plants, etc. Investments in all basic industries suffered because of expansion of manufacturing industries for current consumption.

Further, the Government has been giving to the sector producing mechanised industry a set of facilities which, in quantum, is manifold times that of the labour-intensive sector. The large firm gets land, civic amenities, road networks, railways transport, facilities of ports, airways and aerodromes, of telecommunications, of banking and credit, of computer installation, of access to raw materials and availability of foreign exchange — all at highly subsidised rates. They get technologists, and accountants and managers (who have been educated almost entirely at public expense in colleges of higher education). They get capital allowances and rebates in direct taxes.

Let us look at an important component of the Heavy Sector — Power used at the Consumption Sector. The electricity tariff rate is, in some states, less for large industrial units than for consumption, while it is higher for shops than for residences. The very small firms are treated as commercial establishments and equated to shops in this regard. Hence, the very small units pay at a considerably higher rate for electricity than the large firms do. The large capital-using firms are also users of the products of the small suppli rs of intermediate products with whom they have, one may say, a sort of patron-client relationship. The network of industry instead of being diffused as regards control in many hands, forms a complex with the large firms dominating the destinies of the small ones. In some recent studies of the relationship of large firms with small ancillaries (carried out under my supervision, by Dr. Nisha Srivastava at the Motilal Nehru Institute, Allahabad), it may even be observed that the former also pass off some burdens for a long time (like interest on borrowed working capital through the process of delaying payments) to the captive ancillaries.

The large firms, have an unfair advantage over the small ones (in spite of pronouncements to the contrary), while their products appear to be cheaper only because of these concessions vouchsafed unto the large sector by the Government, and the exploitation of the smaller firms in their *potestas*.

However, a further consideration in support of the capital-saving sector is to be taken into account. The highly-mechnised techniques yield lower employment opportunities. They are so highly capital-intensive that the rate of growth of the product and of employment both, become low. They take us further away from the objective of full employment (which is one of the basic aspects of social justice which formed part of Gandhian economics). Hence, when our objective of achieving growth and social justice together was implemented through mechanised techniques it put the economy at a disadvantage on both these grounds.

When we follow a strategy of using capital-intensive machinery in the consumption sector (C-Sector), on the one hand, (because of the drain of product of the self-reproducing Heavy-sector towards current consumption) we cannot get a high rate of growth of Heavy-Investment sector itself. We lose on the ground of long-term growth which we do not get (in as high a measure as we could have got). We thus achieve a low payoff on the count of equity to the next generation.

Professor Yadava Reddy at Osmania University calculated the ploughback of Heavy Sector achieved during the first four plans. Mr. T.V. Ramamurthy of the Institute of Applied Manpower Research, Delhi, has done this calculation for the 5th and 6th Plans using the input-output tables. Using his own methodology, Dr. P.K. Chaubey of the Benares Hindu University has supervised the operation of similar calculations in his department upto almost current time. All these three scholars have, independently, found H-Ploughback ratio to be of the order of 1/5th only (whereas it is surmised that the potentiality could be as high as 4/5th). The ratio of long-run investments to production of equipment (for short-term consumption needs) emanating from Heavy-Investment capacity is thus 1:4. The ratio of technological time-preference for the future over the present actually achieved was thus 1/4, while its potentiality has been 4:1. The Index of Achievement of Priority to the needs of the future is then the ratio of these (the actual and the potential Ratios of Technological Time-Preference, 1/4 and 4 respectively), that is merely 1/16th, or 0625.

One may compare this with the situation in a regimented socialist policy in a labour-shortage economy. The rate of recycling of their H-Sector could be taken to be about 60 per cent. That gives the Actual Index of Future Preference as 60 per cent (1-60%) that is 1/5. The Potential, however, for a non-inflationary re-cycling would be much less. We may take it as a hypothesis compatible with a non-inflationary manner of growth that it would be 40 per cent. This gives a Potential Index of Future Preference as 40 per cent (1-40%), that is 2/3. It is through considerable Real Inflation enforced by regimentation that the Actual can become so much higher than the Potential Achievement. The Index of Priority to Heavy Investment is then estimated to be (3/2) / (2/3) that is 2-1/4 or 36/16, compared to the Indian estimate of 1/16. This the degree of comparative inadequacy for the Indian Priority to the future.

Due to lack of surplus manpower, the regimented economy's potential for non-inflationary growth is so much lower than India's, while the actual is so much higher. It is no excuse to say that we, mercifully, have no regimentation. There do exist efficient substitutes pertaining to a Free Society, which we shall discuss later, which are available to India with respect to the working of Liberal Democracy, and they have to be followed if long-term growth is to be attended to seriously.

On the other hand, we do not also get the objective of potential creation of employment opportunities realised at present at a pace which is rapid enough. So we lose also on the ground of social justice to the present generation. When the forms in which investments get embodied pertain to highly-mechanised equipment, the Index of Priority for the Future settles down at a low figure; and correspondingly is the score of attainment of social justice for the current generation depressed to a low level. High mechanisation in the C-Sector results in high diversion of H-capacity from its further expansion towards short-run requirements; hence, it yields low priority for the future. Paradoxical as it may seem, low priority for the future engenders a strategy which succeeds in yielding a low priority for the present generation also.

The Unfavourable Social Consequences

We come next to the criterion of social justice on the basis of generating a favourable distribution of income. If we take the case of workers producing with the help of handlooms, the wearer is the person who is generally also the producer. The profit margin is small, and his own subsistence out of it (including what is needed for his family's maintenance, forms a large proportion of the revenue; hence, the Wage to Profit ratio is high.

Let us take, on the other hand, the case of the large-scale factory producing textiles. The profit margin is very high and the wage base is low. Therefore, the distribution of income is unfavourable to the working class, and is in favour of the capitalist producer. On this count also, the highly-mechanised techniques run counter to the criterion of social justice. Not only do they create less employment opportunities for a given investment, but they also create functional inequalities of income through higher profits in relation to wages.

When large functional-inequalities are associated with large-scale production, personal-income inequalities follow. Now if the income is not equitably distributed, huge volume of purchasing power (both current and accumulated) rests in the hands of the top echelons of society (composed of say one-tenth of the population, or even less). Following from these inequalities of income, one gets a demand vector which is oriented towards more luxury consumption. The main components of the consumption of the affluent are luxury items by definition.

This has the unfavourable social consequence of creating a Glass-Curtain Economy where the privileged few enjoy good living, while the deprived ones watch, and desire to be admitted to the inner circles. All this we see around us if we visit big market centres, and the consumer goods of luxury variety one can see on display therein. There is no scarcity of luxury consumption-goods; one only notices that for ninety per cent or more of the population there is lack of purchasing power to buy these goods.

As the luxury items (from videos to household gadgets) draw away almost half of fresh investments (as per the estimates of Professor C.H. Raghuram of Osmania University), there is diversion of resources away from production of necessaries. If necessaries were to be strictly interpreted (as in Gandhian thought and analysis of the late eminent economist Professor J.K. Mehta regarding the Doctrine of Restriction of wants) then items like modern effervescent drinks and films would be excluded from necessaries, and substituted by the traditional cooling drinks and live folk classical and contemporary drama and culture — what the moderns call classical dancing was a folk art when our culture was a living one. In that case the degree of diversion would go up from half to a figure nearer four-fifths.

There is created thus, artificially, through malallocations, a scarcity of necessaries of consumption. For instance, unadulterated rationed sugar is not available to the extent necessary for the middle-class consumers, while high grade sugar is available to any extent desired by an individual who can afford it. This scarcity of necessaries causes their prices to rise, which counters any valid moves to achieve non-inflationary growth as a constituent of social justice. The act of catering to the demands of the rich causes Real Inflation for the less-advantaged.

The techniques of high degree of mechanisation are also those which are generally (though, as shown by the late Professor K.T. Rama Krishna of Osmania University in his Ruhr Lecture not, by any means, exclusively) associated with large-scale production, or with the units which act as ancillaries of the large firm. In agriculture, the mechanised farms form part of the holdings of the very rich farmers. The mechanised industrial-units of production (operating upon a large scale) get concentrated in and around the metropolitan centres and make them into megalopolitan complexes. The large firms also give rise to the possibility of monopoly and exploitative elements in industry. Production on a large scale in a firm, as we have seen, yields a large volume of profits, and the high degree of mechanisation yields a high Profit-to-Wage ratio. The two together tend to yield an aggravation of the skewness of personal-income distribution or concentration of command over purchasing power. This, further, leads to the demand for modernised luxury goods (which again can get satisfied only by using machanised techniques).

Hence, the income distribution becomes skewed even further, and a Vicious Circle of Affluence forming a Glass-Curtain Economy gets entrenched. The whole structure is opposed to social justice.

Hence, the manner in which we have implemented our planning has not taken into consideration the basic aspect which Gandhian economics taught us (which was that we must have social justice as our primary objective). Nor has it taken into account the basic aspect of planning which Prime Minister Nehru wanted, namely that planning must give us long-term growth in addition to social justice. We neither got a high enough level of growth rate of capital goods for the future, nor did we get enough social justice on any of its criteria—namely of higher employment-creation, greater equality of personal-income distribution, more favourable functional-income distribution, reduction of disparities in consumption, absence of shortage of necessaries, absence of monopolism and of metropolitanism, spatial diffusion of industry in rural areas, etc. We have, thus, lost on both the counts — of growth and of social justice, of the benefit of looking after the future and after the present.

Indian long-term planning was designed by Prime Minister Nehru to be a case of the future benefit as well as the present. The theory formulated by Ricardian classicism would give us either future benefit or of the present. The strategy accepted preferred the future benefit to the present. The strategy as followed yielded benefit neither for the future nor for the present in as great measure as was possible. From a possibility of this As Well As that, it was translated into Either this or that, and then transformed by the touch of planners into Neither this Nor that.

Social Justice and the Heaviesque Strategy

This opens out the alternative before us that through proper planning, it is still possible for us to salvage the economy from the grip of non-achievement in both fields — of growth and of social justice. We can very well have a system in which, as regards the Heavy-Investment Sector is concerned, we can use modern technology as well as efficient forms of existing techniques. We can use the technology as we have it in USA or in Czechoslovakia or the Soviet Union or Japan or anywhere else, and also use the technology which was developed over centuries in our own country and which has been improved upon recently. Thus, in the Heavy-Investment Sector we can have capital-intensive techniques as well as labour-intensive ones. Both these types of technologies are permitted for this sector; and hence, one can have, on the one hand, a scheme which can be of multipurpose nature like the Bhakra-Nangal Project which used a highly-mechanised form of dam-construction (where cranes were used to haul up steel, cement, and concrete, and imported manpower skills were used at the highest level).

One can have, on the other hand, a mainly capital-saving form of Irrigation-cum-Electricity-generation project (which can be like the Hirakud Project). One could have even a less-mechanised and more labour-intensive form of construction (like the much wider Pochampad Dam) in which earthworks may be raised in a region where one gets unemployed men and women who can be put to work using baskets and poles, building the whole dam, step by step, without using any scarce-resource capacity of the economy. Such irrigation dams can, by redesigning and use of non H-scaffolding, also generate electricity as was done for much higher Nagarjuna Sagar Dam. When, in the Heavy-Investment Sector, it is possible to have both these types of techniques (the capital intensive and the labour-intensive ones) the latter method is preferable whenever labour and the other real resources are available or can be easily procured or fabricated.

But when we come to the production of consumption-goods, in this particular sector (as has been observed earlier) if we use mechanised techniques they will not allow our Heavy Investment Sector to grow fast, because they draw away all the scarce resources which could have gone into building capital goods industry. Hence, the best techniques to use are those which conserve the scarce resources of the Heavy-Investment Sector's inputs and products — foreign exchange, minerals in short supply, mechanical and electric power, etc.

The labour-intensive and animal-using techniques usually do not take away the resources of the Heavy-Investment Sector to any substantial extent. For instance, they do not put a draught upon high-grade steels or fuel inputs of a very scarce nature (like diesel and petroleum, or metals which are in limited quantity beneath the earth's surface), or upon power which ought to be preserved for the self-reproducing Heavy Industries own growth. The further prevention of use of such material for luxury goods — as bamboo for nylons at Mavoor — increases the capacity of H-Sector growth and of H-serving consumption necessaries sector. This is the logical basis of the priority for Heavy-Investment through eschewing highly-mechanised techniques in the consumption sector for both luxuries and necessaries, and even labour-intensive techniques for the luxury-consumption sector. When it results in a rate of ploughback of H more than 50 per cent it is referred to as the Heaviesque Strategy; when less than half, the Lightesque strategy.

Now, therefore, the techniques which conserve the H-resources are also those which tend to create employment. They are all very similar to the techniques which used to be advocated in pure Gandhian economics (before its adultration by the nylon fibres — which are an adjunct to the mechanised-sector for consumption-good production). The quality of H-conservation is not adduced to the machines which use scarce forms of capital (when they are used in the consumption sector they do not permit the growth of long-term capital thereby). Hence, only the pure Gandhian techniques qualify for helping in generation of growth pertinent to long-term technology perspective being helped.

The pure Gandhian type of techniques also possess the characteristics of a low degree of mechanisation which is associated with the miniature scale, and consequent distribution of entrepreneurial opportunities (and dispersal of economic power) widely. It thus prevents monopoly conditions from developing. As they pertain to optimum capital-intensities, they do not aggravate the inequalities of income. The Heaviesque Strategy requires a large proportion of H-products to be re-cycled into that sector. It keeps the degree of leakage of H-products into the consumption-sector low, (and consequently, of the Nehruvian H-Priority high), and at the same time compels the latter sector to confine itself to the use of H-conserving techniques (which are identified as Gandhian techniques).

The use of Gandhian types of methods of production in the consumption sector would create a more favourable functional distribution of income in the consumption sector, and it would prevent inequality. The ratio of Ransoms to Subsistence-Wage would be low in these techniques (corresponding to the concept of Surplus to

Socially-necessary Consumption or the Rate of Surplus value as in Marxoid analysis). In advanced countries where mechanised technology is used Profits-to-Wage ratio could become low but this would be because of high wages demanded by organised labour in a Near-Full-Employment situation. In less-developed countries ultra-high wages of the privileged and organised workers (as well as high salaries of the executives) could diminish the Profits-to-Wage ratio. But that does not give the full idea. The ideal index of functional distribution is not Profits-to-Wage ratio but Ransoms to Subsistence-Wage ratio. In mechanised techniques and labour-market conditions of scarcity of skilled manpower, or of high degree of labour organisation, the Ransoms to Subsistence-Wage ratio would not be low but very high; and to the income inequalities as a result of Profits obtained as a ransom, there would be added income inequalities as a result of ultra-high wages (of organised labour, of executive managers, of technicians and technical experts — whether appropriately employed, or misemployed, and of professionals as well as the earnings of the commercial underworld — all income classed together as Ransoms.

Consequently, the Gandhian techniques have the equity advantage of not producing the effect of adding to the demand for luxury goods and aggravating disparities of consumption. Nor is the further effect manifested of satisfying the demand for luxury goods through mechanised or professional-skill-intensive methods of production (which are both prone to creating further inequalities of income and disparities in wage levels, and hence generating further demand for luxury and semi-luxury goods). Thus the techniques advocated in the Gandhian model prevent the vicious circle of consumption disparities to be generated. The Gandhian techniques are seen, therefore, to yield the essence of social justice through all the above criteria; and they, at the same time, strengthen the capacity for the long-term Heavy-Investment Sector to grow.

The pure Gandhian techniques indicated in the aforesaid argument yield equity to the present generation precisely because they aim at equity for the future generations. These techniques have a proper place within a modern economy, in the process of building up long-term capital (as a most important and desirable part of our planning system). It is really the other types of techniques — the mechanised ones for the production of consumption goods — it is those which are irrelevant to our system at the present stage of development; for they aim at modernised growth — and in that process they deny not only equity to the present generation, but whittle down the capacity to achieve growth for the next generation, in the 21st century.

The pure Gandhian techniques form the proper technology in our planned economy for the consumption-good sector, and form the foundation on the strength of which the edifice of modern self-regenerating Heavy-Industries can grow. Therefore, in this sphere, Gandhian Economics is not only relevant today, but is one of the most important constituents of a properly-planned developing-economy. The Heaviesque strategy can succeed only by relying upon pure Gandhian techniques in the consumption sector.

The pure Gandhian techniques, on the other hand, get new life because they are mainly the ones compatible with priority to Heavy Investment. Without the H-sector priority, the principle of H-conservation is not applicable, Hence, in the absence of H-priority, the encouragement to Gandhian techniques (for social justice in the short-run) gets denied the support of a still-stronger justification (rooted in considerations of long-term growth).

Proper planning (based on the Heaviesque Strategy), was and is capable of giving a large volume of employment as well as rapid growth of meaningful goods. It was, and is, capable of giving subsistence to a much larger number of people employed in the various sectors in the rural and urban economy. It is the Heaviesque strategy which would rapidly lift the oppressive burden of poverty from the deprived sections, by giving them employment, purchasing power and the consumption necessaries in simple measure. Contrary again to a generally believed proposition, it is the Lightesque strategy which imposes the burden of oppression on the non-employed and poverty-stricken masses. What is called Heavy rests lightly on the deprived, what is dubbed Light sits heavily on them. The paradox arises because of wrong nomenclature popularised by the Planning Commission in the fifties. The Heavy-Sector ought to have been called, as described by Prime Minister Nehru the Parent-machine sector or the Machine-Reproducing Sector. These are Higher-order machines. The Light-Machine Sector should have been referred to as the Consumption-Machinery sector. These are what Capital Theory calls the Lower-order Machines.

The Heaviesque Strategy is in fact the Policy of high Recycling in the Parent-machine-Reproducing sector, and Low-Diversion of its Product into Highly-mechanised Lower-order machines for production of consumption goods. It, therefore, uses in the consumption sector technique which force, a low content of the Higher-order machinery. The latter are the Gandhian techniques which are compatible with High Priority to the Parent-Machine Sector's growth.

The Lightesque Strategy, on the other hand, requires High Diversion of the Product of the Parent-Machine Sector into Consumption-good manufacture. It, therefore, yields Low Recycling of the Parent-machine sector and a high content of the higher-order machine renders possible a high degree of mechanisation in the Consumption Sector. These machines are the enemies of the Gandhian techniques, because the former compete with and force the simple products of the latter out of the market. The Gandhian economists who do not recognise that the policy of Heavy-sector Priority is through the Principle of H-conservation a means of implementation of the Prescript of High Employment and Social Justice is doing injustice to its supporter.

Therefore, we are constrained to state the general proposition that it is what was supposed to be antitheses of Gandhism—the Heavy-Investment Sector—which (to the perceptive minds) is the greatest ally of Gandhian techniques, and leads to the Gandhian objectives of employment and favourable income-distribution to be best realised for the less-privileged classes.

Conversely, the suppression of the (supposedly anti-Gandhian) Heavy-Industry Sector encourages the mechanised machinery in the consumption sector which is the antithesis of Gandhian Precepts. It is the policy of low priority to the recycling in the Heavy Sector which eradicates Gandhism from the sector which most needs it, and where it has the greatest economic potentiality of being diffused — the production of consumption goods.

II. AUSTERITY

The Place of Austerity

The Second aspect of Gandhian economics was that our base must be an Austerity-oriented economy. That also is a highly relevant aspect for two reasons — one based on long-term considerations and the other on short-term priorities.

The first reason stems from equity to the future generations. This follows because of the reason that if one wants long-run accumulation to take place, it requires investment in basic industries. To fulfil this requirement, it is further necessitated that scarce physical capital resources should go into further production of capital goods to produce capital goods (and to reproduce themselves rather than the output of the Heavy Industries going towards consumption-goods manufacture). But one has also to supply the consumer necessaries for all the people employed; and hence capital accumulation should not impose a curb on the consumption of necessaries. The act of capital accumulation and production of consumption necessaries should thus both be encouraged together—simultaneously, and in balance. It is for this reason that the stress on agriculture in the Third Five-Year plan is to be taken as a manifestation of restoration of balance to a lop-sided situation of priority to Heavy-Investment, and deserved commendation. It is the undue stress on consumption of luxury commodities in the later plans which needed to be deprecated.

The second reason for austerity depends upon equity to the present generation itself, and this prescript is independent of the objective of provision of equity for the future generations. According to this viewpoint, the important consideration is for inequalities in consumption in the present generation themselves to be removed. But in implementation of the first objective of long-run accumulation, the independently-obtained second objective of short-run equity dictates that for accumulation, as well as for production of consumption necessaries to be enhanced, the physical resources must come from a source depriving the more affluent section of its luxury consumption. Hence, the cut in consumption ought to be imposed only upon the luxury-good purchasers.

The analysis of both the considerations leads to the conclusion that there should necessarily be a curb imposed on the growth of the standard of living of the more affluent entrepreneurs, and following that, of the employed and organised operatives. Both are privileged sections of the community. A policy of prevention of cost escalation and cost-push inflation requires as one of its important constituents,

Restraint upon ultra-wages (above the subsistence level which the Non-employed require for entering the circle of the Employed). This can be asked to be implemented only if we submit ourselves firstly, to fiscal legislation which ordains high consumption out of income (and investment in support of that) to be restrained; and secondly, if entrepreneurial consumption and executive manager's consumption is curbed as a pre-condition.

At the same time, to implement these policies the society must be imbued with the cultural environment conducive to designing and working an Austerity-oriented Economy. Gandhian austerity is clothed in the form of self-restraint, but it requires a social constraint as well. Similarly, the Doctrine of Restriction of wants was worked out in formal terms by the most original and independent of Indian theoretical economists — the late Professor J.K. Mehta of Allahabad University who was a lone human voice in the wilderness of modern economics inhabited by birds which fly with wings borrowed from abroad. This philosophy also was a socially-imposed persuasion to restrain one's wants, amounting to Social Constraint. The Socialist ethos is, of course, an externally-imposed constraint on consumption through either egalitarian legislation or fiscal obligations.

The basket of consumption goods for workers and entrepreneurs in a perfectly-competitive capitalist system would also be differing little between three classes, and that too for functional considerations, as evidenced by quaker form of capitalism. The external constraint on the untrammelled consumption in this case is the force of fierce competitiveness in capitalism. An individual's scale of preferences and his Liberty to do what he wishes, is thus conditioned by external compulsions. In the capitalist economy in the time of past Wars (for annihilating enemies of the free nations) there were a lot of constraints on consumption which were imposed; and no votary of Liberty held up the implementation by talking of market demands favouring automobiles rather than butter for the troops. But in our present war (for preservation of the lives of the poor) the market demands are brought in with impunity (by economists holding brief not for the national interest but for class of holders of the purchasing power), to defeat the implementations of Social Constraints.

The Austerity economy materially differs from the economy which promulgates the obligation to achieve a High-Savings-ratio.

The latter is a condition which neo-classical economists (with genuine regard for the national interest, but with mistaken analytical framework) wish the Government to foster (and in which they have succeeded, as for as our country is concerned, to a substantial extent— whatever the nature of Government at the Centre or at the State level). But the effects of a high Savings ratio is that financial savings may increase. However, these Savings in money terms largely come out of higher profits; and the latter, further, are generated by a choice of techniques in favour of high degree of mechanisation. The latter has disastrous consequences to social justice and to growth, as we have already analysed. Out of the higher profits, savings may be high, but so also is consumption of the entrepreneur increased; and it is composed mainly of luxury goods (the production of which then gets encouragement). A situation now obtains, though unwittingly, wherein a higher Savings Effort goes hand in hand with higher Consumption Disparities — and not less of inessential consumption.

The balance of private savings comes largely from provident funds and small-savings schemes pertinent to organised labour. To the extent it falls on the consumption of workers, he is able to shift it to the employer, causing a cost-push inflation. To the extent that his consumption being constant, money savings area higher, the money wage is expected to be higher, which also causes inflation.

Some proportion of Total Savings comes from the unorganised labour's contribution, for example, through the lottery schemes. There are by their nature, a means of revising the direction of redistribution of income and collection of small sums from a lot of poor people and giving the net total in the hand of a few. Lotteries cause the real burden to fall on the poor and shifts their attitudes from earning by work to receipts from non-work and non-productive risk. No wonder that inculcating such an attitude affect the government staff also and is linked to the demand for bonus not linked to higher productive effort. It also generates a culture where non-employed manpower think of seeking placements mostly in jobs on which work effort would be least.

The type of planning which we had undertaken, did not give the non-employed this opportunity to participate in active work. It did not permit even the employed workers at subsistence to get proper maintenance (because the plans do not usually allocate enough for the type of investments which would yield results in terms of higher product of consumption necessaries — to the exclusion of luxury goods).

It is a policy of higher austerity in physical terms which would maintain the consumption of workers at subsistence levels and would curtail that of the affluent . It was not the Growth economist Domar, but the Social-economist Gandhi who had a relevant answer in this context.

The Demand-side Economics

Our growth economists (under the influence of theories of development irrelevant to our environmental context) have hitherto given recommendations to Government for supply to cater to demand. It required that whatever the market demand (of a skew income-distribution) showed as requirement, had to be supplied. The governing factor was demand, the determined variable was supply. The practice thus opposed the Theory of an Austerity-oriented economy which rejects the dominance of market demands and substitutes it by social restraint. During the course of even the present (early) stage of our development, while looking for models to imitate, they have taken, as photos of demand creation, the advanced economies, in which there are huge income differentials, and large disparities of consumption.

Nor did the system, as we have seen, yield enough growth. With use of H-oriented machinery for the manufacture of consumption goods, the consumption sector uses up resources of the capital-goods industry and reduces the H-sector rate of growth. If a larger chunk of our resources is, further, going into luxury consumption and their equipment, then the rate of growth of Heavy Investment is still further reduced. We may take the example of an important constituent of the Heavy-Investment sector — the Export Activity producing foreign exchange. We were all the time saying we have very little foreign exchange and we should do some import substitution. Import substitution took the form that what we were importing from abroad previously, we would produce now within the country.

Firstly, we tried to think out as to what are the goods to be manufactured within the country. When the planners drew up a list of such goods, it was found that this was really a set ranging from machine tools to steel and metals, from electricity and power to mining equipment, from defence to heavy-chemical plants. It was, for economics as well as strategic reasons, confirmed that basic-machinery and all ancillary products form a collection of goods which need to be manufactured within the country.

Secondly, we were given to understand that there was another huge list of consumer products which were being imported, and these also had to be substituted by domestic production.

The latter list of goods was the result of demand-oriented planning to augment the supply of what was commanded by purchasing power. These goods, according to the Doctrine of Restriction of wants, come under the category of luxury consumption (like tape recorders, refrigerators, televisionsets, video recorders, airconditioners, decorative laminates, terylene cloth, cosmetics, beverages, etc.). We decided we would not encourage the import either of German or British or American or of Japanese brands of these goods, but we would produce the goods here. But to produce them here one requires modern high-technology equipment. From where was this equipment supposed to be coming ? This equipment, at that time, had to come from foreign countries; so that in the first few years, to set up nylon factories one required a huge amount of physical capital from abroad. When one had to get these machines from abroad, one dissipated foreign exchange (which was earned, say, by exporting cashewnuts). A lot of foreign exchange was thus misutilised — in bringing equipment for the luxury goods — for decorative laminates or for synthetic fabrics, etc.

We did the same with regard to the other requirements of the top few percentiles of the population. If ladies and gentlemen of fashion required modern cosmetics, these used to be imported from abroad. Then we said that they will not be imported from abroad, but as our social-elite classes cannot do without face lifts, we shall allow the same foreign companies to put up factories, in collaboration with indigenous industialists, to prepare these products in India from equipment which is imported from abroad. But the effect as regards drain on the foreign exchange for import of capital (or borrowing it and then allowing the proceeds within the country to be continuously repatriated abroad) was detrimental, and in many instances it was even more pronounced (because the market catered to was for non-essential goods). These were industries which could be identified as belonging to the non-austerity group. These industries took up not only a huge chunk out of our foreign exchange resources, but also diverted the capital resources within the country from essential uses.

Supply-side for the Affluent

It is under the influence of Demand-side economics, to cater for all the goods which the affluent classes (supported by their purchasing power) demanded, that we invested in luxury-good production. We thus implemented the Supply-side economics much before the current wave in some countries abroad to frame policies with its help. Whether one uses Demand-side economics or Supply-side economics, the theory accepted by authorities of many countries is that Supply is the dormant and Effective Demand the active variable. In economically-advanced countries, Effective Demand refers mainly to the volume of purchasing power generated by the employed workers. In the less-developed countries, even with so-called planned mixed-economies, Effective Demand refers to the volume of purchasing power released on to the market by the rich. Thus supply-side Economics is as in the countries abroad, clothed under the grab of supply catering to urgent Market Demand, but was a device to supply goods demanded by the affluent.

A small number of people having a very high standard of living, and a very large number of people having a very low standard of living (even below subsistence) has been the situation which was foisted upon the country by some of our academic economic economists misadvising the Government. This was not the proper format of planning, because the benefits of this make-believe system of planning could not be expected to reach the common man.

Along with these, we did not invest sufficiently in the necessaries of consumption. It was not possible to do so side by side (as scarce resources were competed away by the more profitable luxuries and the industries catering to necessaries were permitted to be de- rived of facilities). There was a malallocation in the form of too much investment going into luxuries catering to the top echelons of the population, and too little investment going into the necessaries required by the rest of the people.

The result necessarily was that prices showed a consistent rising trend, because the necessaries were not easily available, and the situation pertained to Real Inflation. With price inflation, the purchasing power of the subsistence-level workers or iso-workers got reduced to below subsistence, so that they were converted from the category of the "employed" to that of the "sub-employed". Consequently, when the supply of particular consumption necessaries did (at some future time) increase, there was inadequate purchasing power with the poorer workers to buy the essential goods. Their deprivation, therefore, continued.

The economists in general, are apt to side-track this aspect and to blame the price increases upon additions to the quantity of money (which, in reality, would not be inflationary if the increased liquidity were used for increasing production of necessaries). The neo-classical economists have been maintaining that there was a lot of inflation being generated, and every one experienced that inflation, but the general public were indoctrinated by the traditional economist to get used to believing that this was due to monetary causes — that inflation was due to deficit financing or to too much money in circulation. At other times (with somewhat greater validity) they found another target for side-tracking the aim — and blamed black money as a cause of inflation. In both cases the root cause was not being attended to.

The supply-side economics is neo-classical in nature and expects money to earn a high rate of interest. The rate at which banks lend must, therefore, be even higher. The producers of necessaries in poor country are faced with a situation of wanting to possess the necessaries of subsistence but lacking the purchasing power. They need to and wish to buy, but are wanting in the means for the same. The producers then get discouraged in these lines and give way to producers of scores of new types of products which a supply-side economist and his establishment colleagues point out as profitable. The sale outlets shift from sale of cotton textiles to polyester. This creates a deficiency in the supply of necessaries and their raw materials and an inflation for the low-income consumers at the subsistence-wage level.

The supply side economists forget that the basic reason for the inflation is that the Planning System does not channel enough investment into the field of necessaries, and does not create enough deficit finance (as needed for that purpose). Too many luxury goods are being produced, and the physical resources of investment are going into that, monetary resources (including deficit financing and high-interest borrowings) are going into that; and this mal-allocation, therefore, produces a scarcity of necessary goods which basically are meant for the common man.

Unscrupulous blackmarketeers have been taking advantage of the scarcity situation generated by deficiency in production, and have added to the scarcity by illegal hoarding. It would be necessary for the State to take firm measures to deal with these unsocial elements through mobilising the help of the civil authorities, but economic action would be required to hit at the root cause which acts against the weaker sections.

This can be done by shifting from the Demand-side as well as the Supply-side economics — both meant for the benefit of the affluent and both supporting the enslavement of supply to the Skew-Demand vector for the inessential goods — and attending to supply for the common man and for future needs only.

It is not a matter of shifting from Demand-side economics to Supply-side economics in order to be up-to-date in policy and practice. The dispute is neither on existence of demand nor on the desirability to increase supply of certain goods. It is with respect to what goods are to be supplied and what is to be the price of its inputs that the question arises. Demand for luxury goods should be curbed; and merely in response to demand, the supply of these goods ought not to be augmented.

On the other hand, the demand for necessaries at the level of subsistence-maintenance for all the employed population ought to be encouraged and purchasing power provided. The supply also of these goods must be increased. Whether one is a Demand-side man or Supply-side economist the two must get integrated and reverse the causation from Supply as a Dormant variable to Supply as an Active variable, through attending to social priorities not to market structures. In Effective-Supply Planning one confines investment to the field of necessaries and long-term needs. No valid imperative for State action to permit supply of luxuries (just because they are demanded by the affluent) is recognised in the principle of Effective Supply.

Effective-supply Conditions

External constraint on the free play of Market imperfections is inherent in the concept of a regulatory mechanism. The capitalist will take the aid of the force of competition, the Fully-planned State of the force of Authority. The socialist pattern in a mixed economy will take the help of compulsions of Egalitarian measures, the Restriction-of Wants School of the force of Persuasion, the Divines of the force of moral Restraint, the Gandhians of the means of evoking the force of Self-Restraint in an environment of Social Restraint.

Whatever the means, it is the business of the Planned Economy to exert the Force of Restraint on the market, and to produce goods only according to the austere basket of goods included in Effective Supply vector, alongwith consumption-good equipment and capital-good parent-machinery for priority to long-term needs. Effective Supply ensures the neutrality of the market, and eliminates the baneful influences of skewness of Income Distribution, for in all cases it emanates from Imperfections leading to Rents and Ransoms.

As a result of any Investment, simultaneously two effects take place. Firstly, there is the creation of Effective Demand, because incomes are created thereby (which require consumption demands to be satisfied). This was the special study to which Lord Keynes devoted his attention. Side by side, the Investment which takes place creates supply. This was the field of attention of (and the lasting contribution of) Sir Roy Harrod, as the prime Post-Keynesian.

From the point of view of development, a spectrum of investments in proportions such that non-inflationary growth takes place, and Effective Demand created is satisfied by the supply of goods has been termed in Capital Theory developed in India, the Effective-Supply vector. Effective Supply requires allocation of resources in a non-inflationary Balanced Allocation Ratio.

Effective supply, therefore, firstly requires that only socially-relevant type of goods ought to be manufactured, and hence Investment would have to be only in relevant forms. Secondly, the relevant investments are to be only for production of necessaries and for long-term capital needs. Among the relevant investments those for long-term need, or of long gestation create demand, but no supply of essentials of consumption or their intermediate inputs in the short-period. This part, no doubt, puts inflationary strain as a parasite sector on the productivity and growth generated by the other relevant part of the Investment sector — for consumption necessaries in the short-period. But, these inflation-creating investments are necessary in the Heaviesque Strategy. However, the vector should not be indiscriminately added to, for inessential purposes. Perhaps much of Defence expenditure could be justified on Security grounds as essential. But luxury consumption and inert education cannot be basically justified by equity considerations or by social necessity. The Effective-Supply vector thus excludes as the inessential element of luxury consumption or of waste, inactive education and other parasite sectors which are not socially-essential as a part of the Investment vector.

The production spectrum would not be dependent upon demand backed by purchasing power but upon demand of goods needed for production in the Self-reproducing H-sector and the Consumption-good Sector under Austerity conditions of growth. The investments would also be in balance regarding yield of product of consumption necessaries being sufficient to cater to the demands created at constant prices. Further, the quantum of investment must be sufficient in size to create enough employment to achieve a state of high-employment creation.

To ensure Effective supply one must have a spectrum of goods for non-inflationary balance. In order to contain inflation, it is not sufficient to say that a Basic-Needs Programme may be put into practice. It can succeed only when the planners also decree and implement the policy that there will be no Afluence-Oriented production. It is necessary to decrease the production of luxury products which cater to the satisfaction of demand of a very small proportion of the population, and to divert those resources to investment in necessaries and their equipment.

It is not simply desire to save more or invest more for the future which should primarily prompt the policy for restriction of consumption of the affluent. There is no desire to reduce aggregate consumption while non-employment continues or later. The springs of the policy originate from a wish to re-distribute consumption (as of value in itself from a moral point of view), and to increase consumption of the sub-employed and the non-engaged (as a part of functional requirements of Employment Policy). The reduction of affluent consumption is for equity to the weaker sections of this generation, not for the next as the Higher-Savings School would advocate.

This prescript would then aim at reducing disparities in consumption standards. The large disparities in consumption, at present, gives a score against social justice. They run counter to the Austerity-oriented economy (and also, incidentally, yield less for accumulation, and consequently of growth). The diversion of resources to the production of luxury consumption goods must be entirely eliminated from the system, if it is to yield both social justice and relevant growth.

Therefore, having failed to implement, up to now, two of the main aspects of Gandhian economics (namely, that social justice is obtained through distribution of employment amongst all people, and equality of consumption amongst all people, at a level of austerity), what is required to be done for the future is to have an austerity-oriented economy permitting high accumulation in the appropriate industries (including the H-sector). This stress on H, itself dictates an employment-creating consumption-sector (based on growth only in the sub-sector of approved industries of that sector; namely that producing necessaries only — and that also with H-conserving techniques).

To get sufficient long-term growth we must change the strategy which we have been using, and look for new ways to secure the implementation of Gandhian precepts as well as of Nehruvian objectives (both of which we have missed benefiting from, on account of doctrinal opposition of adherents of each of these two philosophies to the views of the other). Having come to understand that our influential (traditional) economic-views have, till the present time, given us tools which have only made us succeed in our economy losing on both the grounds of growth and social justice we must now shift to the Heaviesque strategy which will take us out of the present situation. Nehruism is, therefore, an ally of Gandhism, not in conflict with the main precepts. Gandhism is the mainstay for the Nehruvian objectives of long-run growth to be achieved. Not only are the two compatible with each other and not opposed, but separately neither of them is viable in the context of present-day economic planning.

If we wish to shift to the type of policy which Gandhian economics taught us, namely, Equity-oriented Economy through Austerity and through Employment creation, it will be implemented best by adopting the Heaviesque strategy which gives greater employment through priority to Heavy-Investments. As discussed earlier, the high rate of ploghback of that sector within itself — the Nehruvian aspiration — will not only yield the rapid growth of that sector, but H-conserving techniques for the consumption-good sector would yield the equity required by the Gandhian precepts. This indicates — or rather dictates — a lower degree of mechanisation in consumption-goods production; and employment creation will follow out of it.

It is not possible to obtain as much employment directly which the Social-policy Priority school (basing itself upon Gandhism alone) recommends — as through the methodology of taking advantage of the indirect consequence of the Nehruvian path of investing in the H-sector. By going in for employment-creation directly, one would tend to invest outside the Heavy-Industry Sector. One may introduce thereby a lot of inferior technology in the economy, and one would miss the massive employment-creating sources of investment which lie in the large projects of the Heavy-Investment sector, for instance, the Autobahn network of roadways, the Railway-track honeycombs, the linking of River-systems and the formation of Windmill - Water fall generation feeding a national Super-conductive Power-grid, etc. If we take the Heavy-Investment Sector and make it grow fast, then by adherence to the prescript of non-inflationary growth, it must necessarily require rapid growth of the sector for consumption necessaries to maintain growth without inflation; and thus it would give a fillip to employment creation and to production of necessaries in the latter sector also.

Modernity and traditionality are intermingled in this process. Progress takes place through proper growth being fostered; but proper growth does not come about at the expense of social justice; nor is social justice looked for without long-term growth. Proper Growth which is through the adoption of the Heaviesque strategy takes place along with social justice. Further, this growth takes place in an equity-oriented fashion. Thus the Heavy-Investment sector is an essential part of the Effective-Supply vector.

The Pure Gandhian model gets investments done only in relevant forms for a village economy. It creates full employment in the village economy. There is no place in it of mechanised techniques in the consumption sector and of luxury consumption goods. This model conforms to Effective Supply conditions without Intergenerational consideration.

The Nehruvian requirement was of long-term development to be added as a necessary part of development. The Heavy sector in the Mahalanobis formulation and the Feldman plan implemented in Soviet Russia concentrated upon highly-mechanised techniques. Both sectors using machinery capital goods and consumption goods being mechanised, the model departed from the very beginning from the capacity to generate sufficient employment. Hence, it did not qualify for being included as an Effective Supply Model.

The Heaviesque Strategy includes the Nehruvian long-term consideration but retains the Gandhian techniques in the consumption sector and, therefore, generates employment rapidly. It is, therefore, an Effective-supply model with Intergenerational Equity. It replaces Demand-side and Supply-side economics with a meaningful alternative which keeps Gandhism not only alive but vibrant and integrates it with Nehruvian aims.

III. TRUSTEESHIP

Equity-oriented Private Sector

To obtain relevant growth in a spectrum of Effective-Supply product, a system of instruments of implementation has to be established. The system of instruments should, therefore have, as its immediate objective, the creation of Effective Supply. The instruments we have for implementing a plan could either be controls of the physical type, or instruments of guidance. In a Parliamentary democratic frame, with avoidance of regimentation, the Instruments of Guidance are preferable to Physical Controls. But the former set of instruments have to be of as powerful a type as regimentation, as an alternative, would have been.

For this purpose, the monetary instruments are not sufficient — though they form a most essential constituent of the system of supplementary instruments of implementation. These days the matter is being considered by academics, for purposes of advising the government to change over from Physical to Monetary controls. My considered view is that the requirement of the instruments is for purposes of shifting not merely monetary but real resources (manpower, materials and equipment) from one set of uses to another and for this task monetary instruments are going to be ineffective. The monetary instruments are Condensers — weak instruments — because even a large change of interest rates would not be able to shift allocations (except marginally).

What is required to achieve the allocation of resources for Effective Supply is a set of Magnifier Instruments, so that a small change in schedules of inducements may shift a large volume of physical resources from unapproved to approved fields. For such a task, fiscal policy must be brought in, and not only used but modified, so that powerful Allocative Taxes may be introduced. The present structure is incapable of performing the task of shifting Real Resources from one set of uses to another; especially as high profits may be in the process of being earned in the existing set of uses, because of high demand (existing or created through advertisements) for luxury goods by the affluent sections. The present system acts in the opposite direction to that optimally required for approved investments to grow, and unapproved ones to be curbed.

If the spectrum of production has to be made austerity-oriented, the Kaldorian Expenditure Tax has been recommended at various times. However, in my opinion, it would not suffice for that purpose, because it primarily acts from the demand side and does not directly tackle supply. Any fiscal instrument which purports to act from the Effective-Supply side should be one capable of evoking investments in the required uses and discouraging fresh investment in the unapproved industries. But the Expenditure Tax has no mechanism for it, nor was it designed for evoking Effective-Supply. It is a powerful instrument of demand control, but a condenser instrument for allocation.

The production spectrum can only be changed (from the present day emphasis upon profitable luxuries) by using a Misexpenditure Tax. One of its forms constitutes the most powerful Magnifier Fiscal instrument for ensuring allocations known — the direct Misallocation tax called the Disparity Tax.

In the Disparity-Tax system (as a comprehensive and socially-purposive direct tax) misearnings, misinvestment and misconsumption (together constituting misallocation, but the latter two only constituting Misexpenditure) are all penalised while the proper and approved forms of earnings as well as of investment and of consumption are highly encouraged. The use of the surplus of the Private Entrepreneurs, then, is channelised towards the approved industries — that is, the H-Sector with a high ploughback, and the Consumption-goods sector with less mechanised techniques. It is to be channelised away from being used in the unapproved activities like wasteful or luxury industries (and their equipment), as well as mechanised equipment for consumption necessaries to eliminate the inessential portion of the Investment-vector and to ensure adherence to the bare minimum Investment for the maximum size of non-inflationary growth, which is included in the Effective Supply vector.

Private Enterprise as well as the Public Sector, are then both given the responsibility of looking after the social good in their respective fields of earnings and spendings. The Gandhian idea of the Trusteeship of owners of capital as holding the funds (and real resources) on behalf of society for its long-term social good, is then possible to be put into practice through the Allocative-Tax System. The whole exercise is a means of implementation of the Trusteeship formula drafted by Professor Dantwala and fully tuned to the precise Gandhian phraseology. The Disparity Tax does not, however, depend upon voluntary change of heart which the formula envisaged — and whereby it remained a generally unimplemented wish of Gandhians. In the same manner as for the other two Precepts of Gandhian economics, this essay has throughout searched for the practical ways of getting the conclusions and wishes in forms feasible for implementation.

In implementing Austerity and in Trusteeship also the State depends not upon goods grace of the individuals, but on legislation and planning for ensuring implementation. If the moral force of social constraint generated by Gandhian precepts is brought into being, this would certainly aid the implementation through fiscal means, for an Austerity culture is a more propitious environment for the Allocative Taxes, as would be the case for the prevalence of Quaker ethics.

This Tax system supplement with legal authority what Gandhian philosophy expects through moral persuasion. If the latter were adequate, by itself, in the present-day cultural and moral environment, there would have been no need of devising Magnifier Allocative-Tax systems for the channelization of resources.

To conclude, it may be emphasised that equity (for the current and future generations) is not obtained merely through redistributing tax-revenue. It is obtained through the adjustment of composition of the spectrum of types of goods, types of equipments and types of manpower skills, in the exact relative quantity of each (in relation to needs of equity in the optimal long-term strategy of development). The strategy is designed by using economic principles which are analogous to the Gandhian concepts integrated with Nehruvian ideas. The implementation uses another principle — that of channeling of resources for approved investments. It can be shown that according to the present state of knowledge, the real allocation is best accomplished through the allocative tax called the Disparity Tax. This tax makes use of the principle of responsibility of the Private entrepreneurs (as much as it does so of the Public Sector) to act in support of the social good. The Gandhian precept of Trusteeship gives the moral counterpart to the re-allocative devices, and brings the Private Sector into the fold of social responsibility (in which sphere the Public Sector has been supposed to be for many years right from its inception under the Nehruvian ideal).

The concept of the Heaviesque Strategy (leading to Employment generation) of the Austerity Economy and Allocative Taxation (implementing the goal of Trusteeship) together constitute the base for a Proper Planning system based on Effective Supply. All three use Gandhian Precepts integrated with Nehruvian planning objectives.

Revitalisation of the Planning Process

Sometimes it is said that the actuality of our low achievement of the objectives should lead us to ask for a Plan Holiday, because it is alleged that we had earlier, as a Nation, messed up our economic affairs by resorting to Planning. Others have demanded that we should give up planning altogether. The critics of planning are, in both cases, blaming the wrong factor. When we say that our administrators have not implemented the strategy, we are again blaming the wrong agent; for if the strategy is itself by its nature incapable of delivering the desired goods (even with the best administration) it must necessarily prove a failure. If one blames the politician for it, again we are passing off our shortcomings, as a people and as a Nation, upon our elected Representatives. If we blame the Government for it, we do not realise the limitation under which it works, for the plans were based on a national choice — upon a consensus expressed through Parliament right from the early fifties. To change their basic framework, the orientation of the Nation itself and of the Economic Orthodoxy must change.

Around 1972, in oral evidence given in an interview, to the Bhagvati Committee for Unemployment, the then Prime Minister had been asked by me as a member of that Committee, as to why should the planners permit the producers to cater to the consumption of the elite class. She answered clearly that this class was comprised (to a large extent) of the professionals who are not ready to give their willing services without the comforts of good living, which some of them can get abroad. She wanted, she said, to implement Austerity but required help and support from the Nation, and its vital professional classes. When asked further, about re-emphasising priority to Heavy Investment, again she said that one could whole-heartedly wish to do it, if the people were to express their solid backing to that policy.

The present contributor had no doubt then (nor has any now) that should the hypothesis and argument presented in this Lecture get communicated to the masses by the elected representatives belonging to the dominant party (in terms which the electorate can comprehend), the members of the public cannot fail to appreciate the value of the conclusions with regard to how it affects them in this generation and their children in the next, and consequently to give overwhelming electoral support to the party which promises to implement it.

Hence, we ought not, in the first instance, to put the blame upon the shoulders of the politician or the Government, but to take it upon our own selves. We should, in particular put the responsibility for indifferent success squarely upon our traditional economists for advising the nation in an unimaginative manner. It is not in the proposition that what is wrong is the idea of Planning itself, but in as much as we have, under the influence of inapplicable theories, applied planning in the wrong way, that the sources of our ills are to be looked for.

It is not that the remedy for that lies in a 'Plan Holiday', but in discarding such invalid theories. The remedy for the present situation does not lie, as is canvassed strongly by misdirected minds, in getting rid of planning or reducing its scope — because if one denigrates planning even that which is being done aright will hardly get done — but in giving it a new shape, a new orientation, and a new life. It is 'Plan Revitalisation' which is now required.

The planning methodology of the future in attempting to be relevant to our common man should insist upon its being divorced from the dicatates of the upper income-groups, and their demands, and supplies for fulfilling their requirements. It would, then, have to be based upon the type of Heaviesque strategy required for Intergenerational Equity which I have just outlined. It would have to be a happy intermingling of the principles of traditionality (which we have already got in Gandhian economics) and of modernity (as were introduced by Prime Minister Nehru). Modernity would not indicate a move to highly mechanised techniques of high productivity for the Consumption Sector.

These fusions will really be capable of giving us growth and social justice along with a new planning system, with new corrective instruments, a committed administration, and a Firm State with immensely larger powers with the government to deal with those who are holding back implementation of national policies for the good of the common man. In that case, we shall not have the tendency of talking against the idea of Planned economy; but we would have better methodologies of planning — and on the basis of that revised framework we shall be able to secure the objectives of our National Policy for the masses.

The yield will be measurable primarily in terms of higher growth. Firstly, it will be evidenced in terms of growth which will give better potentiality of a higher standard of living in the future, and more employment in the meantime. Secondly, austerity would rule in the shortrun. Thirdly, emphasis in growth would be observed to be in sectors giving more consumption necessaries for the common man, and less of luxuries for the affluent. The existing capacity in that sector would be allocated for exports. The framework would yield the effect of current-equity in addition to the long-term growth for the future. This would be achieved on a permanent basis through production and distribution of the baskets of goods which would be considered, at each stage of development as consumption necessaries. Consequently, there would be no fixed standard of living for all times, but elimination of luxuries from the point of view of the common man (of each Age) would be insisted upon for all times to come, and more equality in consumption would be experienced.

The strategy of priority to Heavy-Industries would continue till the country has accumulated enough Heavy-Investment capacity to give full employment to all our people at a low, but steady, rate of growth of population (but at a high standard of living, rising at a steady rate as relevant technical progress takes place). The high standard of living could then be given to all, and not only to a few. This is the concept of the Golden Age as visualised by the late Professor John Robinson, and economic philosopher imbued with the spirit of equity.

The path to Golden Age requires that rapid absorption of the non-employed, austerity and uniformity in consumption standards (among the workers, executives, administrators, industrialists and now academics also, alike) and allocative responsibility of the public and private-sector enterprises in the socially-meaningful channels, should all continue in full measure. At least till that state is reached, all the main Gandhian precepts remain applicable — and in an extended form even thereafter.

The Urgency of Revitalisation

My submission is that it is the type of capital theory of development outlined here which provides the rationale for relevance of Gandhian thought in the context of planning for the future, and it is this which is neglected to be studied by Gandhian economists. It is the growth of the self-regenerating Heavy-Industrial Sector (through allotting to it a considerably higher priority than was envisaged even by Professor Mahalanobis or the Soviet planners) which gives justification for considering the entire consumption-goods sector as the preserve of Gandhian techniques rather than the reservation of merely a small proportion of textiles to it (and that also diluted by incursion of the polyester yarn and other materials using products of the Heavy-Industries' Sector in the handloom fabrics).

It is austerity in physical terms, through restraint in real standards of consumption (as linked to the Gandhian precepts) which, at the present time, provides the basis of ensuring proper growth (by preventing malallocation of physical resources in luxury products).

But the economic methodology of achieving this very result gets ignored by the Gandhian economists; and we have to depend solely on moral exhortations for exercise of selfrestraints. For a small number of the well-to-do, such moral precepts work (unless they belong to the second generation of tycoonic heritage). Under the spell of an over-whelmingly-towering moral personality like that of a spiritual leader who works no miracles and rides no airplanes, many more recalcitrant elite could be induced. But neither is our universe of canvassing small, nor is it limited to the middle class; but it is primarily addressed to those at the very top, so that the vogue of austerity may be adopted and may percolate downwards. Nor, indeed, do we have now the very rare personalities deserving the title of top moral leaders of the masses in prescript and precept both.

It is the duty of evoking involvement of the whole of the private sector (apart from the public sector) in the proper forms of investment, and for production of proper goods in the austerity-oriented economy, which ought to form the basis of our attention for channelling of real resources. It would be these actions which would convert the private sector into a trustee for the nation's resources from a state of private ownership. It is the study of the form of the economic system — the Composite Economy (as a Mixed Economy) with social relevance of both its constituents — which will permit and help such a transformation to take place, but it is this very study which, upto the present, has not been well-assimilated into current Gandhian studies.

About nineteen years ago, for the Gandhi Centenary number of Interdiscipline the journal of the Gandhian Institute, on the invitation of its then Editor, Visiting Professor Hans Rieger (who had come to Varanasi from the University of Heidelberg), the present contributor (while he was with the Osmania University) had examined the whole question of intermeshing of modern Capital Theory and Gandhian Economics. This suggestion was taken up by the late Shri Pitamber Pant in the Planning Commission, and separately by Dr. I.G. Patel at the Union Ministry of Finance for further study of the economic doctrines being propounded at the Osmania University (which had been first published by the said Gandhian Institute). On these topics, Reports had been prepared under the project directorship of the present contributor namely the Perspective Plan 1970-2000 A.D.(1974), and earlier Fiscal Policy Reform ((1970), by Dr. Yadava Reddy and Mr. H. Venkateswar Rao.

The subject was also fully discussed at Andhra Mahila Sabha Hyderabad under the chairmanship of Shrimati Durgabai Deshmukh in 1973. Twelve years ago, in a lecture at the fifteenth Anniversary of the foundation of the Gandhian Institute at Varanasi, the position had been re-examined and the text is published in the Inaugural Issue of Gandhian Perspectives, April 1979, under the editorship of respected Professor Amlan Datta at a seminar in Allahabad, ten years ago, under the auspices of the esteemed Institute of Gandhian Studies, the thinking upon this subject had been presented and had been reported by the learned Professor J.S. Mathur in the esteemed journal edited by him. The theme was also presented and discussed at a session of the Annual Conference of the Indian Society for Gandhian Studies at Muzaffarpur on the invitation of Professor Surendra Prasad Sinha, then Pro-Vice-Chancellor of Bihar University.

Thus, the government and the economists in general and progressive Gandhian economists in particular have had some opportunity to take note of the strategy which indicates the possibilities of Gandhian principles being made an integral part of modern economic planning. There has been once a government in power at the Centre which stated it believed in Gandhian Austerity and Equity and Planning — but it did not implement it. The ruling party at the Centre has for the last four decades pronounced itself in favour of Austerity — witness the many types of drives for saving — and its resolute determination to implement good Planning. But they have not come to grips with the crux of the problem which is to achieve equity through a spectrum of production which itself is a by-product of efficient growth for the future. But leaving aside the broad-minded Gandhian Economists there has not been even a ripple of activity regarding follow-up upon these lines in the closed precincts of Gandhian philosophical and scholarly circles as for as integration of Gandhian and Modern economic values (through long-term strategies of equity) are concerned. Is the methodology of interaction of the traditional with the modern going to be confined to practical considerations of utilisation of Gandhian technology in conjunction with mechanical power (and raw-materials as products of mechanised-industrial-origin) — or is a philosophical integration needed?

The scholars of Gandhian philosophy on a narrow interpretation will not find this presentation to be a part of orthodox Gandhian thought, which it is not, indeed, claimed to be. It is an application of economic theory of the Intergenerational-Equity School to development planning, and finding parts of it capable of identity with some important elements of Gandhian thought. Conversely, it could be viewed as application of Gandhian principles to long-term development and obtaining conclusions which coincide with the propositions indicated by modern Capital theory. Whatever the way the matter is viewed, the resultant opens a way for at least one part of modern economic theory not being considered an opponent to Gandhian thought, but as an ally capable of being integrated with it.

I fear that any further delay (through doctrinal opposition to one's allies) will take the matter of reform of the mixed economy and plan restructuring from the hands of the democratic processes to the arena of explosive upsurged of the deprived youths of our mother earth. Before the eventuality arises, let us take some steps to put the planning process on to the proper tracks through a re-evaluation of the whole structure and concept of the mixed economy, the choice of strategies, the choice of goods, and of techniques in which sphere to talk of high technology as highly productive per man and in which sectors to consider it as highly productive per unit value of scarce capital (including human capital skills natural non-reproducible endowments, and the capital required for production for the future).

Further, we must decide the instrument of the regulation of the system by supervision over millions of transactions, by physical controls or by inducements. This re-evaluation must take place well before the start of the Eighth plan and must be on the basis of a national consensus — for the Government will need cooperation from all quarters in this fight against human deprivation which is no less than fight against aggression in its import. Only in such a Revitalisation of Planning on the lines indicated in this essay, will the Gandhian precepts have a hope of surviving as parts of the Planning process (rather than as preserves of the learned antiquarians). Only such an integration would be a tribute to the vision of our first Prime Minister in his Centenary Year.

7

EQUITABLE TRANSFORMATION FOR NATIONAL INTEGRATION

I. TRANSFORMATION FOR NATIONAL INTEGRATION

National Integration requires that the divisive sociological forces be countered by economic action favouring cohesion. With such action, greater cquity is established as a norm, and is visible to people. The will to strengthen the body politic as a whole is then created, rather than for betterment solely of one's own interest or that of one's class or group. But this action must be of a form which establishes equality of interest, for in the absence of that there is a high degree of resentment, and hence the divisive forces — of community, of region, of caste, of creed, of class — take advantage of that situation and play upon emotions of those who perceive discriminatory treatment of their group. The emotional appeal is backed by an ideology, howsover sectarian it may be. It can only be countered by an emotional appeal, not merely by strenthening law and order.

Whatever may be the emotional appeal of National Integration, it must be supported by economic action which:

(a) generates employment;
(b) reduces visible inequalities (in holding of land, in consumption standards);
(c) controls real inflation;
(d) reduce disparities between regions;
(e) builds up capital for the future generations;
(f) gives entrepreneurs, as well as managers and workers, the feeling of participating in this national investment and managing it;

Published in *Nation Building in India—Socio-economic Factors*, Dutt, R.C. (ed.), Lancer International, New Delhi, 1987, pp.140-80.

(g) gives educational opportunities equally to those who require it and can benefit from it; and
(h) yields a comparable basic standard of living irrespective of educational qualifications, and higher talent, or productivity, apart from what is required for each specific job for functional purposes.

These aspects are captured in the ten Prescripts of Equity; and the planning system if it is geared to achieving them, would also create the Ideology of Equity which is required for National Integration. These Prescripts—five of Consumption Equity, three of Production Equity and two of Distributive Equity—are presented here to show that with their help the emotional appeal of National Integration will be strengthened, and whatever sacrifice of individual benefit is required will be forthcoming because it will be for the social good rather than made visible through disparate living standard.

The classical model of growth is basically a closed system. The conditions for a Golden age are described in terms of an economy without an international environment. This is so for the Sraffa[1] and the von Neumann[2] closed linear systems[3] also. In the Sraffa-Neumann Input-Output Analysis (using the Robinsonian framework) the external environment enters through the objectives of the planned growth of an underdeveloped country as being the attainment, over a long period, of the Golden Age state[4] (which less underdeveloped countries, usually miscalled advanced economics, are capable of achieving in the short or medium term). This is to be achieved in minimum time.[5]

The choice of investment in type of equipment is governed by the choice of techniques for the optimum strategy. The choice of techniques should be governed by this optimum strategy for International equity (which is determined by prescripts of production equity), and the demand for consumption goods ought to be determined by the prescripts of consumption equity.

This essay presents the point of view that following the dictates of Social Justice or of Growth, as long as both are in their proper frames of reference, the planner would be led to describe the same profile of Equitable Transformation. According to this view, the so-called conflict between growth and social justice arises out of using inappropriate frames of analysis.

Inequity is traceable in each case to either wrong choice of goods or of techniques. In either case, it leads to deviation from true employment and, in particular, existence of non-employment, sub-employment[6] (in occupations not giving even subsistence wage) or malemployment (employment in the inappropriate goods or techniques).

The essay is based on the author's work over a number of years. References are given at various places to articles and books on which the arguments are based.

II. CONSUMPTION AND PRODUCTION EQUITY

We start with the consideration of Consumption Equity.[7] There are five prescripts of Consumption Equity. The first one relates to insistence on the growth process not resulting in depression of the standard of living of employed workers at subsistence. The second one seeks to prevent a rise in the wages of those already employed so long as there exist manpower units who are non-employed and who could, by alternative use of the consumption resources; be brought into the fold of the employed. The third prescript seeks to discourage disparities of consumption standards among the employed workers. The fourth one relates to the reduction of disparities between managers and executives (as also professional experts) and workers. The fifth prescript enjoins the industrialist or the large shareholder to spend upon his personal consumption only in his capacity as a manager, and not out of the surplus which should, ideally, be reinvested in totality.

These are followed by three prescripts of Production Equity.[8] Thus the sixth prescript of Equity (and the first one of Production Equity) relates to the attainment (in minimum time) of international equity of standards of living at full employment; and for this purpose considers that particular strategy as optimum which permits rapid accumulation in the Heavy-Investment sector (H). This yields intergenerational equity or long-run growth.

The rapid accumulation in the H-sector requires the rate of H-ploughback (or H-Recycling) to be high. This immediate aim enjoins the planners to use H-conserving techniques[9] in the Consumption Sector which forms the Seventh Prescript of Equity (and the second one of Production Equity). It allows the H-Sector to grow fast, and it also yeilds current social justice. The Eighth prescript (which is the third and last one of production Equity) indicates that the instrument of achieving the earlier seven prescripts must aim at change of spectrum of production in conformity with the prescripts. Hence, instead of deferring the search for equality of consumption-standards till only after redistribution of income and wealth (the egalitarian state) has first of all been effected—which is a circuitous method—it is felt that straightaway there should be the discouragement of consumption disparities[10] effected. The two methods—of circuitous action and short-cut in consumption control—are alternatives to each other. But in the latter method, the Demand-side methods and Supply-side methods are compatible and capable of being integrated, and they support each other.

Consumption equality or the equalitarian state as it may be called, should be achieved through eliminating the luxury goods from the production spectrum (as well as through fiscal policy directly restraining the demand for excessive consumption). The elimination of luxury consumption goods can and should be achieved through inducive instruments rather than physical controls. Among the former set we can have direct fiscal instruments which correct the unfavourable distribution in consumption standard (and the distortions in production spectrum simultaneously).

The contravention of the prescripts gives rise to an inequitable profile of economic transformation. We shall consider these in the next four sections of this essay. In the further next three sections we shall consider the situation where the inequities are absent or less conspicuous. In the last two sections we shall consider the two prescripts of Distribution Equity, and the means of implementation of the Optimum Strategy.

III. EFFECTS OF MAL-EMPLOYMENT

A high degree of current social justice is indicated, firstly, by the extent of spread of true employment, and, secondly, by the prevention of real inflation. In the former category, we have further two sub-categories, firstly of removal of non-employment, and secondly, of the low level of mal-employment at one place and over various regions. Among the employed, those possessing the four characteristics of:

(1) working with equipment corresponding to the non-inferior techniques,
(2) for production of goods of social relevance,
(3) at the appropriate degree of mechanization in each activity,
(4) in balance allocation ratio[11] required for development, are termed as the "truly employed".[12]

True employment requires firstly, the proper type of equipment (i.e. belonging to the optimal strategy), and secondly, physical consumption goods (at subsistence level, neither less nor more) as wage fund in advance of production (composed also of proper type of goods compatible with consumption equity) and thirdly, training of manpower in the skills required for operating the appropriate equipment. Fourthly, it requires a person to be in true productive work rather than enjoying a concealed dole (because there is no well thought out scheme of purposive work as a part of optimal strategy or complementary to it, but he has been guaranteed employment as a welfare measure).

Hence, mal-employment[13] on account of wrong choice of goods or of techniques is excluded from the figure of those who are found to be engaged in production or investment, to arrive at the figure of the truly-employed.

Those who get from their employment, a subsistence level wage or marginally above it, are called "iso-employed". Those workers who are provided with jobs (i.e. they are "engaged"), but they do not get therefrom even subsistence level wage (because of using inferior techniques, who may be called the "infra-employed", or on account of real inflation), are termed as the "sub-employed" (rather than their being included among the "employed"). Hence, inflation converts employed workers at subsistence or just above it from what may be termed as the "iso-employed" into the "sub-employed".

The remedies for sub-employment are interlinked with the analysis of its sources and causes. Apart from lack of appropriate equipment of a highly-productive nature (for a given capital intensity), one of the important causes of the state whereby a large mass of people (who are capable of being better off) are afflicted by sub-employment (and consequently, poverty), is real inflation. This is itself traceable (to a certain extent), firstly to a large degree of mal-employment and secondly, to Spontaneous Inflation[14] (created by adherence to classical fiscal devices).

Mal-employment stems from the demands of the affluent[15] (and also of the anti-social elements) which attract away both skilled labour and physical resources, from the task of producing necessaries with the optimum techniques towards producing inessential goods or enhancing unproductive activities.

Due to materials and skills channelled away in mal-employment from essential uses, there arises consequent shortage in production and supply of essential goods. The prices of necessaries thus tend to rise. This is known as real inflation arising out of a parasitic origin[16] — and it is manifested through mal-employment. It depresses the standard of living of those who are in true employment, and in particular when it affects those who are just within the circle of employment (with wage near subsistence) it impoverishes them. It also converts the status of those at subsistence from one of being in employment — or more specifically in "iso-employment" (which has been defined by us to be for a wage at, or marginally above, subsistence level) — to workers in sub-employment, or workers merely occupied (which is distinguished from being in employment on account of its yield for labour being a wage below subsistence).

The consumption of the affluent has a similar effect, and also converts the employed into the sub-employed, because of lack of real consumption goods to yield subsistence level consumption to the workers. Austerity in consumption standards and the balancing of allocations both separately and together act towards eliminating mal-employment; and they convert simultaneously the sub-employed into the employed, and the mal-employed into the truly-employed (or at worst the infra-employed — these producing the socially-appropriate goods but with inferior techniques).

Even if employment in luxury goods production offers wage higher than subsistence (called ultra-employment) or equal to subsistence, the investment being in industries which do not produce necessaries, it is inflationary and hurts the rest of the employed population at subsistence. In placements yielding a wage at or above subsistence (as also in occupations giving wages below subsistence), the higher is the amount of expenditure on goods and services which have a large element of inputs of organised industry (like bus transport, kerosene, housing) the more are the workers adversely affected by increased mal-employment in mechanized techniques for production of inessential goods, because of the competing use of resources and consequent lowering of production of consider necessaries. Where there are non-competing physical resources, prices still rise because effective demand is created and supply of necessaries is not increased.

No strategy has been shown to be feasible in a mixed economy by which poverty[17] can be removed quickly without first of all attempting to channel the resources of the economy to use more purposive than the consumption of the affluent within the country. Mal-employment is the key to existence of poverty and ought to be reduced first as a pre-condition of anti-poverty programmes. Employment offered in providing luxury consumption is at the expense of a larger scope for true-employment. The latter ought to be offered through providing optimal equipment for long-term growth and for necessaries of consumption in balanced proportions. In that manner we shall get a planned reduction of real inflation, and conversion of these merely occupied (the sub-employed of the variety classified as infra-employed) into those engaged with non-inferior equipment. They will then be counted among the iso-employed.

Employment with consumption equity eliminates the consumption of the more well-to-do-persons—of the "ultra-employed" workers as well as of the managers and professional experts, and of the industrialists who use their profits for basic consumption standards higher than subsistence (to which only they are justifiably entitled on a footing on equality with other units of manpower). The part of the ultra-employment wage (or salary or consumption out of profits and rents) above subsistence—which is the just due for all manpower units irrespective of their qualifications productivity, efficiency or talent—is called a Ransom. Removal of Ransoms has an effect opposite to that of Real Inflation. To the sub-employed who are occupied in jobs with non-inferior techniques, it restores the erstwhile status of the employed.

IV. INEQUITY OF THE GLASS-CURTAIN

The affluent group can be stratified by consumption levels which may be represented by concentric rings and mapped like contour lines (each with a higher consumption in relation to the ring adjacent to it on the outer side). The persons in the outer ring have their eyes directed towards those in the next inner ring. Some of those who have been in the outer ring are now enjoying a position in an inner ring and it is this which causes social tensions among persons in the outer ring. The consumption of the person in an inner ring is visible to those outside, and the goods are also displayed in showrooms in various markets. But entry to the inner ring is possible only with a higher purchasing power which is the result of past accumulation or for the ultra-employed a current drawal of Ransoms or both. The lack of purchasing power acts as a barrier to improving one's status. The set of those rings has been called the Glass-Curtain Economy.[18] There are psychological pressures of securing availability of a better basket of goods and achieving equality of living standards with the group of persons just above one in the consumption hierarchy. The innermost rings of the Glass-Curtain Economy contravene the fifth Prescript of Equity that the entrepreneurial consumption should not be higher than managerial consumption.[19]

These impulses of spending compete with the desire to save, but the impulse to be at par with the people in the inner ring has the character of a force, and is stronger, in most cases, than the logic of following the morality of austerity. In other cases the persons desirous of the higher consumption standards seize the opportunities of making extra incomes, through fair or unfair means. It leads to skilled manpower either weakening its moral fibre or to changing the character of their interests from their own professional work to subsidiary money-spinning activities to the neglect of their proper professional jobs. Teachers looking for tuition and examinerships to the utter neglect of instruction in schools and colleges, and causing the time of 40 young men or so per class to be wasted in formal schooling, is an example. Government doctors in private practice neglecting their official duties, is another example. Whenever there is a conflict of duty towards their proper jobs and the subsidiary activity, it is expected by the authorities that the former should prevail, but the reverse is the actual case, for extra incomes (so necessary to counter real inflation or to go to the inner rings of the Glass-Curtain Economy) can only be earned in the subsidiary activity. The educational and research sector, and the administrative sector being among those less well-paid are specially prone to this malady, and hence their inefficient performance in most situations. This is equivalent to mal-utilisation of Human Resources.

The demands created by the members of any ring of the Glass-Curtain Economy are for some variety of the luxury goods, and mal-employment is caused by catering to that demand. Equity suffers on account of the very existence of consumption disparities and by the diversion of resources from employment-creating investments for long-term accumulation and production of consumption necessaries to current consumption of the affluent. The key to the conversion of the employed into the sub-employed (arising out of inflation caused by Parasitical consumption), and for the continued poverty of the masses, is, hence, the consumption of the affluent. The well-meaning prescriptions regarding Basic Needs Programmes[20], Guaranteed Employment Schemes, and Distribution of Goods among the poor can only offer palliatives (but cannot cure the ailment)—because they attack the symptoms of poverty while they refrain from tackling the real cause which lies in the continuance of the prime inequity embodied in the Glass-Curtain Economy.

It can thus be noted that mal-employment of some workers (by the entrepreneurs) for catering to the demands of the affluent, keeps other people in sub-employment when they could be in employment. The contravention of the fourth Prescript advocating elimination of divergence between the consumption of professionals and executives and workers, apart from creating primarily poverty (through real inflation diverting resources from necessaries) also induces secondary poverty (income above subsistence but expenditure mis-directed). The more existence of goods of a luxury character which are on display and beyond the reach of the employed persons at subsistence, sometimes (through Salesmanship tactics of publicity[21] and marketing persuasion) induces these to be bought by the non-affluent sections, thus manifesting itself in secondary poverty. The worker and his family have then to cut their essential consumption items somewhere else—for, the more there is Coca-Cola for the college going boy, the less will there be milk for his school-going younger sister in a lower-middle-class family. Mis-employment and mis-expenditure are two sides of the same spurious coin.

Hence, on the one hand, the problem of providing avenues of higher employment is linked to efficiency (which is geared to, firstly, producing equipment which offers true employment to the non-employed, and secondly, imparting training to the uninitiated in the use of that superior equipment), and on the other hand, the problem of raising the real wage of those below subsistence upto the subsistence level (called iso-employment level) is that of producing more consumption necessaries. These problems are different in character. The former is of offering greater employment (i.e. it is the problem of increasing investments in equipment and in human capital with Active Education—minimum content of formal education necessary for performance of given operations and maximum amount of practical training and skill creation). The latter is of producing more consumption goods (and thus of balancing the expenditures between investment of long gestation and of quick yields in production of consumption necessaries, and consequently countering real inflation). But both of these aspects are parts of one integrated field of Investment and Employment Strategy for Non-inflationary Growth. It is these which will engage our attention in the next two sections.

V. THE PERCOLATION INEQUITIES

A. Inequalities

Before we study various alternative strategies, we note that the strategy in practice in most countries is the Percolation Strategy and one would like to list its characteristics. The Percolation Strategy aims at planning a small sector initially of modernised machinery, and hopes that this will, in time, expand and cover a large sector of the working population. In this strategy, because modernized consumption-good technique is derived from the use of Heavy Investment, the consumption sector uses a high degree of mechanization. It is thus a strategy of priority of Mechanized Light Machinery. Hence, in the consumption-good sector, less employment is created in general (and less purposive employment in particular). This affects the benefit to the present generation also (apart from mechanized light-machinery taking away a large capacity of self-regenerating Heavy-Investment sector, and thus affecting the latter's accumulation for providing consumption goods to the next generation).

The degree of mechanization and capital intensity of investment in such a strategy being high, the ratio of profits (-cum-extra wages of the ultra-employed) to earnings of the iso-employed at subsistence wage (to be referred to hence forward as Profit-cum-Ransom to Wage ratio) is also high, for there is a bias towards medium and large scales of production in the micro-economic system. Thenceforward, starting from micro-economics and going to the macro-economy, as a side effect, one notices an unfavourable Functional Income-distribution (measured through the above ratio of Profits-cum Ransoms to Wages, rather than as simple Profit to Wage Ratio). One also notices a tendency for inequalities in Personal Consumption-distribution (by deciles) to be increased towards the two or three top deciles (above the per-capita consumption) and away from benefit to the less-advantaged median consumer. This also creates in a micro-economic system the element of tendency towards adopting larger scales of production favouring the distribution of income to the privileged. This tendency also permits creation of monopolistic combinations.

B. Ultra-Employment

Observing these privileged workers as regards their standard of living in relation to subsistence level workers (the iso-employed), one sub-specifies them (within the category of the employed) as the "ultra-employed". There is an even greater inequality of consumption standards among the skilled workers, when the situation is coupled with scarcity of skills. There is a general misemphasis placed by employers favouring education given by elite schools, and there is an invalid tendency to give preference to managerial skills over technical ones, sometimes because those in decision-making position have the former type of skillls. A higher standard of living is claimed, as of economic right, by the operatives in favoured positions and it is granted because of the scarcity element in the supply of skilled personnel. The claim and its acceptance contravenes the fourth Prescript of Equity.

Among professional experts, a couple with both the spouses in the category of those so-called highly-skilled operatives can pool their benefits arising out of the supposed. The situation becomes even more incongruous when the woman's claim is further supported by considerations of equity towards that weaker section—when it is extended to cover all women-folk (irrespective of the previous background being the low-income section). The earning couple is capable thus of gaining an even better payoff in terms of a combined purchasing power of each, allowing (in the absence of direct taxes on consumption) an even higher standard of living for the nuclear family.

C. Non-inflationary Employment Creation

For underdeveloped countries the exercise is a matter of converting the Percolation Strategy (where the simultaneous achievement of giving more employment and countering real Inflation cannot be effected), to some other strategy (where employment generation and non-inflationary growth are secured together). In the school of development economics which derives its strength from applying the methodology of Platinum[22] Age economics (of Professor Lord Kahn and of Jaon Robinson) to underdeveloped countries, there is no conflict between higher employment (through higher investment) on the one hand, and removal of inflation on the other. Both problems— of eliminating inflation and offering true employment are capable of simultaneous achievement through reduction of real inflation and increase of true-employment by investing in the optimal activities (in which production of consumption necessaries in balance with other goods is an essential component). This is achieved through non-inflationary growth of the Platinum Age type.

According to the traditional literature of advanced countries, for full-capacity periods, the two actions (of offering more employment through investment and of producing more consumption necessaries for countering real inflation) cannot be achieved simultaneously — for higher employment comes from greater investments which will cause the burden of real inflation to be increased rather than being reduced.

This is not true even for advanced countries even in non-depression conditions because consumption necessaries can be simultaneously increased with high investment by reducing at the same time the production of luxuries. Even at the high level of their standards of living of average working class members, silver-lined hubs for limousine-wheels are not unknown, and could perhaps be dispensed with in those societies instead of depressing the consumption of butter of working-class school-children and simultaneously increasing investment and employment.

The level of true Employment actually achieved can be enhanced through proper deployment of resources (which includes reduction in investment for production of luxuries, and increase in investment for production of necessaries) without depressing the standard of living. Larger investment can take place without bringing down the real wage of the employed by keeping a balance between investments in quick yielding processes, on the one hand, and in long-gestation projects, on the other. For this reason, in an underdeveloped country undergoing proper planned or guided growth, it is less meaningful to talk of a payoff between inflation and unemployment, for the latter can be reduced without necessarily depressing real standards of living. There is also no equation describing, on the one hand, necessarily the relationship[23] between depression of the real wage (supposed to be caused by investment) and, on the other hand, increasing employment. This is contrary to what some theorists in advanced countries claim through depicting the famous Philips Curve. Therefore, the proposition is firmly maintained herein that the act of generating employment for some need not in a proper planning system cause the inequity of sub-employment to be created for others.

VI. CONTRAVENTION OF THE PRESCRIPTS

The contravention of the fifth and fourth Prescripts causes the organized labour to demand, very naturally, a higher proportion of the product in the form of higher money wages. This is supported by successful organized action in collective bargaining.

In the process of development, Real inflation causes, ultimately, a forceful demand for higher salaries for workers and the staff in the commercial field of Government activity. From there it leads to the Public-sector concerns having wage agreements to neutralize the rise of cost of living, followed by similar arrangements even in non-commercial Government departments at the Centre and in the States. This is effected either through collective bargaining backed by organized action, or through the mechanism of averting a confrontation by a timely revision of dearness allowances (through the good graces of the Honourable Finance Minister) or rise in the pay-scales themselves (with the assistance of the esteemed Pay Commission).

The neutralization of the contravention of the first prescript is done through an act which itself contravenes the first prescript of consumption equity (pertaining to non-inflationary character to growth); because a large volume of purchasing power is let loose on the market as a result, without corresponding increase in Effective Supply. Hence, prices start rising immediately afterwards, or in sure expectation of it. A self-defeating remedy[24] is then set afoot for rectifying the effects of contravention of the first prescript (relating to non-inflationary growth).

The cycle of price-rise and wage-increase (occurring in retard), which is so generated, is further reinforced by wage increases in advance of price increases. These could occur in the private sector industries where profits are unusually high, or where technical progress tends to be pronounced. Workers who are in this category may be called "Privileged workers". The neo-classical theory of wages supports such increases, because the so-called marginal productivity of workers goes up in these industries due to technical progress. The government departments welcome these wage rises as being (supposedly) non-inflationary.

As a result, there is a disparity created in the real-wage structure of the workers in organized and unorganized industry; and among the former there is a further differentiation between workers in the rapidly-innovating industries (or in more profitable ones — called the privileged workers)[25] and the rest of the employed and organized workers. This contravenes the third Prescript of Equity (uniformity of wage levels among workers).

The contravention of the third Prescript causes the second Prescript of Equity (of no wage rises for these within the circle of the employed as long as there is non-employment outside) to be violated. The consequent rise of money wages of the organized labour who then become ultra-employed, is neutralized by the private-sector entrepreneur understandably (and in the public-sector sometimes unjustifiably) through rise of prices of products to a certain extent. It is unjustifiable for the public sector to seek to create profits at the expense of the cousumers of their products in essential activities and thereby to engender a general and spontaneous price rise.

One would like to believe that one could have, alternatively, a discriminatory price-system depending on the use of the particular material product of the public sector for essential and inessential activities in terms of their use. When this discrimination between essential and inessential activities is not practised, and prices are raised by the public-sector enterprises for all consumers, price-inflation would be expected to spread, as a result, throughout the economy causing a real inflation through a decline of the real wage for the workers in other sectors of the economy.

The present author believes that this argument is fallacious as far as distinction is made between prices of luxuries rising and of necessaries. Even when discrimination is practised and the prices of luxuries produced by the public sector rise, this is transmitted to the semi-necessaries and necessaries. All public sector profits raising prices up are injustifiable as they are causes of Spontaneous Inflation.

On the other hand, with rise of wages of the ultra-employed, the demand for goods following from the rise of purchasing power of privileged workers would lead to shifts in production pattern to semi-luxuries from necessaries, causing a shortage of the latter. Thus money wage rise for a few ultra-employed workers leads to inflation directly and produces real inflation (through shortages) for workers in general. It is for this reason that for Profit-Wage ratio one substitutes the ratio Profits-cum-Ransoms to Iso-wage as a measure of functional distribution. The ultra-employed workers is an ally of management and not a protagonist of the Labour Movement in the broad socialist sense.

Thus, because of contravention of the fifth, fourth, third and second Prescripts of Equity through high consumption of a few persons above subsistence, Real Inflation necessarily arises for the rest. This acts through upsetting the balance through higher unproductive expenditure, and lesser investment in quick-yielding activities for production of consumer necessaries. The real inflation leads, first of all to a depression of the real wage, converting the iso-employed into the sub-employed, thus contravening the first Prescript of Equity, and secondly to distortion of the production spectrum with larger proportion of luxuries and semi-luxuries to necessaries (which latter are the socially-relevant goods).

Departures from Prescripts of Equity are material for social tension; one ought to strive to prevent the departures; and if they occur, to correct them instantaneously—otherwise they are dangers to national integration.

VII. THE INTERACTION OF PRODUCTION AND CONSUMPTION INEQUITIES

From the percolation strategy is derived the Production Inequity which, as we have seen, produces consumption disparities. A large quantum of consumption by entrepreneurs, combined with rise of real wages for the privileged workers, managers and professional experts, leading to choice of goods favouring the affluent and semi-affluent classes, as well as a high degree of mechanization (creating higher Profit-cum-Ransoms to Iso-wage ratio, with lesser employment opportunities) is responsible for a further conflict of interests, i.e. between the employed and the non-employed workers. In this conflict, the employed workers are converted into malemployed workers, on the one hand, as regards their channels of employment either lying in production of socially-irrelevant goods, or in production with socially-inoptimal techniques of production.

Corresponding to the creation of the ultra-employed, there is (through real inflation) deprivation of the unorganized section of the employed workers converting them into the sub-employed. The working class then breaks up into various tiers — the ultra-employed, the iso-employed (at subsistence), the sub-employed, the infra-employed (at subsistence), the sub-employed (having inferior type of equipment), and the unoccupied. Each class has a different set of interests, which is in conflict with the rest of the working class.

Even when employment opportunities are created, in organized industry they become, to some extent, the preserves of patronage and right of that type of influential worker (labour-leadership) which does not abide by the concept of labour movement for the benefit of the working class as a whole, but seeks benefits for itself. Those who are employed in organized industry, consequently, have a better chance of getting their dependents into prized employment positions, or getting others into employment on payment of a consideration. Either the burden of dependency falls for such workers, or the receipts rise, and the per capita real wage in the family rises, thus enhancing the disparities in living standards among the members of the working class, and as indicated earlier, breaking them up into four categories, namely the ultra-employed (consisting of the influential workers, the privileged workers and the organized workers), the employed but unorganized workers, the sub-employed workers (including the infra-employed, and especially those without other family members in employment or occupation), and lastly the unoccupied.

The greatest beneficiaries of the system in living standards are, of course, the sponsoring directors[26] of the larger corporations, and other owners of non-human tangible property of a scarce character which give them the capacity of exacting ransoms.[27]

All these tendencies of Consumption Inequality give the benefit to the privileged, and through exercises of the increased purchasing power (partly in consumption expenditure), they are responsible for diverting the real resources of the economy away from production of consumption necessaries. Hence, Consumption Inequity in reverse causation further strengthens Production Inequity. Consequently, it deprives the rest of the population of even minimum subsistence, and thus converts the iso-employed into the sub-employed. In a situation whereby resources of land, equipment and manpower skills have alternative uses with social relevance, the method of achieving prosperity and the show of affluence by a few, leaves the other in a position whereby the latter cannot but tread the path towards poverty and deprivation.

The paradox is that this production Inequity of mal-employment created by inessential consumption is considered to be a favour for the sub-employed or unoccupied. Efforts to restrict the consumption of the affluent through really powerful measures hitting at production are sought to be resisted, firstly, by the producers of such goods (on the invalid grounds of infringement of the liberty to produce whatever one wishes and finds profitable — even though the market is not a perfectly competitive one and has huge inequalities of purchasing power).

Except for extraordinarily enlightened labour leadership, the desire of government to curb the affluent persons consumption is, secondly, resisted by organized labour (on the ground that the curbs on luxury consumption are capable of causing unemployment). If the measures to restrict consumption of the affluent were really adopted, and the resources thus set free were invested in socially-purpose investment, they would, in reality, create greater employment in essential lines and would also reduce real inflation, and hence, they would help to remove poverty and inequity.

We observe that both positive and negative deviations from the standard of equal basic consumption (barring differences due to functional requirements which are a part of kit — like a uniform, or a laboratory apron) are capable of causing social disturbances. In the case of deprivations the social tensions come from those who lack what others have got, and in the opposite case of higher consumption standards having been set, to ask these consumption baskets to be shared by others would also cause actions of resistance. To depart from equity and to allow others to depart from it are situations equally pregnant with forces of disorder.

For national integration it is better to avoid these deviations occurring from the start of the planning process, and to correct them as soon as actions are in prospect which are bound to result in divergences from equitable norms. If they have occurred, it is best to handle them with a firm hand and powerful instruments of statehood, rather than hoping that Time will bring forth a solution. The longer privilege is entrenched or inequity prevails, the more difficult is to dislodge.

Equity requires an Interventionist Government, not a laissez-faire governance; it requires strengthening the process of Planning and Regulation, not of deginerating its importance. It requires a Firm State to implement an equitable plan of development, not a Soft one; nor is a hard one necessary (as the Firm State is feasible and is more efficient).

VIII. LONG-TERM AND CURRENT EQUITY

The first Prescript of Production Equity (and the sixth Prescript of Equity) follows from the objective of Development being International Equality in consumption standards or in possibility of achieving it. International equality requires a rapid built-up of the self-regenerating Heavy Sector (H) which would (ultimately) provide the mechanised equipment for production of consumption goods at a high level per man at full employment of the then-existing working population. This would be called a state of Full Development. It requires, therefore, for the consumption sector a technique which conserves the product of H for its further build-up.

The uses of these H-conserving techniques (which is the second Prescript of Production Equity) are of low-degree of mechanization and do not appreciably reduce the rate of recycling of H from its ideal level. This fundamental idea of capital theory was absent in the Four-sector Mahalanobis model (1955) as the same was not based on capital theory (using the long-term strategies which became known to capital theorists only after that time). Since 1959, when the development strategies based on input-output models were discovered, it has been possible to reconcile growth and social justice (even in a two-sector model provided it is based on H-conserving techniques of low degree of mechanisation for consumption-good production and rise of allocation to the Heavy Sector).

Ignoring the call of the last one of these prescripts, in different underdeveloped countries at various times, Governments have either tried to follow the path of growth (long-run or short-term), and thought that equity would emerge on the way, or followed the way towards equity and expected that growth will be encountered. But neither of these lanes were able to lead to their expected result; for the type of growth or equity selected was deficient.

If we look for growth, and for that purpose follow the type of strategies which rely upon highly-mechanised techniques in the consumption sector, firstly the growth of Heavy-investments (H) which is essential for long-run equity, is adversely affected (because the consumption-sector techniques eat away the product which would have gone to the H-sector). The long-run prospects of growth of capital for the next generation's requirements are then frustrated.

Secondly, as regards the current generation's position, with use of highly-mechanized techniques in the consumption sector, social justice is defeated by lack of employment opportunities, low wage to Profit-cum-Ransom ratio, large scale of production, generation of income inequalities, demand for luxury goods, use of mechanized techniques for the modernized luxury-commodities, the aggravation of unequal income-distribution, concentration of industries in metropolitan area and their expansion to megalopolitan dimensions, regional disparities, and monopolism. Thus by looking for growth through stress upon mechanized techniques, the perspective of long-run growth is automatically shifted away from the long-run built-up of H as well as departing from the current generation's problems of equity. But neither the long-run growth, nor current social justice, gets furthered.[28]

If one does not look for growth, but only for social justice for the current generation and encourages the use of less mechanized techniques, one gets only some aspects of short-run equity looked after. But growth of H-capital essential for long-run growth is not planned to follow, nor does it follow of itself. Thus, firstly, the stimulus which H-growth gives to employment-creation through its labour-intensive projects is denied to the economy.

Secondly, in an economy where the less-mechanized techniques have low output per man, and therefore high money cost per unit of product, the true economic rationale for techniques of low productivity per man in the consumption sector, is that they permit more of H to be conserved and used for its own expansion. In that case they are not high-cost methods of production, but techniques of low social cost. Thus the high money cost of handloom products is possible to be justified on economic grounds only on the principle of opportunity cost in a strategy with priority to Heavy-Investments (H); for a few hundred thousand handloom (rather than powerlooms) allow a few hundred miles more of railway tracks and of electricity cables to be laid and used for respectively transporting and operating cranes. The materials also become available because of lesser investment in mechanized techniques. As H growth is not furthered in a strategy of short-run equity, the employment-creating technique have to justify their cost on their own. If one is only looking for short-run equity, the bottom is knocked off the rationale for use of less mechanized techniques which has very much higher money-costs in comparison with products of the mechanised techniques.

It is by looking for social justice for the future generations — economic justice as it has been called[29] - that one starts to expect the simultaneous emergence of growth and social justice both. It requires implementation of the seventh Prescript through what has been called either the Heaviesque Strategy, or Strategy for International Equity or Strategy for Intergenerational Equity. It is then that we shall get long-term growth; and equity then will follow by itself. Growth of capital for producing for the requirement of the future generation would be achieved through high ploughback within the Heavy-Investment sector, and current social justice would be achieved through the consequent H-conserving techniques in the consumption sector.

IX. THE EFFECTS OF H-CONSERVATION AND H-DIVERSION

This balance is obtained without a payoff between the future and the present, or attaining an optimum rate of discount of the future (and hence, what is called, an optimum rate of savings) and then investing according to that and waiting in the meanwhile. A high rate of capital accumulation is not to be obtained primarily through tightening of the belt for the common man (and consequently converting many of the employed into the sub-employed) because growth with prevention of real inflation will reduce light machinery for the luxuries sector.

Futher, the high rate of H-ploughback is not obtained through reducing investments in necessary consumption-goods (as is apprehended by those who look at the experience of the first plan of Soviet Russia), but through producing a larger output of consumption-goods with the same investment and higher quantum of labour input.

It is, thus, also not true to say that Heavy Investment necessarily draws away the resources for the agricultural sector or the Consumption-necessaries sector of the Consumption Sector, and reduces investment in the latter. It is mechanized light machinery for the luxuries sector which does so. Mechanized Light-Machinery competes with Heavy-Investment, and forces the form of equipment (produced by the Heavy sector) to be oriented towards the production of consumption requirements rather than for further capital goods for the self-regenerating H-sector. In one respect it is H-Diverting in character and from another angle it encroaches upon the Consumption-necessaries sector's resources. In the Mechanized Light-Machinery sector, the highly-profitable Luxury-consumption sector dictates the form of equipment according to its own requirements, and only the residue goes towards production of consumption necessaries. Even this residual equipment is oriented towards the need of the more affluent producer of consumption necessaries, for instance, the tractors and combined harvesters serve the equipment needs of the richer farmers. These techniques further produce the high profits which, in some cases, get further translated into luxury consumption and investment for the same type of goods. The Production Inequity and Consumption Inequity reinforce each other in this aspect also. High-equity production and high-equity consumption go together, on the one hand. On the other hand, Low-equity production and Low-equity consumption, in general, go together in the society's behavioural profile and pattern of activities.

The choice of a somewhat higher or a lower level of subsistence wage (according to biological requirement or moral choice of the State) does not affect the rate of ploughback of H for a given technique in the consumption-sector to that in the H-sector. The consumption of the affluent is sought to be curbed, but not primarily for yielding savings for investment or for equity to the future generation. They incidentally allow investments to aid the future generation to be strengthened, but even if it were not so, it is worthwhile for the sake of consumption equality in the present generation to curb luxury consumption. During the supply of ivory carving for the affluent man's consumption (rather than for exporting) it does not set free much of material resources for long-term accumulation, or investment in H sector, but it has to be done to ensure the dismantlement of the Glass Curtain. Luxury standards of consumption are, therefore, to be primarily reduced not for providing savings for growth (though possibly resources for investment may also be set free), but for the sake of equity for the lower income-groups of the present generation itself — through keeping the consumption disparities low even during the initial phase of the development process.

Nevertheless, it is not a direct poverty-removal programme, but a programme of eliminating mis-expenditure of the affluent for the sake of equity which would, incidentally, set resources free for investment (in essential). It would consequently allow production of capital goods, thereby simultaneously, creating employment, on the one hand, and on other hand, higher availability of consumption necessaries (which would contain the real-inflationary forces). Thus, the undesirable forces of generation of poverty would be affected at its roots towards the containment of the adverse forces in a meaningful manner.

X. PERMEATION EQUITY

In previous section we considered the effect of H-Conservation and H-Dissipation (or H-diversion). Now we go on to consider the profile of the Strategy which has high H-Ploughback in the H-Sector and high H-conservation in the consumption sector.

The strategy for International Equality, or of Intergenerational Equity, permeates the economy with Heavy-Industries and the Consumer-necessaries. The programme of basic needs is a part of this strategy rather than being left to hang by itself without being linked to a programme of Heavy-Investment base of which it is a necessary partner. There is no attempt at percolation of goods (whether of capital equipment of highly-mechanized character in the consumption sector, or of consumer luxuries). Manpower development[30] starts from the bottom of the sector of employed population (or from the immediately prespective persons for employment among the infra-employed) and proceeds upwards. The utilization of this manpower helps to permeate the consumption sector with necessaries. It converts the infra-employed into the employed through providing to them the proper equipment. They are not given a dole disguised in the form of guaranteed employment but they are engaged in well-thought out purposeful schemes of production. Thenceforward when near full-employment approaches, the standard of living of the employed population would be permitted to rise under the second prescript of equity. But it would be recommended to rise first of all for the least-advantaged persons. At the situation of full-employment the least-advantaged would not be the sub-employed, but the iso-employed (at the subsistence wage). There would be, in the ideal situation, no people better off than the least-advantaged. Therefore, the standard of subsistence would rise for all persons in employment (there being no sub-employed for whom to provide consumption necessaries, equipment and training —which section, had it been in existence under different conditions —would have obtained first priority, in preference to the employed, under the second Prescript of Equity).

Thenceforward the rise of the standard of living upwards will be rapidly towards the Golden-Age consumption level when capital for that has been accumulated sufficiently during the Traverse. In no sector and in no phase of the Traverse or the Golden-Age target, one gives to the privileged the opportunity to be better off above the common man by a high multiple in consumption standards.

In terms of and as regards the consumption-good sector the principle of low range of disparities not only pertains to consumption per man but also applies to the value of the equipment (or apparatus for production) per man. There will be no tractors for a few persons in the village and ploughs for the rest, till nearly all persons have been provided with improved ploughs. Combined harvesters would be started to be distributed only after the remote date when all farms have been tractorized. Manpower development is not confined to training workers to be more skilled, but it also includes, according to the present analysis, their employment with appropriate equipment with which they will work, and the consumption goods which at the subsistence level they will expect to be provided and *inter se* equality among workers of different sorts. This type of manpower development can be more easily undertaken as part of a Permeation Strategy because it is employment and equity-oriented apart from stressing long-term efficiency. On the other hand, the Percolation Strategy is based upon inequity of different levels of consumption or of capital resources (or both) per man employed between the mal-employed (these employed on production of socially irrelevant goods, the ultra-production of socially irrelevant goods, the ultra-employed (those paid a wage much above subsistence), the infra-employed (working upon inferior techniques), and the sub-employed (getting a wage below subsistence).

The Permeation Strategy allows the spatial distribution of investment to be larger around the countryside, at least in the consumption sector. It allows the growth centres to be coordinators of growth among a cluster of villages.[31] The Permeation Strategy permits a real rural community to be developed as a part of an integrated plan to develop the country as a whole, because the stress on growth of Heavy-Industries leads to adoption of H-conserving techniques in the consumption sector which can be diffused in the countryside.

The spatial distribution of Heavy Industries could also transform the backward regions, and would moreover decrease the disparities among regions within a country. It will be successful in keeping the rural workers in the rural areas, as they will get employment there itself and the countryside will be no worse than the urban areas as regards amenities for habitation and standards of living. It is on this that the hope of a lasting solution for national integration depends.

One often hears about the paradox that an advanced industrialized country can be identified by its highly developed agriculture. From this witticism many development-economists jump to the conclusion that one has only to machanize agriculture and the country would jump to a state of development. They would not deny the proposition that for becoming industrialized, the country has to undergo a period of capital accumulation. Capital theory indicates that if this is to be achieved in the shortest-time possible it would be undertaken best under a guided or planned regime ensuring conformity to the optimum long-term strategy. For countries with quite a larger surplus population — measured not by number of adult able-bodied heads counted in the census, but by the ratio of working-population to the truly employed being large, the long-term Strategy of Development[32] relevant is the Permeation Strategy of International Equality. But in this strategy, the degree of mechanization in agriculture would remain low till enough H-sector growth has taken place for statisticians to identify the country as one capable of being described as industrialized by any standard—whether the measurement indices are those adopted by mechanizers of agriculture, or of growth empiricists or of Golden-Age growth theory. Till that time, on the path full development, poverty is to be removed through higher opportunities for employment; and after enough capital accumulation in basic industries has taken place there would be a rising standard of living, at full employment, to take advantage of technical progress.

The fallacy of the school advocating primacy for agricultural mechanization lies in making identical the prescription for the path with the conditions which would rule once the objective has been reached. The mistake in logic, is of the same nature as making the observation that developed countries have larger urban to rural population ratio, and then believing that one would become developed merely by sending village folk to seek employment in towns. Or one could notice that farmers in developed countries have lots of household gadgets and consequentially one should subscribe to the belief that a country with large Non-Employment would become developed by encouraging affluent farmers to acquire washing machines. Such remedies are advocated by those who little realize that such a process would increase mal-employment, and would result in retarding of development and of equity both, and would thereby cause poverty to exist for a longer time.

Within the context of strategy of International Equality giving supreme priority to the Heavy-Investment sector (including earning of foreign exchange for essential and inescapable purposes) there is the necessity of providing the essential consumption requirements of the additionally employed population. Then there would be due stress on development of agriculture to satisfy these requirements. There would be need for well-worked out schemes for purposeful employment, for nutrition and child care as part of manpower development, and for educational skills for human-capital formation. There would also be programmes for the energy-sector to harness reproducible sources (e.g. livestock, draught strength, wind power) in the consumption sector.

The Permeation Strategy would ensure, by its implementation in due course, the basic needs of communal consumption (like drinking water) for all, through the development of infra-structure. It would permit the subsistence standards for those additionally coming into employment (the number of whom themselves is kept at a high figure per year). It does not guarantee the immediate provision of basic consumption needs for all, i.e. even for those who are not employed, as there would be no mechanism in the Permeation Strategy to dole out food without work, and apart from emergencies like famine, there is not much capacity in any economy to do so even now. Unless provision of subsistence is linked to earnings for work, which emanate from purposive employment according to a strategy, the Basic Needs Programme or Guaranteed Employment Programme can only create real inflation which would create poverty when it would hit the iso-employed workers (within the circle of employment but only at subsistence wages — or marginally above subsistence).

In the Permeation Strategy, the functional distribution of income becomes favourable because of the low degree of mechanization in the consumption sector, and hence a high Wage of Profits-cum-Ransoms ratio pertains therein.

Within the overall context of Heavy-Investment growth, and for furthering it, other essential sectors grow. If one cuts out priority to H from the integrated programme, the subsidiary programmes also fall, for they cannot get justification by themselves. Thus the Basic Needs Programme cannot validly be the direct focus of the attention of planners in an integrated strategy of development except in a very early phase of development, for capital accumulation is needed to provide for those needs, and hence the allocation spectrum of type of investments must be considered. The crash programmes for employment creation, or schemes of Guaranteed Employment, or Food for Work projects, are not purposive unless carried out in the context of the optimal Growth Strategy. So also would the pursuit of social justice by itself (without inter-generational equity, or what is termed as economic justice) be illusory.

The Permeation Strategy for Intergenerational and International Equity provides the framework through which these plans (which follow from long-term growth) benefit the present more than what would occur if the present alone were sought to be benefited directly. It tackles the supply side in a purposive and socially-relevant manner in a planned regime regulating a mixed economy with use of the powerful fiscal instruments (rather than physical controls in an economy with manpower situation such that effective administrative skills are in short supply). It is, therefore, termed as the Effective-Supply[33] Economics. It denies the validity of unplanned blanket increase of supply of goods — whether socially-relevant or not (which the supply-side economists talk about), for therein lies the root of poverty through diversion of resources from essential investments to inessential goods (bearing high profits), which (like bad money in relation to good money) drive out the socially-beneficial but low-profit commodities from the spectrum of production — as rice land is converted to planting tobacco, as maize is replaced by planting of superior foodgrains like wheat or as growing of foodgrains is substituted by vegetables.

National Integration is furthered by the Permeation Strategy because it deals equitably with each constituent, and provides an ideology of equity on which to pin people's aspirations rather than on consumerism, and on being "one better off than one's neighbour".

XI. INSTRUMENTS OF DISTRIBUTIVE EQUITY

The ninth Prescript of Equity and the first one of Distributive Equity requires the State to consider the prime inequality to be that of consumption standards. In the socialistic pattern consumption is sought to be equalized but the path follows equality of Income and of wealth, and only consequently of Consumption. The ninth Prescript seeks to correct consumption disparities directly rather than waiting for the very difficult and almost non-feasible task of a mixed economy implementing egalitarianism (when incentives are being given in diverse ways to evoke development through creating greater inequality of income and wealth). It does so through a powerful combination of monetary and fiscal policy.

The advancement of National Integration requires:

(a) Following the Prescripts of Consumption Equity;
(b) Allocating physical materials and manpower resources of the economy according to the Prescripts of Production Equity; and
(c) Inducing the Individuals and Corporations to allocate the resources at their command (in the Public and Private Sectors) according to the dictates of the above two, and to elicit the share of the product and its disposal according to Prescripts of Distributive Equity.
(d) Its instruments would be :

    (i) Allocative Monetaty and Fiscal Policy,
    (ii) Worker's Investment Trust,
    (iii) The Firm State, and
    (iv) A Constitutional Structure of Centripetal Decentralization.

These will be briefly described in this section.

A powerful fiscal instrument[34] called the Disparity Tax[35] has been designed to counter this misdirection of investments and to make them conform to the requirements of allocations[36] for the optimal strategy. It would keep the production spectrum in line with the Effective-Supply sector for the optimal strategy, thus implementing the Eighth Prescript of Equity.

The Disparity Tax does not tax income or wealth, but misearning, misinvestment and misconsumption. As a matter of fact income and wealth tax would both be withdrawn when this is in operation. Therefore, it conforms to the ninth Prescript of equity and the first Prescript of Distributive Equity. It performs the task which the Expenditure Tax by itself cannot do — shift the production spectrum from the side of supply.

Disparity Taxation derives its magnifier power from its four schedules — first two representing the difference between the treatment meted out to an assessee in his capacity as income earner who earns his income from lines of low or high-social-priority, and in his capacity as investor who spends his purchasing power in essential lines in contra-distinction to his spending upon investments in the inessential fields. As regards this differential treatment, the pure Income Impost misses out these aspects altogether, in contrast to the Disparity Tax.[37]

The effects of the Income Impost are, therefore, in a reverse direction from that of the Disparity Tax. A general Disparity Tax can be exhibited as:

$$\text{Tax} = f(\alpha Y - \beta \underline{I})$$

(According to the expository interpretation of many concepts commented upon by the distinguished economist Dr. Bhabatosh Datta in 1974 as President of the Indian Economic Conference, Bhubaneswar).[38]

Following this suggestion of Prof. Bhabatosh Datta one may explain that in Income Impost, we have the simple case as part of the generalized Disparity Tax—

$$\text{Tax} = f(\alpha \underline{Y} - \beta \underline{I}),\ \alpha = 1,\ \beta = 0$$

The base of the Expenditure Tax as a special case of the Disparity can be easily seen to be:

$$\text{Tax} = f(\alpha \underline{Y} - \beta \underline{I}),\ \alpha = 1,\ \beta = 1$$

In the case of the Misexpenditure Tax, the base becomes even wider than in the Expenditure Tax:

$$\text{Tax} = f(\alpha \underline{Y} - \beta \underline{I}),\ \alpha = 1,\ \beta \gtreqless 1$$

This last simplification of the Disparity Tax, can be represented in matrix form as follows:

Let Y_i be in column vector of source of Income, Σ_i of outlets of Investments; α_i, a row vector of multipliers of Income, β_i a row vector of Multipliers of Investments ($\underline{i} = \underline{a}, \underline{u}, \underline{n}$), where $\underline{a}$ stands for approved, $\underline{u}$ for unapproved and $\underline{H}$ for neutral.

In the most generalized form of Disparity Tax, with the finest cutting-edge, the base is given by the Notional Consumption NC (as scalar quantity) as follows :

scalar quantity) as follows :

$$NC = \alpha_i Y_i - \beta_i I_i \quad \alpha\, a < 1 \quad \beta\, a > 1$$

$$\alpha\, n = 1 \quad \beta\, n > 1$$

$$\alpha\, u > 1 \quad \beta\, u < 1$$

In the case of Misexpenditure Tax we get the simplifications: $NC = Y - \beta_i I_i$ $\quad \alpha a = \alpha u = \alpha i = \alpha n = 1$ as in the Income Tax $Y_i = Y_n = 1$

$$\beta a > 1, \quad \beta n = 1, \quad \beta u < 1$$

In the case of Expenditure Tax we get the further simplification :

$$\alpha a = \alpha u = \alpha i = \alpha n \text{ (as in the Income Tax)}$$

$$NC = C = Y - \underline{I}$$

further, $\beta a = \beta u = \beta i = \beta n = 1$

the case of Income Tax is a special case of Mis-expenditure Tax when all investments are treated as if they were unapproved, and consequently allotted a zero multiplier. Therefore, its base is

$$NC = Y - \beta u \underline{I} \text{ where } \beta a = \beta u = \beta n = \beta i = 0$$

Thus its base is $NC = Y - O\underline{I} = Y$

Income Tax Base: We observe that the Disparity Tax in full force has $\alpha u - \alpha n > 0$ and $\beta u - \beta n < 0$ $\alpha a - \alpha n < 0$, $\beta a - \beta n > 0$ and both differential treatment schedules existing and possessing all three types of factors (approval neutrality and disapproval). We can then see that as we move from the ideal position of Disparity Tax towards other Allocative Taxes to firstly the Mis-expenditure Tax, then secondly to Expenditure Tax and thence, thirdly, towards Income Impost (which is not allocative at all), the cutting edge of the treatment given to investment (on the criterion of social purposiveness) becomes weaker and weaker. Side by side, the revenue orientation rises; for a weak instrument collects more revenue (but does not strongly disinduce either wrongful consumption, nor wrongful investment for wrongful consumption, type of consumption, nor the right type of investments, and the right type of earnings).

The Orthodox Public-Finance Expert has a strong preference for revenue-orientation, and, therefore, for the Income Impost. Even the Weakest form of Disparity Tax as an Allocative Instrument[39] — the Kaldorian Expenditure Tax — was withdrawn in India for its lack of revenue-orientation (forgetting that its purpose was social disinducement rather than earning revenue for the Treasury — collecting Coopers for the Crown and Commonwealth, as the action may be termed).

It is on similar considerations that votaries of Expenditure Tax simpliciter (who remain wedded to Orthodox Public Finance though seemingly giving a modernized image) would like to introduce that tax as a weak Allocative Tax even while retaining the Income Impost for revenue orientation. It is obvious that this dilutes even whatever weak social purpose is performed by the Expenditure Tax, and the amalgam of the two, a Direct Tax and a Direct Impost, is a very weak instrument of curbing parasitic consumption. It would not have an edge at all, and would be a blunt instrument for the social purpose.

This can be seen in a formal manner as follows:

Expanding these equations of Disparity Tax further and other Allocative Taxes, respectively, let us attach weights $\underline{W}_1$ and $\underline{W}_2$ to the Income Impost and the Disparity Tax.

Then the weighted average of the two Bases

$$= \underline{W}_1 Y + \underline{W}_2 \alpha Y - \underline{W}_2 \beta \underline{I} \; [\underline{W}_1 , \underline{W}_2 < 1]$$

$$= W (\underline{W}_1 + \underline{W}_2 \alpha) - \underline{W}_2 \beta I \; [\underline{W}_1 + \underline{W}_2 = 1]$$

For a given Y and I from individual and for given as fixed by Government, the cutting edge of the instrument comes by minimizing the expression for $\bar{\beta}$ so that the assessee minimizes his payment liability to Government.

Let $Y = \underline{kI}$ where k = Keynesian Multiplier

$$\beta = \underline{I} \; [\underline{k} - \underline{W}_2 - {}^{k(\alpha - 1) + \beta \text{ (Assuming } \underline{k}\alpha + \beta \geq k)}]$$

The expression for $\bar{\beta}$ is minimized where $\underline{W}_2$ is maximum. Hence, $\underline{W}_2 = 1$, $\underline{W}_1 = 0$. This implies that the weight to Income Impost should be zero in the amalgam. If the two are simultaneously imposed, the Income impost acts as a drag and dilutes the efficacy of the Disparity Tax. Thus when the two systems are worked together, the Income Impost blunts the edge of the Disparity Tax in the Field of social purposiveness. It makes the aggregated schedules on the average to have multipliers α and β nearer to unity — whereas the cutting edge lies in their deviation from unity being large for approved and unapproved activities.

This can be accomplished best when Income Impost not imposed and the whole system is governed by Disparity Tax.

When the Income Impost and the Expenditure Tax are put on the cards together, as is often proposed, then if $\underline{W}_3$ and $\underline{W}_4$ are the weights, the equations are:

Income-Impost Base=Y $\quad 0 < \underline{W}_3 \leq 1$

Expenditure-Tax Base=Y-$\underline{I}$ $\quad 0 < \underline{W}_4 \leq 1$

$$\underline{W}_3 + \underline{W}_4 = 1$$

Weighting by W_3 and W_4 and averaging, we get

$$\text{Average of Bases} = \underline{W}_3\, Y + \underline{W}_4\, Y - \underline{W}_4\, I,\ \beta = (\underline{W}_3 + \underline{W}_4)$$

$$Y - \underline{W}_4\, \underline{I};\ \beta = Y - \underline{W}_4\, \underline{I}$$

The incentive effect for Investment (or for Saving) is higher when this is minimized. It requires that $\underline{W}_4$ is maximized, i.e. $\underline{W}_4$ is equal to 1 and, therefore, the system becomes Y - $\underline{I}$, which is a pure Expenditure Tax (unadulterated by the Income Impost);

When Disparity Tax[40] proposal for implementation was first being framed in 1968-71, as an exercise towards the quest of the Planning Commission (Prespective Planning Division under the member Incharge, Mr. Pitamber Pant) and of the Ministry of Finance (Department of Economic Affairs under the Secretary, Dr. I.G. Patel) for an efficient instrument of evercoming industrial stagnation and giving the production spectrum socially-purposive direction, the request to undertake a project was made to the Osmania University upon this theme. The original proposal envisaged by me, as Project Director, was to introduce Disparity Tax over a period of ten years 1972 to 1982 when W_2 would be increased by 10 per cent and W_1 decreased by 10 pre cent every year. At that time Dr. Patel, expressed himself against such a phased plan, for the two taxes having divergent himself against such a phased plan, for the two taxes having divergent and opposite aims, it would create confusion in the minds of the assessees as to what exactly was the social policy of the Government. He said if the system has to be changed to Disparity Tax, it must be changed over at one go, and as single step, not by stages. This wise counsel was accepted by me and the proposal ultimately framed emitted the mention of phasing. The foregoing analysis supplies a rigorous proof of the same.

The matter is relevant, for the last time expenditure Tax was introduced it was in addition to Income Impost — even Professor Kaldor envisaged the continuance of that impost in his report to the Government of India though not in his earlier theoretical[41] presentation. The burden of both was too much for the assesses to bear, and, therefore, the exemption limit was kept pretty high. Thus it affected only the case of the innermost rings of the Glass-Curtain Economy where Income Tax rates were pretty burdensome already, and where the group provided the bulk of personal investments. The reform was bound to be a failure for an administration looking for revenue from the Expenditure Tax.

The matter is also relevant from the point of view of long-term fiscal policy. If the proposal is to introduce Expenditure Tax in the form of Kaldor's Personal Consumption Expenditure Tax it would be a condenser tax— a very weak instrument of shifting the materials and manpower from less desirable ends to activities of greater social-priority. The Mis-expenditure Tax would be the minimum necessary for tackling the matter from the Supply side (as well as the Demand side) as is envisaged in this Magnifier Instrument.

The Disparity Tax would also be applicable to all assessees, not only to individuals, because for tackling the allocation problem, supply side Investment decisions must be changed, and for that purpose bringing in the Corporate Sector is most important. For the Demand and Supply side both it is important to bring in the Religious Trusts also.

If social purposiveness is the objective of the planned regime and equity for the present generation and for the future is to be achieved—which ought to be the function of a long-term fiscal policy—the most efficient instrument is the Disparity Tax, for it is an instrument of channelling investments (from the supply side) according to a Balanced Allocation Ratio. This spectrum of allocations of Investment would yield equity as well as price stability, differences in consumption standards at the minimum, with no limitation for expansion of currency[42] compatible with balanced investment[43] under a system of real-resource planning, and investments for long-run accumulation on a priority basis for the parent-machine sector to have minimum recycling. The private enterprise, as well as the public sector, would be introduced to bear the responsibility of this social and economic restructuring, and physical controls would be entirely replaced by effective and socially purposive Inducive Instruments. Fisco-Monetary policy would then rightfully come into its own as a Magnifier Instrument of Government action to mobilize real resources—materials and manpower—for the ends of equity. Nothing less than that has a chance of success and that would run the danger of being withdrawn for its failure in performance.

XII. WORKER'S PARTICIPATION

Side by side, the expansion of non-governmental enterprise workers' participation in management is to be strengthened through part ownership of the firm (whether private or public). The settlement as an outcome of a strike being withdrawn would not be the increase wage, but issue of new shares equivalent to captalised value of the additional wage. Part only of the yield of this would be for current consumption (ideally none), and the rest would be utilised partly for strengthening trade union organisation in less organised industry, and partly for investment in a Workers' Investment Trust to be set up under an Act of the Central Legislature of the Country. It would be owned by workers and managed by highly efficient professionals, rather than by amateur workers. This Trust would invest the income derived on behalf of workers from settlement of each strike anywhere in the country and derive further funds from the dividends of its past investments. It would achieve a portfolio of investments most profitable and equitable for it after taking into account the schedule of disparity Taxation. They would have resources to buy up firms which do not desist from exploiting their workers.

The Trust would expect, within ten years, to be the largest single financial corporation in the country with more funds at its disposal than either the Unit Trust or the Life Insurance Corporation.

It would be capable of exerting financial power for the betterment of the total economy, and the management role of the working manpower in the production and entrepreneurial process. It would manifest itself through actions in furtherance of National Integration, and in aid of the employed as well as non-employed manpower of the country as a whole, rather than working through a form of Trade Unionism interested only in furtherance of the benefits of its members.

Hence, to establish ultimate ownership and control of manpower on the economic processes is the tenth Prescript of Equity and the second Prescript of Distributive Equity. This together with the other nine prescripts given an internally-consistent profile of equity—short-term and long-run—and its reconciliation with efficiency, background under which the movement for National Integration can best flourish and would encounter the least number of bottlenecks.

REFERENCES

1. Sraffa, P., *The Production of Commodities by Means of Commodities,* 1960.
2. Neumann, J. von. A Model of General Economic Equilibrium, *Review of Economic Studies,* XIII, 1956.
3. Mathur, G., *Planning for Steady Growth*, Basil Blackwell, Oxford, 1965 and American Edition, Augustus Kelly, New York, 1965 Indian Edition, Oxford University Press, 1973, Chapter IV.
4. National Strategy for Economic Development, Golden Jubilee Lecture, Annual Number, Part I, National Academy of Science, Allahabad, 1980, pp. 95-142.
5. *op.cit.* 3 at p. 211, also Investment Criteria in a Platinum Age, Oxford Economic Papers, Vol. 19, No. 2, July 1967 at pp. 213, 202.
   This condition did not appear in the version presented for discussion at the Seminar. The author is grateful to Prof. Sukhomoy Chakrabarty for having pointed out that this assumption seems to be implied and is specifically mentioned in the author's earlier work, of Investment Criteria in a Platinum Age, Oxford Economics Papers, 1967. The moment this objective is brought into the analysis, the importance of capital accumulation in the self-reproducing Heavy-Investment Sector needs to get stressed.
6. True Employment and Non-Employment in a book *Planning for Employment,* Narayana, L., Deshpande, K, Sinha, R.K. (Eds.), Sterling, 1980 pp. 1-9.
7. Equity-oriented Employment Typology, D'Souza Felicitation Lecture delivered at the 67th Annual Conference of the Indian Economic Association, Agra, January 1985.
8. Economic Justice in a Free Society Wheelers - Forthcoming and also in Distributive Shares and Prescripts of Equity by S. Mathur in *The Indian Journal of Labour Economics,* Vol. XXV, April-July 1982 Nos. 1&2 pp.9-43.
9. *The Framework of Planning for Economic Growth and Social Justice*

Interdiscipline, Vol. VII, No. 2, Gandhi Centenary Number, Varanasi, 1969, pp. 130-66.

10. Growth under conditions of Chronic Parasitism, Seminar, Delhi, February 1966, pp. 225-26.
11. Economic Order in a Firm State, *Essays in Honour of Dr. S.P. Verma*, Iqbal Narain (Ed.) - Forthcoming.
12. *op.cit.*, 6.
13. *op.cit.*, 7.
14. *op.cit.*, 8.
15. Percolation and Permeation in an Equalitarian Economy, *Yojana*, India's Silver Jubilee Special Number, New Delhi, August 1972. pp. 609-14.
16. *op. cit.*, 10.
17. The Analytical Dimensions of the Problem of Poverty, in *Poverty - An Interdisciplinary Approach,* Madras Institute of Development Studies, Rao, Sarveswar Deshpande, V.N. (Eds.) Somaya, Bombay 1982, pp.6-15.
18. Planning for a Mixed Economy, Nehru Memorial Lecture, delivered at the Teen Murti House, New Delhi, May 1982 published in *State Enterprise Journal* Vol. 1, No. 4, Oct-Dec. 1982, pp. 339-55.
19. Disparities in a Planned Economy, in a *Weekly Round Table,* Vol.1, No. 46, New Delhi, December 1972, pp. 6-9.
20. Reverse Discrimination in development Policy, *Indian Journal of Labour Economics,* Vol. XXVI. No. 1&2, April-July 1983, pp. 39-70.
21. Minute of Supplementation published in a Report of the Committee on Unemployment, Government of India, May 1973.
22. Little, I.M.D. Classical Growth, Oxford Economic Papers 1957 and also see in Planning for Steady Growth, Chapter XI.
23. *Employment and Intergenerational Equity Employment Policy in a Developing Country*, Vol. I, Robinson E.A.G., Brahmananda, P.R. and Deshpande L.K. (Eds.) the record of discussion by Hehn Teye, Macmillan 1983, pp. 253-75 at p.253.
24. *op. cit.*, 19.
25. Economic Policy Choices, Special Article, *Young India* Republic Day Issue, 1971, and two successive issues Vol. 1, No. 8, pp. 7-10, No. 9, pp. 9-11, No. 10, pp. 7-10.
26. *op. cit.* 8.
27. The Rule of Order, Presidential Address delivered on the occasion of the diamond Jubilee year of the Indian Economic Association, December 1978 published in *The Indian Economic Journal,* Vol. 26, No. 4 & 5, April-June 1979, pp. 1-43.
28. *op. cit.*, 11.
29. *op. cit.*, 8.
30. Active Education for Manpower Development, published in *Manpower Journal* IAMR, Delhi, 1979.
31. Role of Community Development in Economic Strategies in Community Development and Panchayat Raj, *Digest,* Hyderabad, 1970, pp. 9-11.
32. Long-term Development Policy in the *Indian Journal of Social Sciences*, Hyderabad, Vol. No. 1, Sept. 1970, pp. 24-34.

33. *op. cit.*, 20 and 27.
34. *Disparity Tax in a Composite Economy* Macmillan, Delhi 1975.
35. *op. cit.*, 34 and also see in Fiscal Policy in a Composite Economy, contributed in an All India Lecture series organised by the Society for International Development, Jaipur, Bapna Ashok (Ed.) 1986
36. Key-note address and various remarks at the Seminar on Alternative Economic Structure, Shimla, March 1985 - Forthcoming as a proceeding volume.
37. Actuative Development Policy Reprinted from the Recent Developments in Monetary Theory and Policy, Papers and Proceedings of the Seminar held at Bombay, R.B.I. Bombay 1978, pp. 30-55.
38. Datta, Bhabatosh, Remarks of the General President at the session on Public Finance, chaired by Professor Dhiresh Bhattacharya at the Indian Economic Conference held at Bhubaneswar, 1974.
39. *Analysis of Responsibility for Poverty Contributed to Social Science Research and the Problem of Poverty,* Tarlok Singh (Ed.) - Forthcoming.
40. *op. cit.*, 9.
41. Nicholas Kaldor, *Expenditure Tax*, Allen and Unwin, 1955.
42. *The Criteria for Appraisal of the Budget, Perspectives on Economic Development and Thought*, Professor B.N. Ganguli Commemoration Volume, Kamta Prasad and Sinha R.K. (Eds.), Somaiya, pp. 33-53.
43. The Essentials of Planning, *Yojana,* Vol. 10, No. 19, October 1966, p. 37 and p. 59.

8

THE ANALYSIS OF RESPONSIBILITY OF POVERTY

I. CONTINUANCE OF POVERTY

This essay presents the point of view that poverty is mainly the result of :

(a) Continuance of Non-Employment, and
(b) Real Inflation.

While Non-employment is a natural state, Real inflation is an artificially-created state. Even when the former is a natural state, the fact that it might be in our power to alleviate the condition, and it is not done (for insufficient cause) it is still a state in which society is contributing to continued existence of poverty conditions.

This essay will briefly deal with the two separate tendencies mentioned, and their remedies.

Poverty continues to exist because the unnecessarily slow pace at which Non-employment is reduced. The reason why Non-employment is not reduced at a fast pace are:

(a) Inappropriate Strategy of Development
(b) Orthodox Public Finance: Monetarism

II. INAPPROPRIATE STRATEGY OF DEVELOPMENT

The Percolation Strategy followed by the Governments of many underdeveloped countries uses the highly-mechanised equipment in the consumption sector where it is inappropriate, apart from its use in the self-regenerating Heavy-Investment sector (wherein it may be used validly when labour-using techniques are not available). This

Published in *Social Science Research and the Problem of Poverty*, Singh, Tarlok (ed.).

causes employment to be increased at a slow pace, because of the avoidable high capital intensity in the consumption sector. Thus, non-employment remains with us for a longer time in this strategy.

The Wage-goods strategy relies on the less-mechanised technique and creates a lot of employment as a result. But it does not have any element leading to the expansion of the sector of Heavy-Investment (H). Hence, the labour-intensive investments in the self-regenerating H-sector (e.g., multi-purposes dam-building projects) do not figure in it; and hence, all such opportunities to create employment are lost in that strategy.

The Strategy for Intergenerational Equity requires the Heavy-Investment Sector to be built up rapidly. For this purpose, leakage of products of that sector outside it is to be minimised, and within the H-sector also non-employed labour is to be used as far as possible. Hence, in the consumption sector the techniques to be adopted should be H-conserving. Such techniques happen to be labour-intensive and, therefore, employment-creating. This strategy is most important for creating employment as it creates it within the H-sector and outside it[1].

In countries with large surplus-labour, the failure of the State to follow such a strategy contributes to the responsibility of continued existence of high quantum of poverty conditions (through not reducing Non-employment at the rate which is physically feasible, by following an unproved plan design).

III. ORTHODOX PUBLIC FINANCE

The second cause of Non-employment stems from orthodox public finance in its stress on restrictive monetary policy. It is considered that the size of a plan of investments depends upon the financial resources available—impost revenues, borrowing from the public, contribution of the public sector from its surpluses, foreign aid, and permissible amount of deficit financing. The last one is considered to be inflationary. However, when investments are in a Balanced Allocation Ratio[2] this need not be the result, and thus non-inflationary growth is a possibility. The failure of the State to realise this possibility, and its general desire to follow a policy of monetary limitation keeps the size of a plan lower than feasible from the point of view of real resources. The Central organ of societal administration, i.e. the State, thus, contributes to Non-employment remaining for a longer time, and hence to continued existence of poverty.

IV. CREATION OF POVERTY

Poverty can also be created when the marginally employed workers is subjected to Real Inflation. The causes of Real Inflation which cuts the standard of living of the employed at the margin, and converts them to the sub-employed are:

(a) Parasitic Consumption, and again
(b) Orthodox Public Finance : Traditional Sources

Consumption beyond subsistence level (by the ultra-employed—who are defined to be drawing a standard of living higher than subsistence — and the executives, or administrators, or managers or industrialists and any consumption by landowners in that inactive capacity) is termed Parasitic Consumption[3]. Such consumption draws away resources from the sector of consumption necessaries towards the sector for luxury goods, and deprives the lower income-groups of such goods which they can afford to consume.

The conditions of living in which people are constantly facing price rises, along with the condition of shortage of goods, or of purchasing power, is Real Inflation[4]. It converts the employed at subsistence level from the category of intra-employed (within the sphere of the employed) to the sub-employed (outside the sphere of employment), and relegates them to the body of the mass of people who are 'merely occupied with less than subsistence wages[5], but not any longer employed' (which requires that person to have appropriate equipment, skill, pertinent to operation of what equipment and at least a full subsistence wage).

Inflation is also caused by certain planning practices followed by the governing agent of Society (viz. the state). If, along with Heavy Investment in infrastructure, there is insufficient investment in consumption sector, the Allocation Ratio would depart from non-inflationary balance, towards greater emphasis upon long-gestation investments. This distribution of investment would be inflationary.

Lastly, orthodox Public Finance (in its stress upon orthodox sources of finance of government investment) again causes inflation, contrary to the widely-held opposite opinion. This may be termed

Ignited Inflation as State action creates the inflation where it did not exist in the absence of that action. Indirect imposts — whether on necessaries, or on luxuries — are inflationary; the latter through salary rises to cover the high cost of luxury articles (due to higher imposts paid by executives of firms manufacturing semi-necessaries, and necessaries) and consequently raising the cost of production of essential consumption goods.

Borrowing from the public keeps the rate of interest high (or increases it) thus adding to the production costs (including the cost of finance). It saturates the economy with high cost of overhead capital which enters into all activities, industrial or agricultural.

Profits and the Public-Sector enterprises raise the prices of their products (for they seldom emanate from increased efficiency). Government Policy regarding pricing policy (for either raising revenue directly, or through taxes on higher profits of public enterprises — or simply amalgamating these higher profits in the general revenues) are responsible for igniting inflation in an economy and setting in motion a price-wage spiral[6]. If the prices rises are in articles for the manufacture of capital goods or for supply of power or fuel or transport facilities, the price rise is diffused quickly throughout the economy.

Foreign Aid requires the scarce materials and manpower skills paid for in local currency and this demand tends to increase the prices and wages.

On the other hand, deficit financing lowers the rate of interest and keeps the profit rate from rising on that account. It results in a lower interest element in the equipment and other inputs of agriculture. With the low cost of inputs, a profit rate at least equal to profit rate in rural industries can be established in agriculture also and this action would keep the price of the agricultural products low for the urban proletariat. This prevents real inflation in industry and agriculture, and in the urban and rural economies.

The low interest-rate, further, encourages investments in low-profit commodities (among which are necessaries in general). This condition also increases the supply of necessaries, and helps in controlling the price level from the supply side.

Real Inflation is not a natural phenomenon. It is not a product of the economic system being either capitalist or socialist, nor is the

Government ultimately responsible for it though it is an agent of its creation. It owes its origin to orthodox economists[7] who are advising the Government in most underdeveloped countries. They subvert the good intensions of the Welfare State by their restrictive attitudes. Its remedy lies in changing the attitudes of these economists. This requires the economics taught to millions of students in institutions ranging from junior colleges to post-graduate departments of advanced studies — except for a few islands — to be changed in orientation[8]. It also requires the monetary and fiscal experts to be given opportunity to attend rigorous courses in Real Resource Planning.[9]

V. THE ALLEVIATION OF POVERTY

As orthodox Public Finance figures in both causes of Poverty — in continued Non-employment (where there could be every year less of it with the same real resources i.e. natural endowments, physical equipment, manpower skills), and in creation of Real Inflation — it is traditional theories of public finance (particularly monetarism, consideration of impost and borrowings as safe methods of finance of government investments, and revenue-oriented fiscal policy) which need to be tackled as a general measure for alleviating poverty.

When we take the other two elements — one of continued Non-employment as a sub-field of creation of poverty — we note them to be the element of continuance of Inappropriate Strategy of Development, and the element of Reduction in Parasitic Consumption. In both cases, a similar obstruction is encountered (owing its origin to orthodox public finance). The changeover to a system of deficit financing as the normal and unapproved phenomenon) requires that the real resources be put in a Balanced Allocation Ratio between quick-yielding techniques and the long-gestation projects.

The techniques in the quickly-yielding sector have, for this purpose, to be highly productive — not per unit of manpower, but per unit of value of physical capital. Such techniques are labour-intensive and employment-creating in character. They are also techniques conserving the products of Heavy Investment (i.e. they are H-conserving techniques). From a low amount of investment with these techniques a large volume of product is obtained, and deducting the consumption of the workers carrying on the investment, some surplus is obtained. This goes towards satisfying the demand created by the long-gestation investment — parasitic consumption-expenditure being equivalent to investment with an infinite gestation lag (for the product never comes, nor is intended to come, from such expenditures). Expansion of the Defence Sector is another example of the long-gestation investment with almost an infinite gestation lag—very little being ever available in terms of industrial inputs for further production.

Now in the inappropriate Strategy of Percolation, the techniques used are highly-mechanised in the consumption sector. They are capital-intensive and produce per unit of investment. They cannot produce sufficient output for further investment to be undertaken, for the total produce is less then with the techniques where output-capital ratio may be low[10]. Such a strategy cannot benefit from deficit financing being non-inflationary with a Balanced Allocation Ratio. With tractors and automatic looms as the techniques for producing consumption necessaries, all forms of finance are inflationary.

With improved ploughs and handlooms, the method of raising finance by orthodox means — imposts, borrowing of the Government from the public, the savings of public entreprises — may indeed the inflationary (as price rises are initiated by government action in choosing the orthodox form of finance), but were deficit financing chosen as form of finance, this ignition of inflation would not be there. In underdeveloped countries with surplus population the modern (Keynesian) method of finance through deficits can be resorted to with non-inflationary consequences when production of consumption good is with equipment of a low degree of mechanisation (to produce a large output of consumption goods for a small investment). Also because of these techniques being conservists in the use of the products of the Heavy-Investment Sector it can permit a high recycling of the H-products within that sector.

Heavy-Investment priority, therefore, is really associated with non-inflationary growth — both because of investment in H-conserving techniques permitting a huge investment base to be created without using up a lot of H-products, and also because deficit financing can then be used to finance all investments in that case in a Balanced Allocation Ratio.

The Appropriate Strategy of Development is the Permeation Strategy which saturates the economy with self-regenerating Heavy Capital and consumer necessaries in balance, and creates employment rapidly. It is also the vehicle for Intergenerational Equity. Its logic contradicts four clearly and strongly-held propositions of the neo-classical economists:

(a) that priority to Heavy investment is necessarily inflationary;
(b) that H-priority creates unemployment;
(c) that deficit financing is inflationary; and
(d) that orthodox methods of finance of investments are safe because they do not give rise to price rises.

When high H-priority is linked to H-conservation and consequent use of such techniques — as is possible to be achieved in a manpower-surplus country — it firstly, creates employment rapidly (and thus alleviates poverty), secondly it makes possible the use of deficit financing of the Investment Plan (provided Investments is planned to be undertaken in Balanced Allocation Ratio), and thirdly it controls inflation both through supply of consumption necessaries being high, and because a non-inflationary form of finance—deficit finance — is used. No other suggested strategy performs these three tasks together, and, hence, it acquires importance in poverty-alleviation programmes. The said strategy allows employment creation in the manpower-using techniques in the H-sector, and also in the consumption sector.

The State can, thus, instead of contributing to creation or continuance of poverty, do the reverse. Instead of non-employment being went about, it should be made use of in the opportunity to build infrastructive for the future (through H), and alleviating poverty in the meantime through employment creation.

We in India, thus come out to be in a better situation than Soviet Russia was in its First Plan, because we have huge surplus manpower which it did not possess, and use of high degree of mechanisation (which is H-dissipating) was forced on them by initial factor-endowment conditions. We can, therefore, give a very high degree of priority to the H-sector which was not feasible for the Soviet Plan. We also come out better than capitalist countries because State intervention of the proper sort allows non-employment to be removed at a faster pace than what neo-classical laissez faire doctrine would permit.

VI. TRANSFORMATION OF FISCO-MONETARY ATTITUDE

Along with clearing of the decks as regards the appropriate Strategy, a change in our attitude to public finance has the possibility of curbing Parasitic Consumption also. As long as deficit financing is considered to be inflationary, Government exactions are in the nature of imposts — revenue-oriented exactions to enhance the source of general spending by the State rather than taxes (which term was reserved originally[11], in medieval state finance, for exactions with a specific national purpose in view). But revenue-oriented exactions, like indirect imposts, are highly inflationary, on the one hand, and on the other hand, they do not serve the social purpose of a change in real allocations and activities. The increase of prices cuts down the volume of real investment in an economy oriented to financial allocations governing the size of the plan. This reduces employment creation, and contributes to continuance of non-employment (and, hence, also of poverty) for a longer time.

Curbing of Consumption of the affluent by indirect taxes on luxuries is supposed to be for a specific social purpose, and while the idea of this control is undoubtedly of high social approbation, the methodology of implementing the control through indirect imposts on luxury commodities is ineffective. This is so because the affluent can afford to purchase the article by paying the higher impost — witness what those who can afford are willing to pay for an imported car, or for an imported sound system (and that too quite legally, by paying duty at the customs barrier, with a clean conscience and having no grounds to fear social disapprobation of their individual action in a nonausterity-oriented social environment). On the other hand, the incidence of the tax falls on the poor; it creates sub-employment, and diminishes employment.

Now when there is expansion of money for investments in a Balanced Allocation Ratio (which reformed attitudes in administration might permit), it takes the burden of the financial task — that of providing finances for investment (in the public sector, or in the private sector by expanding bank credit) — off from the shoulders of Government exactions. The instruments of Government exactions can then take up its rightful tasks — which is to serve a national purpose. If we give it now the task on curbing parasitic consumption, then the Direct Income Impost (mis-called the Income Tax) can be converted to Direct Consumption Expenditure Tax.

A form of Direct Consumption Tax in the Personal Consumption Expenditure Tax (proposed by Professor Lord Kaldor[12]) as a direct application of the Keynesian remedy of curbing Effective Demand and its extension through Lerners[13] principle of Economics of State Regulation. In this tax, one takes off all Investments and Savings from Income and Capital Receipts, to derive the base of the Expenditure Tax after the deduction. It is no burden for assessees to keep vouchers of their capital transactions, and the banking system would be made to gear itself to providing these certificates in time (and without grudging) for a nominal fee to all constituents with big or small deposits.

An alternative form of direct exaction would be the Direct Misexpenditure Tax which does not originate from the side of curbing Effective Demands but from the side of ensuring Effective Supply[14]. In this form of tax, one weights the investments upwards for high social approval (like investment in growing food) and downwards for low social approbation (like investment in production of luxuries) before deducting from Receipts, and thus deriving the base of Misexpenditure taxation. This not only acts upon the consumers — for curbing their Effective Demand (as is the purpose of the Kaldorian Tax) but also on producers and investors.

The task is not simply of curbing excess monetary expenditure, but of not producing the goods upon which the excessive expenditure takes place. It is by this method that the conspicuous consumption of the owners of secret wealth, and of small (but affluent) operators in trade, industry or agriculture, can be curbed. The Pure Expenditure Tax does not touch this class.

The task, therefore, is of setting allocations aright attuned to socially-purposive investments (rather than to those which the market finds to be profitable in any economy which has a large component of wealth outside the purview of tax authorities — either because of impost concessions, as in the case of agriculture, or because of evasion which may be creating secret wealth and secret expenditures upon luxuries). It hits at wrong production even in an economy with lots of undeclared money, which the Kaldorian Expenditure Tax does not affect.

The Misexpenditure Tax historically, and logically, followed from the Robinson-Sraffa[15] Capital Theory of Growth, and not merely from Keynesian Public Finance (curbing Effective Demand). It would be the instrument of implementing the Kahn[16] Prescript of Equity and other similar prescripts[17].

VII. THE REDUCTION IN PARASITIC CONSUMPTION

The Direct Misexpenditure Tax gets its vigour not only from simultaneous action against consumers and producers (both of whom may be wrongly channelising the physical resources of the economy), but also action in favour of those who are investing in the right lines. Thus the differential treatment becomes very large. This is called Actuative Development[18]. But it derives its teeth from the fact that a high and increasing rate of marginal taxation is possible in the Allocative Taxes. The marginal rate of mis-expenditure, in a progressively progressive tax schedule — and not, as in income impost, a regressively progressive schedule. The penalty increases with the quantum of mis-direction which an individual assessee inflicts upon the resources of the nation — just as the penalty is higher for the second and still higher for a third violation of traffic regulations leading to successive convictions for socially-disapproved conduct of an individual bus driver[19].

A schedule of low rates of expenditure tax does not have this set of teeth, and would be ineffective in providing a discouragement. This is especially so because the higher degree of discouragement to unapproved activities (in relation to the treatment for approved investments), may also be viewed as provision offering differential encouragement for the channelling of resources into right sorts of uses (by individual assessees who are correctly directing the resources of the economy into socially-approved channels). If at the assessee's notional expenditure level there is 200 per cent rate of additional taxation then fifty thousand rupees higher misexpenditure tax is the penalty for putting an extra twenty thousand repees in investment for production of domestic refrigerators with disapproval factor of 1/4 (rather than for manufacturing baked-earth coolers with approval factor of one and a half). That much (fifty thousand rupees) would also be taken to be the reward for doing the reverse (putting twenty thousand rupees in baked-earth products rather than in producing refrigerators) and earning exemption from the penalty of the additional tax.

The rates of returns would then tend to be governed by the Scissors Effect — they would be decreased in less socially-purposive channels (in which they are usually high), and increased in highly-approved directions (in which they are normally low) till the latter exceeds the former in quantum of profitability. Physical and manpower reosurces would then exhibit a tendency to shift from less approved to more approved channels — which is the social object of the Misexpenditure Tax and not directly so far the Kaldorian Expenditure Tax).

It is because of this highly socially-approved function that this fiscal measure is a powerful instrument of a democratic policy against misdirection of resources, and in favour of channelling the real resources according to the requirements of an Effective-Supply vector of socially-approved investments in balanced allocation.

VIII. MAGNIFIER INSTRUMENTS OF SOCIAL PURPOSIVENESS

We have seen that investments are weighted upward or downward in a Misexpenditure-Tax Systems to derive Notional Investment which is then deducted from Receipts to derive Notional Consumption, as the base for the Misexpenditure Tax. In a more general form of this tax, incomes are also weighted upward or downward depending upon the social disapprobation or otherwise, respectively. This is called the Disparity Tax[20], and the Notional-Consumption base that is ultimately derived, as a multiple of the common man's consumption (at the median) is called the Disparity Index.

The schedule of tax is the degree of tax (measured as a percentage of the base) to be paid in relation to a particular Disparity Index. Once established correctly, it is to be kept constant for a number of years to provide certainty to the tax-planning investors. In a long-term fiscal policy this is the element which provides stability of expectations.

The two differentiating treatment schedules (one each for Receipts and for Investments, and one sub-schedule each for Social Approval or Disapproval or Neutrality) would provide material for annual change to guide enough quantum of investments in each line as per the response of the investors. This is an instruments of annual control in the hands of the Finance Minister.

The tax planner would be encouraged to avoid tax, for thereby he would be following the socially-desirable directions of investments and earnings (which is a welcome step for national benefit). The less tax such a person pays, as a result of tax planning, the greater hero he would be, and is not a person to be decried, or complained against — because the social purpose in a tax (as distinct from an impost) is to channel physical and human resources properly. Its purpose is to change people's actions in investments and consumption. The purpose of a tax (as distinct from an impost) is never to collect more revenue for the Treasury. It is not even correct to say that collection of revenue is one of the socio-economic purposes of fiscal policy or it is a side-purpose. The collection of revenue ought not even to be included in the list of social and economic purposes. Only a tax administration not afraid of a deficit (if physical resources are properly channelled for a balance for a non-inflationary growth) can digest the purport of this powerful instrument for social equity and growth.

A tax in which a small change in the schedules produces a large shift of resources from less approved to more approved channels, is a Magnifier Instrument (in contradistinction to the reverse case which is called a Condenser Instruments).

The Income Impost is not an instrument of shifting resources at all. The Expenditure Tax has a rather indirect and slight effect of shifting resources in the right direction and it is, therefore, elevated from the status of an Impost to that of a Tax. But it is still a Condenser Instrument.

The Misexpenditure Tax — and more particularly the Disparity Tax — are magnifier investments (for alleviation of poverty) to which we have been logically led by a stop-by-stop analysis.

It is for this reason that analytically the responsibility for poverty continuance, its creation, and its removal has been traced in this essay to wrong type of State action and, therefore, society itself has been found to be responsible for this phenomenon. A large share of the blame rests on the intellectuals who permit this state of affairs to continue — without perceiving the problem amongst themselves, and reorienting their minds.

It is necessary to think of measures which will prevent creation or unnecessary continuance of poverty by appropriate and radically-different State action from that undertaken in the past. The composite instrument of firstly, the Strategy for Intergenerational Equity and, secondly, of Allocative Public Finance (encompassing unrestricted Monetary expansion to the extent necessary for physical resource mobilisation and Disparity Taxation) ensures :

Firstly, the acceleration of employment,
Secondly, of not permitting lack of finances to be a bottleneck to the higher growth-rate, and
Thirdly, the eradication of Real Inflation by curbing parasitical consumption.

By not following orthodox means of finance it also removes the contribution of the State to higher inflationary tendencies. It is by acceptance of and implementation of these processes that Poverty will be alleviated most rapidly, and ultimately eliminated.

REFERENCES

1. "Planning for Steady Growth", Basil Blackwell Oxford; American Edition Augustus Kelly, New York, 1965; Indian Edition, Oxford University Press, Delhi 1973.

— "Investment Criteria in a Platinum Age", Oxford Economic papers, Volume 19, No. 2, 1967, pp. 199-214.

— "Framework of planning for Economic Growth and Social Justice" *Interdiscipline*, Vol. VII, No. 2, Gandhi Centenary Number, Varanasi, 1969, pp. 130-66.

2. "A Defence Exercise" *Economic Weekly,* February 1963, Annual no. pp. 225-6, comments by Krishna Bhardwaj, March, 16, 1963; Rejoinder of original author through an article on "The classification of Basics and Non-basics" *Economic Weekly,* June 29, 1963, at pp. 1041-42, and rely thereto by Krishna Bhardwaj pp. 1041-2.

3. "Growth under conditions of Chronic Parasitism", in the Seminar, Delhi, Ferbruary 1966, pp. 225-6.

4. "Minute of Supplementation on Employment Policy", Report of Central Committee for Unemployment, (Bhagwati Committee) Government of India, May 1973, pp. 722-806.

5. "Equity-orientation of Employment Typology", D'Souza Felicitation Lecture delivered at the 67th Annual Conference of the Indian Economic Association, Agra, January 1985.

6. Economic Policy Choices", *Young India*, Republic Day, as also February 4, and February 11, 1971 Issues.

7. 'The Criteria for Appraisal of a Budget' in perspectives of Economic Development and Thought, Professor B.N. Ganguli Volume, Prasad, Kamta (Ed.), (Forthcoming 1985).

8. "The Rule of Order", Presidential Address delivered on the occasion of the Diamond Jubilee year of the Indian Economic Association, Bombay, December 1978,

Published in the *Indian Economic Journal*, Volume 26, No. 4-5, April-June 1979, pp. 1-43 at p.4.

9. "Choice of Planning Framework", The Indian Economy: Performance and Prospects, Golden Jubilee Volume, Deptt. of Economics, Sandesara, J.C. (ed.), University of Bombay Publications, Economic Series No.23, 1974, pp. 60-70 at p.66.
10. Sen, A.K. "Choice of Techniques", Basil Blackwell, Oxford, 1960 Chapter II, pp. 25, 26 wherein the Galenson Leibenstein Technique (more mechanised) has been shown to be less productive of output of consumption-good than the Polak Technique (the less-mechanised).
11. 'Actuative Development Policy' Recent Development in Monetary Theory and Policy (with special reference to Developing Economies), Papers and Proceedings of the Seminar, Reserve Bank of India, Bombay 1978.
12. "An Expenditure Tax", 1955.
13. "Economics of Control", Macmillan, 1940.
14. 'The Rule of Order', *op.cit.*

    Disparity Tax in a Composite Economy, Macmillan, Delhi, 1975.
15. Joan Robinson, 'Accummulation of Capital' 1956. P. Sraffa, The Production of Commodities by Means of Commodities, 1960.
16. Professor the Lord Kahn 'Challenge of Development' Jerusalem Lectures, 1956.
17. 'Employment and Intergenerational Equity' in *Employment Policy in a Developing Country*, Vol. I, Robinson EAG, Brhmananda, P.R. and Deshpande L.K. (Eds.), the record of discussion by John Toye, Macmillan, pp. 253-75.

    'Equitable Transformation for National Integration' India International Centre, New Delhi (Forthcoming 1986).

    'Economic Justice in a Free Society', Wheeler, 1976 (Forthcoming)

    Mathur, Shantanu : 'Distributive Shares and Prescripts of Equity', *Indian Journal of Labour Economics*, Vol. XXV, April-July 1982, Nos. 1&2, pp. 9-43.
18. 'Actuative Development Policy' *op. cit.*

    'Plan Formulation in an Economic Democracy' in Socio-Economic Development Problems in South and south-east Asia, Manzoor Alam S, and Rama, Reddy, G. (Eds.) Popular Prakashan, Bombay, 1978 pp. 5-35.
19. Disparity Tax in a Composite Economy, *op. cit.*
20. 'The Framework of Planning for Economic Growth and Social Justice' *op. cit.*

9

SOCIAL RELEVANCE IN TRANSFER OF TECHNOLOGY

I. TECHNOLOGY

When a set of processes is integrated into a technological system in such a way that the inputs of any process are produced somewhere in the set, then they form a technique. The process-intensity vector or distribution of manpower vector for non-bottleneck growth can be worked out, and it shows the ratios of manpower deployed for various activities. Correspondingly, the relative values of capital goods and other commodities are possible to be worked out. A technique is thus a self-regenerating system of process capable of non-bottleneck growth. Such a system can exist only as a steady-growth state at a particular time. Any commodity not in the steady-growth equilibrium-ratio becomes a bottleneck good, if in shortage, or a redundant commodity, if in excess.

All the techniques known can be displayed on a graph with value of output of consumption goods per man, and the value of capital per man employed. The scatter diagram so obtained is a set of known techniques. Out of these, the outer envelope consists of techniques of mutually non-superior and non-inferior variety. These form the production function and the set of techniques together is known as the Technology. Inventions leading to a newer set of techniques with outputs per man and outputs per unit of capital both higher, form a new technology.

Technology Transfer is the reduplication of a particular new technique, once a prototype has been established, so that a self-

---

Published in *Technology Transfer and Social Transformation*, Campbell, M. J. (ed.), pp. 103-117.

regenerating system using that type of technique is set up, and it grows at a steady pace to cover the whole working population or labour force.

Any odd invention sought to be introduced in an under developed country merely because it was found to be—

(a) useful abroad, or
(b) profitable abroad, or
(c) even, as in pharmaceuticals, harmful abroad but capable or being sold easily in under-developed regions to earn profit on the capital invested,

is not a part of the Economics of Planned Development, although there will be many agencies who will be ready to support its introduction on various seemingly-plausible grounds.

The part of technology chosen depends upon the optimum strategy of development. This depends, further, upon the degree of unemployment.

The phrase non-employment does not refer to a small population counted by number of heads. The total working population is composed, firstly, of those using non-inferior technique for producing the relevant goods and drawing at least a subsistence wage. Secondly, it includes workers who are using inferior or inappropriate techniques and those altogether unemployed. Low non-employment is indicated by and calculated from the ratio of the total working population to the numbers using the optimal technique being low. Thus level of non-employment indicates the degree of advancement achieved before the start of the Strategy. Non-employment includes malemployment (those working with inappropriate techniques or making socially-irrelevant goods or both), as well as under-employment (working for a part of the year), and also sub-employment (people who are working but paid a wage below the subsistence level).

II. THE CRITERIA

The evaluation of the type of advancement of technology can only be looked at in the framework of the optimum long-term Strategy of Development. This implies that one has to be highly selective about what type of technology-improvement one evokes from the laboratories of one's own country, what type one imports, and what type one rejects. Questions of Transfer of Technology arise in either case—whether of popularisation of the inventions of indigenous science, or of those of which the patents are secured from abroad. The aspects of technology which require an examination regarding introduction of improvements are, therefore, the following:

(a) which goods are to be manufactured with the help of the new technology;
(b) what capital intensity is to be chosen;
(c) what place has each of the above in the Optimum Strategy of Development.

The subject of Technology Transfer to underdeveloped countries has been clouded over because of lack of application of proper criteria for selecting the invention. It is not that criteria were not known to economic science, but there have been streams of thought among influential experts in which the known criteria has been ignored. These experts have not looked at the economic effects in the context of long-term planning. The myopic among scientists, the technologist for a single industry, the productivity expert who looks for labour-saving and capital augmentation in a labour-surplus and capital-scarce country, and the management man who knows that his subject is governed by objectives but does not know the proper objective may be, these are all examples of sections of experts who have ignored the criteria. They have taken the easier way out by not caring to study the subject from the angle of social profitability. They have not acquired mastery over understanding the methodology of selection, and have looked at the issues from the side of micro-economic benefits to one industry. These may appear to be huge and positive, whereas the effects upon the economy as a whole may not be in the favourable direction. Secondly, the investor may consider the matter from the point of view of his firm's profits and in this case private profit may be positive but social profitability may be negative. The criteria which one should adopt must relate to social optimality—long term benefit to society as a whole.

III. THE OPTIMUM STRATEGY OF DEVELOPMENT

For answering any of these questioning the prior issue which has to be taken into account pertains to determining what Strategy of

Development is to be considered to be optimum. For countries with low surplus population, the optimum technique would be based on the use of Mechanised Light machinery as in the following Chart:

CHART I

The Technology for the Percolation Strategy

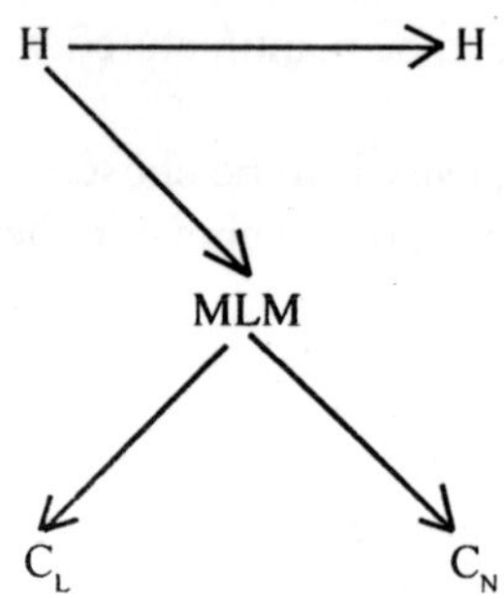

The self-reproducing Heavy-Industries Sector (H) produces itself as well as the Mechanised Light Machinery (MLM) which makes the consumption goods (C_N as consumption necessaries, and C_L as consumption luxuries). The techniques of advanced countries are introduced for use by a small percentage of population who form a privileged section, as capital equipment of the consumption sector and in some cases even the consumption goods introduced are those in common use abroad (but which are luxuries for the underdeveloped country). The expectation is that these goods and equipment of capital-intensive nature will both percolate to the rest of the population and will cover all the people ultimately. The strategy is, therefore, called "Percolation Strategy".

However, for countries with quite a large degree of non-employment (i.e. of surplus population), the optimum strategy pertains to maximisation of ploughback of the Heavy-Investment Sector (H) and minimisation of the leakage of its products to the consumption-goods sector (C). This is usually seen to be an economy with a modern H-sector (with high capital intensity, if necessary) and an improved C-sector (but with low capital intensity, because it uses H-saving techniques).

This may be depicted in the following Chart :

CHART - II
The Permeation Strategy

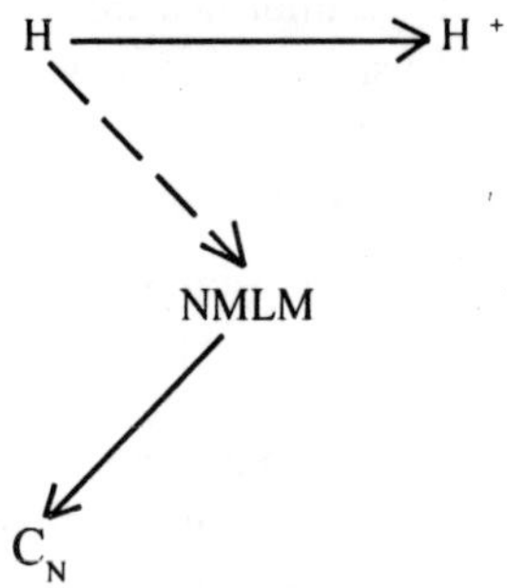

In the strategy optimum for an economy with quite a large surplus population, the route H → MLM is not to be followed. Instead, one should use a path H → NMLM → CN by virtue of which Non-Mechanised Light Machinery makes the consumption necessaries and requires only a trickle of H to manufacture it. On account of this property of H-saving machinery, this is the only S Strategy compatible with priority for Heavy-Investment. This is termed as the Permeation Strategy due to its property of building up H for the future generations and of C for the present one.

In countries in which the Permeation Strategy is optimum, the transfer of technology from abroad to be socially-relevant must be in the field of the cluster of industries and ancillaries consuming the self-reproducing Heavy-goods sector. This is depicted as $H \rightarrow H^+$, where H^+ represents the improved technology.

For the second level of processes consisting of the activity NMLM → CN. Transfer of Technology from advanced countries is of little help any way, for such techniques are not used any longer in advanced countries. The technological innovation should eschew the route H → MLM in the labour-surplus underdeveloped countries. However, this (because of the wide demand and the prospects it opens up) is precisely the field in which the protagonists of Technology-Transfer press for its acceptance and introduction in all the underdeveloped countries. The planning anthorities are all shown various micro-advantages like increase of productivity, scientific advance, replacement of out-dated technology, maximal modernisation, elimination of back-breaking efforts, export orientation keeping abreast of other countries, demand by public, rapidity of operations, etc. The industrial-licensing authorities are induced to permit the use of highly-mechanised H-using techniques, thus draining out the products of the H-sector into current production of consumption goods, and bringing down the growth rate of the H-sector.

IV. THE SOCIAL EVALUATION OF TECHNOLOGY TRANSFER

The effect of transfer of technology depends upon the character of the inventions proposed to be introduced and the nature of the economy where it is to be introduced. The following Table sums up the categories noted above.

Table 9.1 : Place of Innovations

Efficient innovation having:	High Mechanisation		Low Mechanisation	
Type of Country having:	H Sector	C Sector	H Sector	C Sector
Labour Shortage	√	√	X	X
Labour Surplus	√	X	√	√

It can be seen that whatever the category of the economy, an advance in H must be furthered, and adopted at the earliest for new investments. One cannot afford to go slow on the transfer of technology for improvement in any process which forms part of the self-reproducing H-sector. This is because trasferable technology is to be that wherein the new technique after adoption of the transferred technology becomes a superior technique on the criteria of output per unit of manpower and also per unit of capital. The principle applies whether the transfer is on the basis of imported technology or indigenous inventions (e.g. programmes like "Lab to Land"). In case of indigenous technology, the proper type of research can be evoked through the right ingredients in Science Policy.

The social evaluation of a change of technology depends upon the transformation of society observed from the point of view of social justice. These effects can be judged in terms of (a) Real Inflation; (b) Unemployment; (c) Unfavourable Distribution of Income; (d) Concentration of Industrial Power; (e) Urban Concentration; (f) Disparities in Consumption.

V. THE PERCOLATION STRATEGY

The Percolation Strategy depends upon transfer of technology for production of consumption goods relevant to conditions in advanced countries. This type of machinery draws away the products of the H-sector into production of consumption goods. It reduces the ploughback of H for its own expansion. It gives, therefore, a low payoff regarding long-term growth for technology transfer when introduced in a labour-surplus country. From the point of view of short-run benefits or social-justice, from the manner the strategy is implemented (to get a particular output for consumption goods needed for organised workers in industry), there is large investment in H-using processes needed. The consumer goods needed by executives, managers and other operatives (including unorganised labour) draws away the physical resources from manufacture of consumer necessaries. The use of mechanised machinery for manufacturing these also leads to the effect of low output per unit of capital invested, and hence shortage of consumption necessaries, resulting in Real inflation. This converts the employed (at subsistence) into the sub-employed (earning from their respective occupations a wage below subsistence). This creates further an unfavourable distribution of income.

For a given subsistence wage, the degree of mechanisation being high, there is a high profit to wage ratio, and an unfavourable distribution of income is created by the use of the technology in addition to the effect upon distribution noticed earlier, of Real Inflation.

The high degree of mechanisation also implies low creation of employment opportunities. There is moreover, the possibility of association of high degree of mechanisation with the larger scales of production which is liable to lead to concentration of economic power or monopolism. The large-scale industry is, further, likely to cause urban concentration and metropolitanism.

The unfavourable functional income distribution and large scale which is associated with a high degree of mechanisation, create a larger degree of skewness in personal-income distribution. This induces demand by the top echelons of society for a basket of goods (classed as consumption luxuries) which are used in advanced countries by a section belonging to middle range of incomes. Thus, along with technology and mechanised machinery for consumption-goods production, the consumption goods of foreign advanced countries are also transferred to the underdeveloped countries to satisfy the wants of a small percentage of the population with high purchasing power.

It is expected that these two strands (mechanised equipment and luxury goods) will percolate to the lower-income group. In the Percolation Strategy, some of these goods (being modernised consumer-goods) are manufactured again with highly-mechanised techniques. They create a high profit to wage ratio in relation to the low near-subsistence wage, and a distribution of income follows which is yet more unfavourable. This again creates greater disparities in income, and thence in consumption, thus creating a vicious circle. The Percolation Strategy yields a low payoff in terms of social justice, on this count of avoidance of consumption disparities also.

The transfer of a technology which was designed for an advanced country is appropriate to a situation of low non-employment only.

VI. THE PERMEATION STRATEGY

The transfer of improved technology in the H-sector in underdeveloped countries (with quite a large degree of non-employment) permeates the economy with H-capital and side by side it increases the rate of growth of the consumption necessaries sector. The high rate of ploughback of H (which the Permeation Strategy indicates), generates employment and opportunities for working in that sector itself rapidly. Thus, the correct manner of giving priority to the H-sector through H-conserving techniques in the consumption sectors generates both growth and social justice. Both these factors of growth and equity lean on the H-sector growth and depend upon priority to it.

The C-sector processes are of a low degree of mechanisation, because they are H-conserving techniques. Hence, high employment is a by-product and not the reason for their adoption. They have a low product per man and low surplus over the wage. Consequently, a high wage to profit ratio is established, and the techniques helps in functionally distributing income favourably. The low surplus is, however, connected with a very low capital intensity. Hence, rate of profit can be large if the technique is not an inferior one for a given capital intensity. The techniques are associated with small and miniature scale, and do not form the natural base for monopolism. They can be diffused in the countryside among small growth centres, and the cluster of villages surrounding each. They do not create a skew income distribution which would generate demand for luxury consumption goods, and in manufacturing which goods a further skewness of income distribution would be created. There is thus no vicious circle of consumption disparities created by the consumption-sector production in this Strategy.

VII. COMPARISON OF THE TRANSFERRED TECHNOLOGIES

The results of social justice can be displayed in a tabular form, a low performance earning a zero score, and a good performance a unit score, as in Table 9.2.

Table 9.2 : Results of Social Justice

Social Justice Effects	Percolation with Priority of H	Score	Permeation	Effects Score
(1) Tendency towards Non Inflation growth	Low	0	High	1
(2) Employment Opportunities per Unit of investment	Low	0	High	1
(3) Functional Distribution (Wage to Profit-Ratio)	Low	0	High	1
(4) Avoidance of creation of monopolism	No	0	High	1
(5) Avoidance of metropolitanism from C-sector	Low	0	High	1
(6) Avoidance of disparities in consumption	No	0	High	1
		0		6

When social justice effects are considered along with the economic effect of growth, we can summarise the result as in Table 9.3:

Table 9.3 : Social Justice and Economic Effect of Growth

Strategy	Percolation	Score	Permeation	Score
Effect:				
Growth of H	Low	0	High	1
Social Justice Content	Low	0	High	1
		0		2

In the Permeation Strategy, the scientific advances in the indigenous laboratories for improvement of techniques would be of H-saving nature and would be diffused at the same pace as the growth of H, for a balance growth.

Inventions made a few years back for which capital exists for manufacture and production generally continue to produce for some years more till they are found to be edged out because of unprofitability. In a capital-shortage country this need not cause anxiety for it avoids the problem of low service-life of equipment in relations to its natural life.

When the equipment is finally discarded (on account of repair costs raising beyond a threshold point which gives adequate profitability) there will be ripples of different techniques of different vintages. At that time, the equipment ought to be replaced by the newest well-tested invention. The targets of canvassing the sale of new technology will be the owners of both quite old type of equipment and new entrepreneurs (or investors), but not owners of recently-acquired equipment.

VIII. SOCIAL TRANSFORMATION

The sociological effect of this procedure is that there is a phased transition from primitive techniques to modern machinery. The mechanical and electronic inventions are easy to churn out in workshops and laboratories. Their assimilation is a difficult process and offers mental blocks on account of the cultural Field being different, or education or training having created a long-lasting impression which is difficult to obliterate. To the Civil Engineer who was taught to use logarithmic tables for calculations, the use of the slide rule was a bothersome device. To those used to adjusting the marker of a slide rule, mistakes creep in while pressing keys of pocket calculators with their fingers. To the watchman used to bars and bolts, the self-locking sealed-door is a mystery, what to talk of push button devices. He cannot be trusted to operate the freezing chamber of an ice-factory without considerable reorientation and safety precautions. The operation of an elevator would require a further cultural readjustment. The cultivator can shift from a wooden plough to one with an iron frame, and from there to a tractor. But he cannot understand, without prolonged training, the meaning of the salinity coefficient, or the degree of humidity as analysed by a micro-processor; and it would be a long time before he lets his sowing and harvesting decisions to be directed by the computer.

One further consideration of great moment must be mentioned. As a result of pressures of transfer of technology from abroad, some forces wrongfully induce the Government in a labour-surplus country to adopt the Strategy of Percolation, and to engage workers in the inappropriate techniques (because the strategy itself is inoptimal). Hence, it is not employment but malemployment which increases. But this creates the illusion of low unemployment, and on that basis, the mechanised techniques and further transfer of technology of high capital-intensity is tried to be justified. Similarly, through transfer of inappropriate technology for socially-irrelevant goods, resources are diverted from consumer necessaries and there is a shortage of these, and real inflation is created. This drives employed workers into the category of the subemployed. Yet, by traditional methods, they would continue to be counted among the employed, and yield a low statistical figure for unemployment or surplus labour.

To malemploy people by popularising inappropriate techniques, and to describe as "employed" those workers who are merely "occupied" at a wage below subsistence, and then to say that the degree of employment is large and the reserve of labour small, and hence to justify mechanised techniques, and on the basis to ask for more transfer of technology of inappropriate sort, is not a valid procedure.

Another effect of malemployment of a few people and at a higher wage than is obtainable elsewhere, is the imitative effect. One transfers technology which is not appropriate. Under a theory of wages which makes them equal to additional product yielded by employing one more labourer when capital and technique are constant, it is thought that with product per man rising on account of even change in capital, wages ought to rise proportionately. In violation of Prescripts of Equity, in the presence of huge non-employment, wages are increased and create "Ultra-employment" for a small section of organised workers and for the privileged workers in the high technology areas. Many of them produce goods socially less relevant and with techniques which are inappropriate. High wages of the malemployed and the supra-employed create a demonstration effect which not only induces the non-employed to join the concerns which use the inappropriate technology, but attracts other employed workers to shift to them. Further, after introduction of the labour-saving technology, sociclogical barriers crop up which dissuades the new entrants to the work force from using the traditional equipment or its appropriate modernised form. Thus, tractors have been introduced in surplus-labour countries, and bullock-drawn ploughs then become primitive technology, even if they have appropriate modernised innovations.

This is followed by what has been put as a hypothesis by Professor Nurual Hasan whereby young members of families in such places are observed not to be relishing the hereditary occupation of cultivators or putting their hand to the plough, and they are looking forward to sitting on the seat of a tractor which is a highly-expensive equipment. The cultivating families, according to the said observation, become increasingly dependent upon the richer peasants who hire out tractors at exhorbitant rates.

In place of social transformation of the country-side as a dynamic rapidly-progressing entity, the millenium does not come, and the old virtues become out of fashion, inviting disaster. The problem is brushed aside as one of ''manpower maladjustment'', not realising that is causation lies in Social Transformation of Technology Transfer itself.

The transfer of technology is not a matter of physical duplication alone. It is a psycho-educational process of acculturation of one's mind through a gradually changing environment. If there is too rapid and too frequent change, (as has taken place in educational systems in many countries), the system loses vitality and purposefulness, and becomes a mechanical one in which (though examinations are passed) learning is low, and (though formulate are memorised and reproduced) the significance of concepts is not understood. Statisticians so taught can calculate the median, but do not understand what it denotes. It is a mechanical process to redesign equipment every ten years. To reorient one's mind to the implications of that new technology every ten years is not a mechanical process, and is liable to encounter mental blocks. The adverse effects of transferred technology upon Social Justice get exhibited more quickly, than social and cultural transformation.

INDEX